Objectifying China, Imagining America

Objectifying China,
Imagining America

Objectifying China, Imagining America

Chinese Commodities in Early America

Caroline Frank

The University of Chicago Press | Chicago and London

Caroline Frank is an independent scholar, visiting lecturer in the Department of History at Brown University, and historian for the Greene Farm Archaeology Project.

Publication of this book has been aided by a grant from the Neil Harris Endowment Fund, which honors the innovative scholarship of Neil Harris, Preston and Sterling Morton Professor Emeritus of History at the University of Chicago. The Fund is supported by contributions from the students, colleagues, and friends of Neil Harris.

The University of Chicago Press, Chicago 60637
The University of Chicago Press, Ltd., London
© 2011 by The University of Chicago
All rights reserved. Published 2011.
Printed in the United States of America
20 19 18 17 16 15 14 13 12 11   1 2 3 4 5

ISBN-13: 978-0-226-26027-3 (cloth)
ISBN-13: 978-0-226-26028-0 (paper)
ISBN-10: 0-226-26027-5 (cloth)
ISBN-10: 0-226-26028-3 (paper)

Library of Congress Cataloging-in-Publication Data

Frank, Caroline.
    Objectifying China, imagining America : Chinese commodities in early America / Caroline Frank.
        p. cm.
    Includes bibliographical references and index.
    ISBN-13: 978-0-226-26027-3 (cloth : alk. paper)
    ISBN-10: 0-226-26027-5 (cloth : alk. paper)
    ISBN-13: 978-0-226-26028-0 (pbk. : alk. paper)
    ISBN-10: 0-226-26028-3 (pbk. : alk. paper)
    1. United States—Relations—China.   2. United States—Commerce—China.
    3. China—Relations—United States.   4. China—Commerce—United States.
    I. Title.
    E183.8.C6F73 2011
    327.73051—dc23
                                                                                            2011025254

♾ This paper meets the requirements of ANSI/NISO Z39.48–1992
(Permanence of Paper).

Contents

     China in Northern Colonial Homes   *143*

5   Manly Tea Parties
     The Idea of China in Boston's Rebellion   *175*

     Epilogue: An East Indies Trade for North America   *203*

     Notes   *209*
     Index   *253*

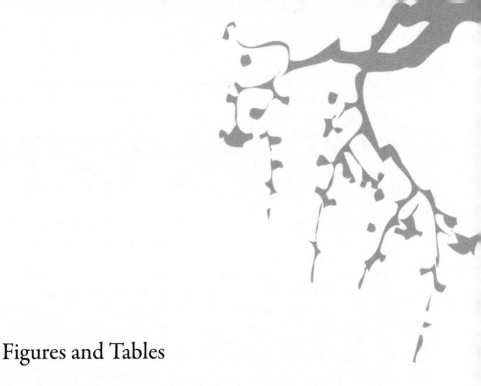

Figures and Tables

Figures

Tables

Acknowledgments

This book would not have been possible without the support and expertise of a small army of folks dedicated to moving American history out of the Atlantic and to better understanding the Chinese objects found in early America. Patrick Malone and Bob Lee in Brown's Department of American Civilization oversaw my initial work on a porcelain collection at the Rhode Island School of Design Museum and offered direction throughout the project. Seth Rockman, who fortuitously came to Brown University at the right moment, provided invaluable guidance and expertise. Brown University curator Robert Emlen has helped me better understand the material side of history. Sucheta Mazumdar, a Chinese historian, brought a keen global perspective and knowledge of Asia to the project. Robert St. George offered excellent suggestions, criticism, and methodological guideposts. I am honored to have worked with each of these scholars.

Kathy Abbass and Rod Mather introduced me to the shipwrecks of Narragansett Bay and revealed an astounding world of global trade. Tom Michie, Alice Westervelt, and Henry Brown brought the social life of porcelain in Providence, Rhode Island, alive. Jim Egan trod the discursive paths of early American Orientalism ahead of me and led me along. I am grateful to Christina Hodge for sharing the artifacts from the Pratt site and her important dissertation. In Rhode Island, I would also like to thank the late Margaretta Maganini Clulow, Pat Rubertone, Dick Gould, John Carpenter, Charlotte Taylor, the staff of the Rhode Island Historical Society, Bert Lippencott, and Adams Taylor.

The librarians and curators at the John Carter Brown Library have been enormously helpful. I am grateful to Norman Fiering, Rick Ring, Susan Danforth, Allison Rich, Val Andrews, and Nan Sumner-Mack. This project was greatly enhanced by a series of fellowships at other important institutions. At the Gilder Lehrman Institute of Early American History in New York City, I am thankful to Sasha Rolon and Ana Luhrs. Nan Rothschild at Barnard kindly shared with me her rich artifact collections from Lower Manhattan. At the Winterthur Museum and Library, I would like to thank Leslie Grigsby, Ann Wagner, Linda Eaton, and the library staff. At the Library Company in Philadelphia, I am grateful to Jim Greene and the staffs of the library and graphics collection. The Franklin Tercentenary was launched while I was in Philadelphia, and I am appreciative that Constance Hershey took time to share her knowledge about local porcelain collections. At the Massachusetts Historical Society, Conrad Wright and Anne Bentley were especially helpful. I would also like to thank Polly Latham and Crosby Forbes for consulting with me in Boston. The Peabody Essex Museum has one of the most extensive collections of Chinese export porcelain in North America. I was grateful to be able to spend a month in the PEM's Phillips Library, and would like to especially thank Bill Sargent, Karina Corrigan, and Kathy Flynn. A number of other people willingly shared their expertise of porcelain and material and visual culture, including Amanda Lange at Historic Deerfield, Kee Il Choi in New York, Jim Bradley in Boston, Patricia Johnston in Salem, and the late Chuck Fisher at the New York State Archives. Elizabeth Mancke and Joe Cullon offered insights into early American history. Thank you to Robert Devens and the superb editorial staff at the Press. My greatest debt is owed, ultimately, to an anonymous reader who slogged through two drafts, providing a fount of valuable criticism word by word!

A special thanks to Jean Wood, Krysta Ryzewski, Kaitlin Deslatte, and Tommy Urban for all sorts of insight in the depths of mud. To Gretchen, Paul, and Conor I owe intellectual nourishment. And without the constant encouragement of Danny, Skander, David, and Olivia, this book would not have been possible. I want to express my warmest appreciation to all of you.

Introduction

Beyond the Atlantic in Anglo-America

The Materiality of a Global History

In 1730 Nathaniel Norden, a Marblehead mariner turned civil servant, died leaving twenty-three "allabaster images," small, pure white porcelain statues made in the Chinese coastal county of Dehua in Fujian Province (fig. I.1). He had perhaps acquired these tokens of global sophistication—or of idol worship, as devout Protestant Americans deemed them—from a mariner such as Captain Andrew Cratey, whose 1680 homestead fronting the fish flake yard Norden had appraised and subsequently purchased. Captain Cratey himself had died in 1695 leaving behind a dozen "lackerd" chairs and couch, a "Jappan case of drawers and table," and a "p'cell of Cheny." Cratey also owned Mediterranean olive and inlaid furniture, "India calico quilts," and an African man named Warwick.[1] Even across the narrow spit of water

I.1. Bodhidharma (Damo), seventeenth century. Ming dynasty (1368–1644). Soft-paste porcelain with clear glaze (Dehua, Fujian Province). Height 11-¾ inches. Gift of Mrs. Winthrop W. Aldrich, Mrs. Arnold Whitridge, and Mrs. Sheldon Whitehouse, 1963 (63.176). Metropolitan Museum of Art. Image © Metropolitan Museum of Art / Art Resource, NY.

that separated Marblehead's ungodly, globe-trotting mariners from Salem's pious pilgrims, we find the stain of East Asian tastes. In the inventory Salem merchant Philip English made of his belongings before he and his wife fled persecution as presumed witches in 1694, there are close to fifty named pieces of "Chaney."[2] Such a large quantity suggests that English, a leading merchant in New England, was holding merchantable stock of Chinese porcelain. In his absence, the family of Jonathan Curwen, one of the prosecuting judges in English's witch trial and a Puritan, confiscated all his property, including the Chinese porcelain.[3]

Further down the coastline in the colony of New York, the evidence for the presence of Chinese commodities becomes overwhelming. The will of Margrieta van Varick, for example, drawn up in the winter of 1696, left hundreds of "Cheenie" dishes of all shapes and sizes to a variety of children, friends, and relatives. Her collection included "7 Indian Babyes," probably the white Dehua statues, as well as "East India" furniture, textiles, trinkets, and pictures.[4] She was the widow of Reverend Rudolphus van Varick, of an old New Amsterdam family. He had been sent to serve the Reformed Dutch Church in Malacca in the 1670s.[5] His religious beliefs clearly presented no obstacle to an accumulation of the alluring Far Eastern goods that streamed past in the heavily traveled Straits of Malacca. In New York of the late seventeenth century, circulation of Far Eastern objects was commonplace, with nearly a third of appraised estates containing Chinese porcelain.[6] But even outside the metropolis of New York, into the rural reaches of Long Island, we are not disappointed by a lack of Chinese wares and Chinese styles. Colonel William Smith, a former English governor of Tangier, Africa, was rewarded in 1693 for good service with a tract of land in Suffolk County. He died on his manor estate in 1705, leaving a large quantity of chinaware and lacquer furniture, in addition to Asian or African rugs, East India sashes, and a scimitar.[7]

Continuing south to the "Stately Palace" of West New Jersey proprietors John and Elizabeth Tatham, we find their estate inventory appraised in 1700. They owned a teapot, brightly colored tin-glazed earthenware, and japanned furniture as well as wampum and beaded jewelry.[8] Their seventeenth-century colonial home presents a true mélange of global taste, spanning English, Chinese, Mediterranean, and Native American commercial aesthetics. The Tathams were known Jacobites, but even among the self-denying reform Protestants of the Delaware Valley we see the seepage of Far Eastern goods. Quaker Ralph Fishbourn of Chester County died in 1708 in possession of "China Ware Bottles &c."[9]

In the face of such material evidence, it is impossible to deny that settlers in North America were involved in the China trades prior to statehood. Prenational British Americans did not view themselves as living in an Atlantic world. Thanks to a growing maritime infrastructure and thriving coastal and inland trade routes, many were cosmopolitan and economically ambitious. Like most Europeans, they saw themselves in a world that reached beyond the Atlantic. American mariners, merchants, and consumers were keenly aware of a place along their sea lanes called the "East Indies," where wealth and opportunity were plenty, where one could make a fortune and retire in security and independence. North Americans collectively were not an independent nation-state, but individually they were undaunted in seeking the sort of authority, power, and self-determination that such a risky and lucrative trade could provide. Their belongings tell us that they had a relationship with China before they achieved independence from Britain. People from diverse regional backgrounds—and the culture-producing responses they have to each other—do not, in fact, enter into relational situations *only* under the aegis of state permission. With significant advances in European maritime transport from the fifteenth through the seventeenth centuries, circuits of trade, commodities, ideas, and people intensified outside the spheres of European government control. This book will examine the significance to early Americans of indirect contact with a place they called the "East Indies," and with China in particular. The large state-sponsored East Indies ventures were, of course, partly responsible for American colonial contact with the countries of the East, but alongside these ventures there existed a vast extragovernmental, transoceanic circulation of ideas and commodities in which Americans actively participated.

While Americans in the seventeenth and eighteenth centuries had fairly precise geographic information available to them in the form of maps, atlases, and published travel descriptions about the regions of the Indian Ocean, Southeast Asia, and the Far East, they, like most Europeans, nevertheless persisted in maintaining an imagined cultural geography contained in the term "East Indies," which lumped together all these regions within one category. Concrete references to routes to Asian countries, their distinct languages, religions, cultural customs, and products are found in the writings and libraries of early Americans.[10] In 1688, for example, Nathaniel Mather in Salem requested a few books of his brother Cotton. "Mr. Higginson," he wrote, "earnestly desires to see Knoxes History of the Island of Ceylon (which lyes on Father's Table) and Taverniers Travels."[11] Knox was a sailor who had been held captive for nineteen years on the island today called Sri Lanka. Mather requested his published memoir, which gives a detailed—some even say ethnographic—account of the people and their language, as well as maps so meticulous that they have been used by today's Tamils to prove their ancient land claims. Higginson, a Salem preacher, had a son then serving in India with the East India Company, who was, a few years later, succeeded by another New England native son, Elihu Yale, as mayor of Madras. We know about these important men, but we know much less about the many American sailors who sailed with the various East India companies and carried firsthand accounts and precise—sometimes printed—knowledge about Asian places back to the western shores of the Atlantic. Despite such accurate information about the countries east of the Cape of Good Hope, an imaginary place called the "East Indies" remained the primary geographic reference for all the distinct regions of China, Japan, India, and Southeast Asia. The "East Indies" took on a geographic reality of its own in the Atlantic, manifested especially in the various East Indies Companies.

China and its exported manufactures were the crown jewels of the East Indies trades. But as we shall see in chapter 1, one did not have to travel further east than the Straits of Malacca, or the coast of India, or even the islands of the western Indian Ocean to participate in the "China trade." In contradiction to nationalist historical paradigms, seventeenth-century Chinese junk trade remained vital in the eastern Indian Ocean, flourishing despite the oft-cited 1656 Qing imperial edict "forbidding even a plank to drift to sea."[12] Superior Chinese trade goods produced within a sophisticated manufacturing infrastructure and vended by commercially sophisticated merchants left the coast of China, easily entering a vast network of commercial streams that circulated the globe. By the time Europeans arrived in the Indian Ocean, this maritime circuit was as dense and as vibrant in disseminating Chinese wares as the better-known "Silk Roads."[13] In the Atlantic, at the other end of these long watery highways, silver extracted from American mines under the auspices of and for the Spanish state sailed away in a hot current eastward, but not always on Spanish ships. In the Indian Ocean, European renegades operating outside political jurisdictions transported and disseminated a host of commodities and prejudices.[14] Regardless of the disposition of states and statehoods, diverse regional peoples living under the Spanish empire, the Chinese empire, the British, Dutch, Mughal, and Ottoman empires were all in material contact with one another by the mid-seventeenth century, competing for global hegemony over raw and refined objects, within both exclusive state rooms and hidden saltwater coves that welcomed any trafficker with goods or specie. Anglo-American coastal settlers became a maritime people at the outset. They tapped into the Spanish silver stream and were energized by the global dissemination of the fruits of a sophisticated Chinese productivity. They were integral players in the maritime flow of raw and refined goods out of and into the Atlantic, even sailing directly into ancient circuits of trade in Asian waters.

Sailing to America in Search of East Asia

The economic and cultural force of China radiated far beyond the limits of an imaginary boundary confining the Eastern half of the early modern globe, a boundary that retrospectively presumes some sort of isolation of the Atlantic from the Indian and Pacific Oceans.[15] While "near Asia" and the eastern Mediterranean have received more scholarly attention as integral components of an "Atlantic World," we need to go further to see the presence of East Asia in the early modern Atlantic as well.[16] The expansion of Europeans into the far reaches of the Atlantic was profoundly intertwined with their awareness of and interest in the "East Indies." Columbus, after all, called his voyages west "Enterprise of the Indies." The desire to find a fabled "northwest passage" that would make America the gateway to the East persisted, infecting even such stalwart intellects as Benjamin Franklin. While living in England, Franklin purchased a sixteenth-century volume by explorer Sir Humphrey Gilbert, describing the northern coast of Labrador and seeking evidence for a "passage to Cataia."[17] In 1753, Franklin rallied a group of investors to mount an exploratory effort, led by Charles Swaine, but like all the other attempts to locate Asia in America, it had little success.[18] But many ordinary Americans knew there were easier ways to get to East Asia. In 1744, a coffeehouse owner in Newport told a Scottish guest he had designed a machine to cut the "American isthmus . . . so we may go to the East Indies a much eaiser and shorter way."[19]

Strident critiques of static Atlantic-bound, Eurocentric economic history begun by Andre Gunder Frank, Kenneth Pomeranz, and other economic historians offer a long list of Asian technological and economic advantages vis-à-vis Europe up to about the time the United States finally entered the China trade.[20] Among relevant products and processes we find not only porcelain, lacquer, and silk, but also printing presses, paper money, guns, ships, metallurgy, hydraulic engineering, and, not inconsequentially, the wheelbarrow.[21] Elite Ottoman Turks had long offered alluring displays of such Far Eastern commodities, but prior to the Age of Exploration Europeans lacked trade capital as well as privileged overland or maritime access to China.[22] As early modern Europe experienced a gradual abeyance of disease, famine, and high mortality, and individual wealth increased substantially, a tremendous amount of European material and intellectual resources went into developing fruitful sea routes to East Asia.[23] Commerce in the Atlantic proceeded apace, and it was never a closed circuit. Demand was growing around the Atlantic for spices, tea, and exquisite Far Eastern manufactures, drawing Europeans to other oceans. Overseas explorers, sponsored by European monarchs longing for prestigious Far Eastern commodities, sailed west across the Atlantic, in search of older, not newer, worlds. In 1497, for example, Sebastian Cabot landed on "New Found Land," which he hopefully calculated at the precise latitude of Chipangu (Japan).

Far Eastern trade goods had rapidly become baroque Europe's most highly valued consumables, for the personal prestige they bestowed as much as for the capital they generated. When explorers gradually realized that East Asia did not, in fact, immediately lie in the western Atlantic, European capitalists sought nevertheless to extract resources from the "New World"—using Native American and African labor—that would enhance their commercial relationship with China. By the late eighteenth century, Asia produced four-fifths of the world's goods but comprised only two-thirds of its population.[24] Over the course of the early modern period, European traders struggled to keep up with a rising deficit. Exchange was frustratingly imbalanced, creating urgency and fierce competition among Atlantic traders. A growing consensus of scholarship alerts us that early modern trade consistently favored China, with specie-based settlements flowing in a rising deficit out of the Atlantic eastward. Even with the help of American resources, there was a constant net drain of specie from Europe to China, with about 75 percent of New World silver ending up in China before 1800.[25] But this did not necessarily leave Atlantic traders high and dry. In struggling to form equal exchanges with East Asians, European traders realized that silver was more highly valued, and gold less valued, in China than Europe. Given New World silver resources, this neat arbitrage allowed them (despite their lack of goods marketable in Asia) to still sail back to the Atlantic flush with valuable gold, capital which ultimately contributed to future purchases in Asia that perpetuated the competitive cycle.[26]

In this global economic and cultural context, the newly "discovered" Americas were valued as a source of precious metals by the Spanish, but for the English, who were less fortunate with their mines, their American colonies came to be seen as a possible source of Asian substitutes—exotic woods, exotic foods, raw silk, even "china clay" and stolen silver—that could enhance the position of London capitalists, judged *always* somehow in reference to China.[27] Competitive commercial frustration pushed Northern Europeans beyond the Atlantic, as traders strove not only to be the first to bring Asian goods to market but also the first to find something the imagined massive Chinese market would consume other than silver. All Americans, including indigenous Americans, participated in various ways in this unquenchable and aggressive exploration. The East Indies trade's importance to early American history, therefore, is not necessarily due to the volume of Chinese goods actually exchanged in the western Atlantic—although there were many more East Asian commodities reaching America than has been acknowledged—but rather to its imaginary force, the sheer magnetism of its economic weight and cultural allure, on traders and consumers alike.

The search for China lingered under the cultural and economic surface of growing English settlements in North America throughout the seventeenth and eighteenth centuries. Even as we acknowledge the relevance of the East Indies trades to the settlement and economies of early America, the significance of this sustained quest for China, and china, to the *political* identity of colonial Anglo-Americans has been largely unexplored by historians. The goal of this study, therefore, is not only to recover the widespread presence of Chinese commodities in North America and the impact of the East Indies trades on the nature of American commerce, but to push the role of the East Indies trade in early America a step further in exploring its relationship to American state formation (compare the East India Company flag to the earliest United States flag in figs. I.2 and I.3[28]). To understand how it was that the English East India Company and Chinese commodities fueled colonial motives behind the

I.2. East India Company flag. *Bombay*, painting by George Lambert and Samuel Scott, 1732, British Library, England.

I.3. United States flag, ca. 1783, from *Bowles's Universal Display of the Naval Flags of All Nations in the World*, London, 1783. Courtesy of John Hay Library, Providence, RI.

opening acts of the American Revolution, our interpretation must take into consideration the intra- and extra-imperial power dynamics of the quest for China and china.

Since prenational Anglo-Americans, as we will see in chapters 1 and 3, were very much invested in long-distance oceanic commercial networks of Chinese commodities, it is not surprising that the trading regions of the northern British colonies would eventually come to blows with an oppressive mercantile elite restricting their movement. Examining their trade for and consumption of Chinese objects, we see that Americans were ideologically relegated to a particular place in the empire that they resisted, and this larger tension within the imperial political economy is visible in how Chinese commodities were deployed and interpreted in local markets and households. These subimperial interactions were culturally implicated in ways that subtly impacted political outcomes. The Anglo-American construction of the East Indies, as discussed in chapters 2, 4, and 5, was as a place where people had been made dopey by despotism, and consumption of East Indian commodities and participation in imagined East Indian styles might leave Americans weakened and effeminate if they did not master the trade. Chinese goods were the sine qua non of the East Indies trades. The desire to be in a masculine, dominant role vis-à-vis trade in Chinese goods, as opposed to (as Americans imagined) an effeminate, servile role vis-à-vis British ministers or East Indian taskmasters contributed to the motivations underlying the American Revolution, as discussed in chapter 5. Notably, it took new U.S. citizens only days to set sail for China once the British redcoats departed New York harbor in November 1783. The groundwork for their prompt commercial and missionary ventures to the East had been laid during the previous century and a half, beginning with the first English settlements in North America.

Using Objects to Tell History

As this argument unfolds in the chapters that follow, we will continually return to the ample material evidence that grounds it, evidence that is in fact often located in the *ground* as archaeological remains. Colonial Americans bought, traded, sold, and used substantial quantities of specific Chinese commodities in their businesses and homes. We need to interrogate, rather than take for granted, costly global commodities such as porcelain, lacquer, and tea. We need to follow the network of meanings, associations, and people these things gathered on the long trail from Chinese cultivator or producer to a western Atlantic merchant and consumer.[29] Far Eastern commodities allowed Americans to demonstrate to themselves and others that they had risen above, in the words of one European tourist critiquing colonial life, "that primitive simplicity practiced by our forefathers."[30] China teacups contributed to a particular sense of self and place, allowing European users, whether nobility or commoner, whether in the colonies or in Europe, a defense against the condescension of a higher cultural authority, be it Moorish princes or genteel British travelers.[31] Historians, archaeologists, and curators all agree that Chinese commodities were the material substance of a superior standard, deployed in contextually specific ways all around the Atlantic, but we need to know more about the content of that standard in early America and more about American participation in the global circuits of trade and ideas that underlay Chinese commodity ownership.[32]

This book builds on the work of cultural historians who use things— material culture—as evidence. Many of these authors have addressed the cultural history of Chinese commodities in Europe; here the intention is to broaden the examination to include the other side of the North Atlantic as well. We must take a critical approach to the perspective that the use of fashionable dining and "new beverage" wares was simply an expression of status and social competition and no more needs to be said about it.[33] Using the more costly Chinese dishes for drinking, serving, and dining often did project a statement of status, especially to visiting observers (whose primary accounts typically form the bedrock of cultural history). But the imaginary complex surrounding the use of Chinese porcelain probably meant more to the user than just an assertion of prominence with respect to one's inferiors or neighbors. Cary Carson's analysis of consumption in colonial Virginia develops the idea that certain objects became popular because they were "socially successful" for their users. He goes on to say, however, that the demand for so many new and different household things in the midcolonial years must have been due to more than just social competition. He points out, "Demand has seldom been satisfied merely by ownership or possession."[34] He urges historians to ask specifically what types of new housewares were "needed" (his quotation marks) and specifically how these objects altered age-old social patterns. This book will try to better animate the social world of tea drinking, porcelain display, and furniture japanning.

In addition to the broken porcelain shards excavated by archaeologists and some well-provenanced old family collections now housed in museums, the study of Chinese porcelain contained here relies heavily on colonial probate inventories to locate Chinese objects in northern Anglo-America.[35] Tax officials had begun itemizing every material possession in a deceased person's estate or household, often grouped by named rooms, in the late medieval period in Europe. The practice continued into the nineteenth century in America. Historians who use these records are rewarded with rich, three-dimensional glimpses into their subjects' worlds and minds.[36] Inventories offer a bridge between the things people kept in their homes and the words they used to describe them, or, to be more precise, how fellow community members imagined them. This book includes a systematic examination of chinawares in over a thousand documented estates from the seaport communities of Salem, Boston, Newport, New York, and Philadelphia from 1690 to 1770. These data reveal the great extent to which Anglo-Americans along the Atlantic seaboard were implicated in the East Indies trades. At the end of the seventeenth century in New York, for example, over 30 percent of surveyed estates contained Chinese porcelain, and about 10 percent did in Newport and Salem. By the 1760s, close to three-quarters of probated estates in New York, Philadelphia, and Boston held chinawares. Silk was even more prevalent in these estates but of less interest to our analysis here as its Chinese pedigree was less obvious than that of porcelain. Indeed, by the mid-eighteenth century, foreign silk was thoroughly anglicized and integrated into the emerging English industrial base.

The material evidence studied here—porcelain, tea, and lacquer—comes to life and enriches our history of the "northern plantations" when it is contextualized within a culture comprised not only of objects but also a wide range of

period writings, from letters to newspaper essays, poetry, broadside announcements, and philosophical tracts. This pairing of material culture analysis and
discourse analysis is further supplemented with visual culture, which includes
primarily decorative arts and portraiture. Like an archaeologist examining
artifacts associated within a stratum, we need to associate the things in question with written and visual metaphors, allusions, symbols, and fragments of
meaning to get at the larger significance of china and China, as object and
geographic imaginary, within Anglo-American society. This interdisciplinary,
intertextual interpretive method allows us to "read" Chinese commodities for
meanings, or for what Robert St. George calls their "indirect reference[s],"
leading us, through these objects, to a more intimate understanding of the importance of the East Indies trades to the character of colonial society.[37] An
object's direct reference would be to its form and function. Here, without ignoring china's material, shapes, and household uses, we will look beyond these
in an attempt to suggest its significant symbolic weight in colonial society.
This is only possible by recovering, within identifiable contexts, those words,
images, and events closely associated with china.

The Soul of the Object / the Sign of the Commodity: Refined China in Anglo-America

Some anthropologists who use material culture to enlighten their understanding of human lives have adopted a biographical approach to the objects they
study, examining the implications all stages of an object's existence—from producer to trader to consumer—have on its overall meaning at any one point.[38]
Since the goal of this study is to learn more about the attitudes colonial Americans had to China, as the star of Europe's East Indies trades, one might ask if it
is important to focus our attention on the "life" of the Chinese commodity in
China, before it enters the export stream and a world familiar to Americans.
Very little attention is devoted here to the "lives" these exported objects had in
China—to the meanings chinaware had for the Chinese potter, for example—
but a glance in that direction is not entirely irrelevant to their significance in
America. By the second decade of the eighteenth century, china ownership in
North America had spread beyond mansion and manor walls, beyond Dutch
cupboards and fishermen's taverns, to almost all sectors of northern colonial
society. According to unanimous consensus among decorative arts scholars,
there was one thing all these diverse socioeconomic groups had in common.
That was an ignorance of the Chinese significance of the decorations on their
dishes (see fig. I.4), or what one literary historian has called "the stubborn

I.4. Porcelain charger, ca. 1730, Imari palette, China. Formerly owned by the Russell-Gerry family (Thomas Russell) of Boston and Marblehead, MA, in the 1700s. Gift of Mrs. J. Alan Gayer and Mrs. G. William Helm, Jr., 1984, E81655. Peabody Essex Museum, Salem, MA. Photo courtesy of the Peabody Essex Museum.

illiteracy of the English when it comes to cross-cultural encounters."[39] This ignorance amounted to an obscuring of the people and the place behind, or contained within, the prized commodity. The Chinese aesthetic was flattened, treated superficially, and in the process the cultural authority of the Chinese potter was deflated.[40] This refusal to scrutinize the real Chinese qualities of the pot was related to the slippage that occurred when geographically literate Americans used such references as "India china" and "India tea," neither of which commodity came from India—and they knew it. Americans were as uninterested in being *too* knowledgeable about the pots' Chinese iconography as they were in showing *too* much regard to its geographic identity.

In the early Qing dynasty (1644–1735), the Chinese potter's choice of figurative, natural, and ritually significant design motifs was not random. Often the designs were talismanic or auspicious symbols originally intended for a popular market of Asian literati. The use of richly textured popular iconography on china, including the less refined export wares made in imitation of domestic wares, became especially common in the mid-seventeenth century when imperial control of the potteries weakened. It was during the same time, therefore, that worldly captains and imperial officials saw land opportunities in North America, that Bay Colony dissenters established trading posts in and around Boston, that the Dutch West India Company was in political retreat in the Hudson and Connecticut River valleys, and that European and American marauders roamed the Indian Ocean, that we see a release of creative energy from Jingdezhen and the establishment of vivid Chinese design traditions that were to continue on export wares for the next two centuries.[41]

The turbulent period that marked the end of the Ming dynasty and the successful conquest of southern China by the Manchu-dominated Qing coincided with one of the most productive periods in Chinese arts (1620–80).[42] Not unlike trends in other parts of the world, a market-oriented, urban bourgeoisie became influential in China at this time. With weaker imperial oversight of porcelain production accompanying the fall of the Ming dynasty and the broadening of an urban, educated, and sophisticated market for porcelains, potters at Jingdezhen experienced greater artistic freedom and inspiration than ever before. Images related to Chinese mythology and religion, such as the Daoist Eight Immortals, continued to flourish. But these were now accompanied by a prolific use of narrative imagery taken from popular Chinese literary works. Potters borrowed from woodblock prints used to illustrate reprints of Chinese classics, novels such as *Romance of the Three Kingdoms*, *Romance of the Western Chamber*, or the *Water Margin*, which were themselves based on well-known historical events of earlier centuries, events that contributed to a Chinese sense of self. This culturally rich imagery, filled with scenes of military figures, rulers, rebels, and men and women at work and at home, proliferated across the surface of porcelain just at the time that the Dutch and English trade with China began (fig. I.5).[43]

In addition to figural designs, the most commonly occurring motif on the general market (as opposed to special order) pots arriving in America was floral, and especially the flowers of the four seasons: peony for spring (see the Russell-Gerry charger, fig. I.4), lotus for summer, chrysanthemum for fall, and plum blossom for winter. All these flowers, and others such as the lily, garden hibiscus, mallow flower, and camellia, appear as decorative motifs on pottery

I.5. Porcelain dish with scene from *Shuihu zhuan* (*Water Margin*), a novel about Song dynasty bandits. Kangxi mark and period (1662–1722). Painted in overglaze famille verte enamels, diam. 6-⅞ inches. E. C. Converse Collection, Bequest of Edmund Cogswell Converse, 1921 (21.175.39). Metropolitan Museum of Art, New York, NY. Image © Metropolitan Museum of Art / Art Resource, NY.

in China dating back to the Tang and Song dynasties or earlier, but it is during the late Ming that they became most popular and that their references to time of year, stage of life, auspicious beginnings, or wealth and rank in maturity became most pronounced. The pine tree, a Daoist symbol of longevity, is another commonly occurring motif found on North American examples. It often occurs with the prunus and bamboo as one of the "Three Friends of Winter," representing in China the peaceful coexistence of Buddhism, Daoism, and Confucianism. The deer is yet another Daoist decoration frequently seen in North America (fig. I.6). In China it is associated with good fortune.

I.6. Chinese porcelain charger, ca. 1740–60, associated with Benjamin Faneuil. Gift of
Mrs. Richard W. Hall. Courtesy of Historic New England (RS 33514).

It is easy to imagine that images of pine trees and deer would also hold
place-specific significance to those in North America. Colonial New Englanders repeatedly used an image of the pine tree in the upper canton of their self-
styled flag, although this tree bore little resemblance to the pine as drawn by a
Chinese artist. Bovine animals also appear on American pots, and this design
motif might speak to the American colonial experience. In China the ox is
featured in both poetic and mythological narratives associated with agricultural health and fruition. In some cases strong associations already existed in
Europe for some common Chinese motifs, such as the dragon, one of the oldest symbols in Chinese mythology and positively associated there with guard-
ianship and the lifeblood of the emperor; in the West, however, the dragon

represents a threat to the royal person. Whereas the dragon might bring to mind sentiments of protected serenity within the imaginative universe of the Chinese potter, it would bring forth precisely opposite allusions in the West of belligerency and bellicosity.[44]

Ultimately we can speculate all we like about what these designs *might* have meant to Americans, but what is more significant is their silence on the subject. In acknowledgments of gifts, in small orders of china, in descriptions of rooms—even descriptions that include china—there is a gaping hole in the primary documents when it comes to detailed descriptions of the china they owned and admired. Rarely did Americans request china with particular artistic designs. They used exclusively a standardized set of adjectival phrases in reference to china. In addition to terms for form, such as "teacup" or "saucer," these adjectives are "blue & white," "burnt," "enameled," and "gilt." After the mid-eighteenth century when potter Josiah Wedgwood and his colleagues in Staffordshire, England, perfected a light-colored refined earthenware that became popular for tea drinking and formal dining, we also see the adjectives "English" and "India." [45]

What does it mean that the china pots valued so highly in many American homes carried a complex universe of Chinese referential signs that were misperceived, ignored, or appropriated for other purposes? How was the china, and the China within the china, figured in colonial homes and used as a prop in defining identity? Americans, like Europeans, remained aloof to the Chinese references in all these motifs. The total lack of evidence we now find for an eighteenth-century engagement with the rich Chinese cultural content of the designs on porcelain is surprising given that Euro-American intellectual pursuits were at this time thoroughly steeped in the deep and probing inquiries of the Enlightenment. Many booksellers in colonial America sold accounts of China and Chinese life, from Marco Polo to Jesuit missionaries, to diplomatic and company travelogues, to translations of Chinese literature. In 1737, for example, the *New York Weekly Journal* ran a series of lengthy extracts taken from *The Morals of Confucius: A Chinese Philosopher who Flourished above Five Hundred Years before the Coming of Our Lord and Saviour Jesus Christ*, a Latin text translated and published in London in 1691. Confucius was popularly viewed in America as an orderly, self-governed, and benevolent person of great wisdom and virtue.[46] This reverence for Confucius is apparent in a compliment paid by Dr. Ezra Stiles to Benjamin Franklin in 1766, in which he compared the future legacy of Franklin to that of the world's greatest known philosopher, whose "Posterity has been honored in China for Twenty Ages."[47] Intense European philosophical interest in and engagement with

Chinese languages and religions date to Matteo Ricci's founding of the Jesuit
mission there in the mid-sixteenth century. Much of this interest began with
the premise that Chinese cultural manifestations resided at the base of a universal ordering, as a more primitive precursor to European culture.[48] From its
founding, therefore, Harvard College required the study of Asian languages.[49]
Voltaire underscored the degree of Western interest in the Celestial Empire in
famously proclaiming in 1768,

> China once entirely unknown, for a long time thereafter disfigured in our eyes,
> and finally better known among us than many provinces of Europe, is the most
> populated, flourishing, and ancient empire in the world.[50]

A pioneering European historian of East-West relations later concurred
with Voltaire, asserting "Confucius became the patron saint of eighteenth-
century Enlightenment."[51] For those Americans who had anything to say
about China, however, the interest revolved almost entirely around either
the issue of religious conversion or the procurement of "useful knowledge."
Cotton Mather, certainly one of the most learned men in the colonies in his
time, wrote about and corresponded with Dutch missionaries in Ceylon and
the Danish in Malabar, studying their work and urging Americans to follow
their examples in converting Native Americans.[52] As we will see in chapter 2,
American newspapers closely followed the papal denunciation of the Jesuits in
China, relishing the insinuation that these Catholic emissaries of Christ had
turned native—which was the dangerous flipside of becoming close enough
to heathens to convert them. As the eighteenth century progressed and philosophical clubs and societies began to emerge in American seaports, we see a
number of enlightened gentlemen turning their attention to pragmatic issues
related to the welfare of the American colonies, such as population growth,
agricultural fecundity, and productive methods and technologies. Benjamin
Franklin, Thomas Jefferson, and other members of the Philosophical Society
speculated about Chinese methods of navigation and their commendable industrial and agricultural practices.[53] Franklin's apparent frustration at his lack
of solid information on the ways of life in China even led him to fabricate a
story about a shipwrecked Portuguese sailor who supposedly spent years living
in China, sending him lengthy accounts. Charles Thomson, a Philadelphian
and Philosophical Society member, wrote in 1768,

> By introducing the produce of those countries that lie on the east side of the old
> world, and particularly those of China, this country might be improved beyond

what heretofore might have been expected. And could we be so fortunate as to introduce the industry of the Chinese, their arts of living and improvements in husbandry, as well as their native plants, America might in time become as populous as China.[54]

This is the sort of interest in China that prevailed in the decades before the initiation of direct trade with Asia. An erudite gentleman of Newport named Metcalf Bowler, who we meet in chapter 3, collected Chinese dishes (many of them taken as booty) decorated with graceful garden scenes. Bowler also participated in a learned veneration of China. After having made his fortune running privateers in the French and Indian Wars, he retired to a private country estate where he elaborated a new identity, turning his attention to farming. In 1786 he authored a treatise on agriculture that opens with a passage praising the agricultural practices of the Chinese emperor, using him as an exemplar and revering Chinese wisdom on such matters.[55] Perhaps he read his reverence of Chinese agriculture back into his flowery plates, but we have no evidence for this and no encouragement from any sort of corroborative accounts from other enlightened gentlemen owning porcelain as to their curiosity about the images on their dishes.

Given the exuberant fascination with not only Chinese aesthetics but with Chinese philosophy and modes of living, it would seem that European and American ignorance of the noisy cultural content of porcelain's design motifs was *deliberate*. What stands out as immediately more important to Americans than the substantive Chinese imagery contained in the potter's painted designs—what one might call the soul of the object—was porcelain's synecdochical quality of remote exoticism, an Eastern geographical identity, and, ultimately, commerce in the bizarre and unfamiliar "Orient." The pot lost its original Chinese cultural identity and became merely a Chinese commodity, emptied of soul and refilled with capitalist insatiability and consumer narcissism. It became a sign of magnificent commerce. The imagery on porcelain was then glossed as characteristically oriental, fueling a derivative style of rococo chinoiserie that debased not only the Chinese symbols on the pot but the Chinese themselves. Chinoiserie exemplifies a deliberate resistance to respect the soul in the object. The convoluted reinterpretation of a so-called Chinese aesthetic emerging in Anglo-American japanned furniture (fig. I.7) is explored in chapters 2 and 4.

Part of the problem of taking a china pot as a stand-in for anything authentically Chinese was the gross decontextualization that transpired in the process of long-distance trade and commodification. English author Oliver

I.7. High chest, 1735–45, owned by Josiah Quincy, Boston, MA, and believed to have been japanned by Robert Davis. Quincy became rich after raiding a Spanish ship and then moved to a country estate in Braintree, with the chinoiserie chest. "Owning a japanned piece meant being part of a cultured elite" (Nancy Carlisle, curator for Historic New England collection, *Cherished Possessions: A New England Legacy* [Boston: SPNEA, 2000]). Gift of Edmund Quincy, 1972.51. Photo: Peter Harholdt. Courtesy of Historic New England (RS 32658).

Goldsmith alludes to this problem in his fictional work *Citizen of the World, or Letters from a Chinese Philosopher*. Here a native of Honan, China, visits an English lady who dutifully points out all her Chinese objects for him, commenting that they are beautiful but have no use. He rebuts that nothing divorced from its purpose can be truly beautiful. In this case they become "flimsy" or as he observes, "precarious." "She took me through several rooms all furnished as she told me in the Chinese manner; sprawling draggons, squatting pagods, and clumsy mandarines, were stuck upon every shelf: in turning around one must have used caution not to demolish a part of the *precarious* furniture."[56] The problem with imports was that they were not tied to the land or one's own manufacture. The china pieces stacked on the lady's shelves had been divorced from their intended use. I would add, more important, that the china had also been separated from its context of production, its maker. In the seventeenth century, Chinese commodities entered an English and English colonial social world that had hitherto revolved primarily around known producers and known consumers. With the vast distances between Europe and China, objects spent a much longer period of time as commodities, traveling in the soulless state between a prized object produced by one's own hands and a prized object owned and used within a domestic setting. The objects we make and the objects we live with become, in some sense, extensions of ourselves.[57] Over time the china in American homes became domesticated, by being repeatedly used in a loving way, by being handed down from parents to children, by acquiring familiar, local genealogies. But in the first half of the eighteenth century most Chinese porcelain was not yet "old" in that comfortable family way.[58] It still retained alien qualities, especially if it had been taken, bought, or pirated from yet another alien, and it perhaps even threateningly displayed another's coat of arms.

Furthermore, the production of porcelain was mystified in the West. Centuries of experimentation had produced only poor substitutes until the Germans perfected a hard-paste porcelain in 1709. But German porcelains did not circulate among Americans at all, nor most Europeans, until late in the century. England only developed a rival to Chinese porcelain in the late eighteenth century by resorting finally to bone ash, yielding a soft-paste porcelain.[59] There was in Europe an obsessive, competitive fixation on their lack of mastery of the technology for producing both porcelain and lacquer wares. The Saxon prince Augustus the Strong—whose name implies a man who could not be left behind—went so far as to imprison an alchemist for years until he developed a means to produce porcelain.[60] Indeed this competitive spirit manifests itself as poor sportsmanship when the European producer, working with a poor substitute, paints the Chinese master producer as a doddering, childlike figure dwarfed by a tropical climate of strange flora and fauna. As long as Chinese porcelain retained its status as an imported commodity, and as a product of an inaccessible, mystified technology, it would exude first and foremost all the desire and risks inherent in the East Indies trade. In other words, throughout the eighteenth century in both England and America, it retained its status as a commodified icon of commerce—an awesome, dangerous, and virile commerce—to the exclusion of any meaning it might have had as a work of art with a genius loci.

Across the Anglo-American world, commercial competitiveness interfered with the intellectual ability to cultivate an appreciation and respect for the beautiful, complex symbolic world artistically depicted on the Chinese pot. Anthropologist Arjun Appadurai defines the situation of being a commodity in the "social life" of an object as that in which the object's exchangeability becomes its most relevant social feature. He also cautions that we should not assume that commodity exchange presupposes "a complete cultural sharing of assumptions."[61] Clearly, in the case of European and American acquisition of Chinese porcelain, very little culture was exchanged, outside the dirty business of commerce between two peoples who were highly suspicious of each other. Western purchasers and consumers were far removed from chinaware's productive source, encouraging a deliberate disregard of the commodity's cultural persona, emptying it of its soul, and allowing it to be appropriated for other imaginative purposes. In this geographically and temporally distended commodity context, the Chinese potter and merchant were debased along with the Chinese figure on the pot.

In an integrated examination of trade and ownership, Chinese export porcelain, lacquer, and tea serve here as guides, leading us deeply into the colonial American cultural landscape. The story line of American colonial history has been divorced from European exploits in Asia. Refined artifacts of Chinese industry and agriculture found in northern colonial homes allow us to see how the two seemingly distinct historiographical fields of Europe's East Indies enterprises and colonial America are related. Americans throughout the colonial period were greatly impacted by—indeed, participated in—the growing European fixation on Chinese commodities and styles. Euro-America's relationship to European activities in the East contributed to the formation of a distinctly American cultural life. The chapters that follow examine the trade for and distribution of Chinese porcelain, tea, and lacquer in the northern colonies in conjunction with an examination of the complex cultural fabric of colonial American interest in China. Without looking at both the macro (trade) and micro (household) engagements with China and the European East Indies trades, we miss an important piece of the American dispute with England—we miss the profound connection between American *economic* and *political* choices at the time of the revolution and England's ambitions in Asia.

The evidence that follows seeks to recover the commercial, political, and ideological significance of the East Indies trades, and of China in particular, to northern colonists during the century preceding the American China trade.

The following five chapters alternate between examinations of trade and domestic consumption of Chinese commodities and aesthetic. This allows us to see the linkages, real and conceptual, between the material culture in colonial homes and colonial American commerce. Americans had a vigorous enthusiasm for trade, necessary to a people dependent on imports from the beginning of colonization, and they were willing to break the law to participate in global trade. Chapter 1, "The First American China Trade," offers evidence for American mariners and sea captains who sailed to the Indian Ocean at the end of the seventeenth century and the repressive response by English imperial power brokers. This chapter demonstrates that, even before the eighteenth century, colonial Americans had broad awareness of the lucrative East Indies trades, an interest in competing in that arena, and a local market for Chinese commodities. Their behaviors and discourses related to these voyages also reveal that Americans had little respect for the all the peoples beyond the Atlantic, who they by and large called "infidels."

Chapter 2, "Imagining China at Home," focuses on a series of chinoiserie wall murals created by a Newport painter in the 1720s. The murals offer evidence that artisan-class New Englanders were completely fluent in the latest metropolitan chinoiserie fashions and were also familiar with authentic Chinese design sources such as lacquer screens and porcelain with figural motifs. Moreover, analysis of the murals' dark content shows that Americans, like their English cousins, had complex, conflicting attitudes toward a geographically imprecise China, influenced by a rich variety of textual and visual sources, including ongoing popular depictions of the medieval Ottomans and contemporary world "histories."

The third chapter, "Islands of Illicit Refinement," returns explicitly to commerce, providing primary evidence for the extent of extra-imperial trade on the part of northern colonials, especially in the Caribbean. There Americans had access to a wide array of "East India" goods as well as to American silver, on which all the China trades depended. This chapter also includes a study of Chinese porcelain found in over a thousand probate inventories from five regions in the north, showing that china was present earlier and in greater quantities than historians and curators have acknowledged. This evidence makes clear that Americans were completely involved with the circuits of trade that reached beyond the Atlantic. In this worldly arena of trade and consumption they ran up against two powerful ideological strains that were inflected in their use of Chinese commodities, that of the *potency* of imperial England and that of the *purity* of reformed Protestants.

How such ideological strains are embedded in the consumption of china is the focus of the fourth chapter, "The Oriental Aesthetic in Old Yankee Households." Here we examine the metaphorical tension mediated by colonists between indulging in the fruits of global capitalist enterprise and the plain living required by a collective xenophobic sense of virtue. American men might fall dupes to the perfidious Chinese commodities they consumed, becoming effeminate and servile like the faceless East Indians who produced them *for* Europeans. But the Chinese pot in the hands of a self-assured Yankee could also be a symbol of commercial and gender conquest, a sign that one lies on the right side of empire. Such a statement of imperial masculinity depended on the perceived Chineseness of the object.

American phobias about the feminizing, slave-making contamination carried in Chinese commodities reached a climax in the years preceding the revolution, just as the mother country became the dominant imperial, colonizing force in Asia. This final chapter, "Manly Tea Parties," puts the Chinese tea back into the mutinous Boston Tea Party. Here we recapture American participation in imperial longing for Chinese material and cultural sophistication alongside their deeply embedded, puritanical prejudices against Asians. Both emotions underlay the revolutionary "spark" of 1773. At a time when American consumption of tea and china was soaring, touching all classes of colonial society, especially Bostonians, resistance to imperial trade policies sprang not merely from their relationship to *British* imports but also from their complex relationship to the most valuable fruits of trade, Chinese commodities. Anxieties about the consumption of specifically East Asian commodities permeate revolutionary rhetoric. For Americans the choice to rebel was deeply connected to the global span of the British imperial world, which was increasingly characterized by a polarity between slaves and masters. At the end of the Seven Years' War, English masters controlled global oceanic trade and Africans, Asians, and *Americans* were destined to serve them. In awe of the power within this empire, Anglo-Americans could let Britain force-feed them tea and other Asian "luxuries" and become slaves themselves, or they could take charge of this high-stakes trade, retaining their masculinity and English heritage as freemen and masters of both themselves and others.

When Americans from Baltimore to Salem fitted out ships to sail to China before the ink was even dry on the 1783 Peace of Paris, they were moved by decades of involvement in the European East Indies trades and early modern orientalism. The American China trade did not begin in 1783 but in the seventeenth century, as it did in the rest of the Northern European Atlantic. Beliefs and commercial markets nurtured throughout the colonial period on American soil gave the American China trade its character. If we are to understand the American China trade that immediately followed the successful war for independence, it is necessary to first acknowledge the decades-old engagement with China and the imagined East Indian realms that preceded it.

1

The First American China Trade

American Mariners in the Indian Ocean, 1690–1700

Since the discovery of the East-Indies, the dominion of the sea depends
much upon the wane or increase of that trade, and consequently the security of the liberty, property, and protestant religion of this kingdom.
— Josiah Child, director of the East India Company, 1681

A World of Wealth across the Atlantic

In the summer of 1693, Jamaica's acting governor Sir William Beeston
wrote a series of letters to the Lords of Trade and Plantations in
London complaining about the "northern plantations." Not unlike
rivalry between children of a domineering parent, the child least
prone to virtue—indeed Jamaica had been called "as Wicked as the
Devil" by one visitor[1]—points superciliously at the foibles of siblings
with more virtuous pretensions. Beeston's complaint extended from
Quaker Pennsylvania to Puritan Massachusetts, including everything

27

reformed, English, and self-righteous in between. Many fine Jamaican mariners, he wrote, had found their way to the Red Sea, and "are now returned with vast wealth to most of the northern plantations of America where they quietly enjoy their ill-gotten riches."[2] Beeston's remarks, however filled with jealousy, were not isolated rhetorical instances.

The distasteful image of northern colonists quietly enjoying wealth from Asia is borne out repeatedly in the official correspondence to London in the 1690s. Two years after Beeston, Peter Delanoy in Albany wrote to the Lords of Trade, "We have a parcel of pirates, called the Red Sea men, in these parts, who get great booty of Arabian gold. The Governor encourages them since they make due acknowledgement." Delanoy also complained of gifts of "jewels" brought by the Red Sea men.[3] In the same month Sir Thomas Laurence, secretary of Maryland, reported on colonial affairs to the Lords of Trade, recounting that these Red Sea men "came out directly to Pennsylvania, New York and New England and from these places fit out again to the Red Sea. Their sharing such large sums tempts the people of these parts to go along with them, and they are a great hindrance to trade, for the seamen run from the merchant ships to go with them, as do also many men from the King's ships. They grow very numerous."[4] Laurence's remarks implicate not only disenchanted Atlantic "seamen," who notably are growing "very numerous," but "the people" as well. The people on the western side of the Atlantic, comprised of merchants, shopkeepers, and all levels of colonial officialdom, used the terms "Red Sea men" or "mariners," not "East India men" or "privateers," or for that matter "pirates."[5] American consumers, like Europeans, in the seventeenth century wanted access to Asian luxury goods and wealth, and they developed and legitimated their own methods and terminology for doing so specific to their perceived role and place within an Atlantic political economy.

Laurence's, Delanoy's, and Beeston's complaints bear a close resemblance to the imperious commentary on colonial consumption and wealth by British officials in the decade preceding the American Revolution, a discourse much more precisely documented by historians than this of seventy-five years earlier. But, as we see in the above remarks, imported goods and consumption were politicized within the English colonies much earlier.[6] Within the emerging power structure of the first British Empire, Americans were to be viewed either as consumers of British manufactures or suppliers of exotic raw materials, never competitors in trade. Although wealth-seeking, globe-trotting Anglo-Americans did not see themselves as subordinate subjects—many, especially those in former Dutch colonies, did not see themselves as English subjects at all—they were indeed considered subordinate and exploitable by the London

metropolis. Yet the range of material goods and worldly sophistication of colonial consumers, and the assertiveness of American traders, reached a high
point in the 1690s, and foreign wealth attracted the attention of the English
government. Colonial consumers became locked in a confrontation with the
English government over their access to foreign goods, including goods coming from beyond the Cape of Good Hope. In all such cases during the colonial
period, new laws were created that allowed English officials to label American
merchants, traders, and consumers as outlaws, whether "pirates," "smugglers,"
or "upstarts." Over the course of the seventeenth century the consumer market
for Asian commodities in northern Europe grew exponentially, and the ruling
English elite became increasingly jealous of this valuable trade, both within
and without England. Through new legal codes and new rhetoric, the English
government sought to obliterate independent access by all "interlopers," including Anglo-American mariners and merchants, to the trade of the so-called
East Indies.[7] The most important and obvious difference between the earlier
and later colonial periods is that, unlike the conflict of the 1760s and 1770s,
that of the 1690s did not end in a revolution but rather in *overt* compliance
to new imperial laws and regulations that forbade Americans direct access to
foreign wealth. Americans acquiring commodities from the Eastern seas were
labeled pirates, and so history has left them, marginalized, ever since.

This chapter examines these American "pirates" and the goods they
brought to America with the objective of demonstrating that, decades before
the American Revolution, Anglo-Americans did, in fact, have direct access to
the porcelains and lacquers of Asia—objects that constituted an early modern
"China-mania" and the aesthetic basis of chinoiserie styles on both sides of
the Atlantic.[8] Evidence for Asian commodities is found in the estate inventories of men who either sailed to the Indian Ocean or supported those who
did. This chapter seeks to demonstrate that Americans, like all Europeans at
this time, were motivated by the imagined wealth of China and a profit-driven
desire to trade in Eastern manufactured exports.[9] They went about setting
up a trade relationship with the East based on the rough-and-tumble English model in use throughout the seventeenth century. American mariners
in the Indian Ocean were acting no differently than English "interlopers" and
"Company"officials had since their first appearance in Asia.[10] If a nationalist
revolution had occurred at the end of this period—say in the year 1700—as
it did seventy-five years later when many of the same trade conflicts between
England and the North American colonies were on the table, these American
"pirates" and their Asian "booty" might be remembered and discussed much
differently today than they are. In fact, they are not remembered at all. Like

its heroes, early American decorative arts might also have taken a different course. Ultimately, we see that the objects and material styles people within a particular region employ to define themselves are as dependent on political power and ideology as they are on numbers of traders, extent of trade, or any other conventional quantification of "direct" economic exposure, especially in the tightly interconnected globe of the year 1700.[11]

American Mariners in the Indian Ocean

Over the course of the last decade of the seventeenth century, references to more than thirty captains sailing between the Indian Ocean and northeast America are found in the flurry of papers sent to London from Indian and American colonial centers (see table 1.1 for a list of thirty-five names sailing at least thirty-seven vessels).[12] Most of the ships were armed and supported an average crew of eighty-five men. From these figures, we arrive at a very rough estimate of about 2,900 Americans who voyaged to Eastern waters at the end of the seventeenth century.[13] This figure may seem small, but its relative strength is impressive. It represents about 15 percent of the estimated number of men able to bear arms in 1693 in the colonies of Pennsylvania, New York, Connecticut, Rhode Island, and Massachusetts combined.[14] Moreover, this figure is probably higher as it is unlikely that every incoming Red Sea man was detected or precisely recorded by British officials, many of who directly benefited from the proceeds of the voyages. In April of 1698, for example, Edward Randolph, the surveyor general of North American customs, reported to the Crown from New York that five to six vessels from the Red Sea were on the coast of Pennsylvania, and a day later that another group of vessels from the Red Sea were on the coast of Connecticut, without ever giving any more specifics as to the names of the captains or their ships.[15] But even counting only the thirty-seven vessels for which we have names and dates, we end up with a very significant source of Asian commodities coming directly into the American colonies.

In the fluid world of seventeenth-century Atlantic maritime employment, it is difficult to identify the first "Americans" who traveled around the Cape of Good Hope. In his study of Anglo-American seafaring, Marcus Rediker points out that the crews and officers of English ships may have called any number of Atlantic ports home.[16] Seamen born in, residing in, or retiring to the North American colonies filled the berths of naval and merchant ships from both England and Holland. A large number had certainly voyaged to the Indian Ocean in East India Company or interloper vessels, or armed as

Table 1.1 Captains sailing to East Indies from America and/or returning to America in the 1690s* (captain's name,† American port[s], vessel name, date, crew size [where information available])

1.	Adam Baldridge:	New York, 1690
2.	William Mason:	New York, *Jacob*, 1689 Leisler commission, 80 men
3.	Capt. Alleson:	New York
4.	George (Josiah) Raynor:	New York and North Carolina, *Batchelor's Delight*, 1691, 80 men
5.	George Paris:	Philadelphia, 1691
6.	William Orr:	Philadelphia, 1691
7.	Edward Coats:	New York, *Nassau*, 1692, 70 men
8.	John Churcher:	New York, *Charles*, 1693, 20–30 men
9.	Henry Every:	Bahamas-Carolinas-Philadelphia, *Fancy (Charles)*, 1694, up to 180 men
10.	Capt. Want:	Philadelphia, *Dolphin*, 1693, 60 men
11.	Thomas Tew:	New York, *Amity* sloop, 1693, 50 men
12.	Daniel Smith:	Bermuda, 1694
13.	Thomas Wake:	Boston, *Susannah*, 1694, 70 men
14.	Joseph Faro (Farrow):	Rhode Island, 1694, *Portsmouth Adventure*, 60 men
15.	William Mayes:	Rhode Island, *Pearl*, 1694
16.	Richard Glover:	i. Boston, *Resolution*, 1693
17.	Richard Glover:	ii. Barbados, *Charming Mary*, 1695.
18.	John Hoar:	Rhode Island and New York, *John & Rebeckah*, 100 men.
19.	Thomas Moyston:	i. New York, *Katherine*, 1695, 20 men
20.	Thomas Moyston:	ii. New York, *Fortune*, 1697, 20 men
21.	Cornelius Jacobs:	New York, *Charles* [carried 19 passengers from Madagascar to New York]
22.	[?, Philipse owned]:	New York, *New York Merchant*, about 20 men
23.	Robert Colly:	Newport, *Pelican*, 100 men
24.	Samuel Burgess (former pirate):	New York, *Margaret*, 1695, 16 men
25.	William Kidd:	New York, *Adventure Galley*, 1696, 150 men
26.	Phillip Babington:	New England, *Mary*, 1696, 90 men
27.	Andrew Knott:	Boston, *Swift*, 1697, 10 men

(*continued*)

Table 1.1 (*continued*)

28. Capt. Stevens: [?]	
29. Richard Chivers:	Rhode Island, *Resolution*, 1698, 90 men
30. James Gillam:	i. Virginia, Rhode Island, and West Indies, *Diamond*, 1680s
31. James Gillam:	ii. Rhode Island & Boston, mutinied on EIC's *Mocha* Frigate, 1698†
32. Robert Culliford:	New York and New England, *Resolution* (*Mocha* frigate), 1698
33. Giles Shelley:	New York, *Nassau*, 1698
34. Joseph Bradish:	West Indies and New York, *Adventure*, 1698
35. John Coaster:	New York, 1699
36. Tempest Rogers:	West Indies, *Fidelio*, 1699
37. Carsten Leursen:	New York, 1699
[Also possibly George Cutler and Thomas Jones]	

*Sources: Legal depositions, declarations, and commissions, reprinted in John Franklin Jameson, *Privateering and Piracy in the Colonial Period: Illustrative Documents* (New York: Macmillan, 1923); *Calendar of State Papers, Colonial Series, America and West Indies, 1693–1701* (London: Public Records Office, 1903); Howard M. Chapin, *Privateer Ships and Sailors: The First Century of American Colonial Privateering 1625–1725* (Toulon: G. Mouton, 1926); Robert Ritchie, *Captain Kidd and the War against Pirates* (Harvard University Press, 1986); S. C. Hill, "Notes on Piracy in Eastern Waters," *The Indian Antiquary*, supplements (Jan. 1923– Oct. 1928); Jacob Judd, "Frederick Philipse and the Madagascar Trade," *New York Historical Society Quarterly* 47 (1963).

†Name spellings can be erratic.

‡See Gillam's own account published in *A Full and True Discovery . . . Capt. James Kelley* (London, 1700).

privateers and outlaws. The spectrum from naval vessel to outlaw, including all sorts of merchant and privateering vessels in the middle, was very blurry, and mariners slipped between different professional and civil statuses as easily as they jumped on and off different ships. A number of the vessels here identified as American may have originated in the British Isles or another part of Europe but ended up in America, at least for a time. While a high fluidity of populations between the American colonies and Europe is characteristic of the early colonial period, and even more so if we look at maritime communities, this has not deterred historians from labeling these people and the events associated with them on American soil as "American." The same rule applies to my use of "American" here.

Although some lightly armed, purely merchant Anglo-American vessels sailed to the Indian Ocean in the 1690s, heavily armed vessels were by far the most common. In addition to the growing presence of Company ships over the course of the seventeenth century, privateers and pirates swarmed into the three basins of the Indian Ocean, the Arabian Sea, the Bay of Bengal, and the South China Sea. Privateers were typically private merchant vessels, manned and armed as ships of war, and licensed by one of the home governments to do its dirty work of economic warfare. Privateers were given letters of marque from a government official allowing them to legally raid ships of the enemy, thereby debilitating that country's commerce. The legal range of privateering licenses varied, and some were issued purely as "letters of reprisal," allowing a captain armed retribution against ships of a country that had previously attacked his ship, if compensation had not been obtained within a specified amount of time. The structuring and restructuring of the rules governing the taking of prizes was hammered out between warring European states at the end of almost every conflict. But despite the great amount of official ink spilled over this topic, irregularities were commonplace. Ships' papers were regularly thrown overboard, cargoes broken open before adjudication, and prizes sunk and crews cast on remote islands.[17]

The key facet of a privateering commission—and the one that made it so difficult to govern—is that the privateer remained *private*. The vessel's owners could personally cash in on most of the captured cargo, after paying tribute, of course, to the official who issued the license. This official, moreover, bore little risk. No capital was required of him, only his signature, and at the end of a successful voyage, he would be handsomely rewarded. While away at sea with a commission to raid enemy vessels, captains were motivated by personal profit and easily fell out of touch with the inner sanctums of state-level treaty agreements. Proclamations of peace hundreds or even thousands of miles away often had little impact on the captain of a heavily armed, heavily manned ship, where every sailor as well as officer intended to pay his debts and live happily ever after thanks to the voyage. The average wages of merchant seamen, 25 to 40 shillings a month for crew members and £2 to £6 for officers, could not compete with £200 to £2,000 earned on a privateering or pirate voyage.[18] As England was officially at war four times with the Dutch, twice with the French, and three times with the Spanish during the seventeenth century—with a multitude of armed disputes and territory grabs occurring outside Europe—it was very easy to avoid peacetime trade altogether for the more lucrative bellicose "commerce."

Warlike behavior at sea became the norm, and, in the Indian Ocean of the seventeenth century, the English were arguably the worst offenders. In the late sixteenth century, English notables such as Francis Drake and Thomas Cavendish—who is said to have returned to England under sails of silk— wreaked havoc in the Pacific and Malay Archipelago, raiding both Spanish and Asian vessels. When the Dutch first appeared in Sumatra in 1596, they received a hostile reception from the natives, who mistook them for English pirates, "who were feared and hated in all parts of the world for the excesses they had committed three years earlier."[19] The first Englishman to sail up the Pearl River to Canton was Captain John Weddell, who had negotiated permission from the Portuguese in 1637. But when the Chinese kept him waiting longer than his patience allowed, he fired several rounds of cannon and managed to return to England with a hold full of Chinese sugar, ginger, cloves, gold, and porcelain. As an early nineteenth-century English historian observed, both Weddell's "excesses" and "rich booty" established a precedent and temptation for generations of English sailors to follow.[20] It also closed Chinese ports to the English for nearly another century. As late as November of 1690, the English Council in Madras was embarrassed by the arrival of twenty English captives sent by the Dutch from Batavia. These men had been caught raiding vessels off Malacca and were either unaware or ignoring the fact that the conflict with Holland, the fourth Anglo-Dutch war, had ended several years earlier. English officials were forced to concede that, indeed, these English sailors were therefore "pirates" rather than legitimate privateers. On such an English ship carousing Eastern waters at this date, there were very likely men who called—or would one day call—the American continent "home."[21]

The *Jacob* Sails East

In New York in 1689, governor Jacob Leisler outfitted one of the first recorded Indian Ocean voyages from America. Leisler had just usurped the governorship of New York following the coup d'état and ascendancy to the English throne of Holland's William of Orange. A German-born American, Leisler responded to his new position like the powerful Europeans: he immediately sent a ship overseas in search of fabulous Eastern trade goods. Leisler commissioned a captured French prize, renamed it the *Jacob*, and gave New Yorker William Mason command over its eighty-man crew.[22] After a stop in Rhode Island, the *Jacob* sailed directly to Madagascar, then on to India and the Red Sea before returning to New York in April of 1693, with its coffers loaded. Exactly what happened on its return is a scenario played out repeatedly in the 1690s.

In the details of the *Jacob*'s voyage, as told principally by crew member Samuel Burgess, we can surmise more about the nature of the inhabitants of the northern plantations and their commerce than from all the subsequent London-based acts of trade, which have provided the historiographical basis for labeling American traders in the Indian Ocean "pirates."[23] Our knowledge of the *Jacob*'s activities while abroad is spotty. Burgess, who spent most of the three-year voyage in Madagascar, does relate being on board for the taking of three ships in the Red Sea. The East India Company also sent letters to London complaining about depredations committed by Mason against Mughal vessels around the southern tip of India.[24] Like so many English ships, the *Jacob* may have been guilty of raiding more Asian vessels than European ones, if any from Europe at all. Although his commission directed him to raid ships from France, Mason, like many American sailors, probably had previous experience in the Atlantic fighting North African pirates, typically called "Turks." Even if he did not, he certainly knew that Leisler did. Sailing in a small pinke in 1678 from New York to Boston, via the wine islands off the coast of Iberia, Leisler, his sons, and nine crew members had been taken captive by Algerian raiders.[25] Leisler personally paid £2,280 in ransom for himself and his crew but lost his ship and cargo. Between 1674 and 1680, 350 English vessels, including many from America, had fallen into the hands of North African pirates.[26] Passengers crossing the Atlantic at this time often related their dread of being taken by the Turks.[27] While the English signed their first treaty with North African rulers in 1662, this and subsequent treaties were never upheld. Moreover, Americans were not protected under these agreements until 1700, when the Lords of Trade finally recommended that colonial traders have the same oversight as English merchantmen.[28]

Given this sort of experience, many American sailors may have shared the sentiments expressed in 1694 by the notorious English privateer Henry Every toward the nature of his "work" in the Indian Ocean. "To all English commanders," Every wrote in a letter to the East India Company, "let this satisfie . . . I have never as yet wronged any English or Dutch, nor ever intend whilst I am Commander." Then, in response to the several ships he had pillaged belonging to Aurangzeb, the Mughal emperor of Hindustan, Every writes, "my Men are hungry, Stout, and resolute, and should they exceed my Desire I cannot help myself."[29] Every commanded a diverse crew of over 150 men that included many American-born sailors as well as fifty-two Frenchmen and fourteen Danes. The distinction he made between European and non-European vessels was a well-established practice among the English by this time, with all Asian seafarers conflated under the designation "Turks" or other disparaging terms referencing religion or geography. Sixty years earlier King Charles I had written a privateering commission for a William Cobb, explicitly permitting him "to range the seas all over . . . and to make prize of all such treasures, merchandizes . . . which he shall be able to take of infidels or of any other

Prince, Potentate or State not in league with us beyond the Line Equinoctial [the Equator]."[30] In raiding "infidels," or indeed *anyone* beyond ideologically constituted geographic lines, Every's crew as well as the crew of the *Jacob* believed they acted within the cultural authority established by their rulers.[31] Every had many such role models when stating that he "fights under the flag of St. George" and "intends to make his fortune at the expense of the French, Spaniards, Portuguese, and Heathen."[32]

That identifiably American mariners also shared this prejudice against Asians is evident in a statement about Red Sea men made in 1699 by Nathaniel Coddington, a clerk in Rhode Island's admiralty court.

> All the vessels as spoken of whilst trimming and procuring victuals (many men came to them from all parts of this Country) and the discourse was Generally that they were bound to Madigaskar but some said they were to go to the Red Seas where the mony was as plenty as stones & sand, saying the people there was Infidels, & it was no sin to kill them.[33]

Whatever the *Jacob* did while in Eastern waters, when she returned to the coast of North America in 1693, her sailors were very wealthy men, claiming each about 1,800 Spanish silver dollars ("pieces-of-eight"[34]) and a certain amount of bulk cargo of East India goods. Mason pulled the vessel into Gardiner's Island on the eastern end of Long Island, where John Gardiner's virtually feudal manor stood. Here, independent of New York governance, Mason began to carefully feel out the political situation in New York after a three-year absence.[35] Indeed things had changed. Leisler had been overthrown and hung in a countercoup, and Benjamin Fletcher, a soldier of fortune and patron of King William's secretary of state, was now governor of the colony. Being uncertain of the validity of the *Jacob*'s commission under the new government and therefore the standing of her prize cargo, the crew took up a collection of 70 to 100 silver dollars each to offer the new governor. This small sacrifice would, in the words of Burgess, "prevent them from being put to trouble." Burgess himself sent the governor "two gold sequins" for his protection. Receiving encouragement from Fletcher, the ship sailed to New York, although about half the crew had already dispersed with their goods while on Long Island. William Nicoll, a New York merchant and city councilman, sailed eagerly out to the vessel and made further arrangements. The remainder of the crew left with their goods, Nicoll was paid 200 silver dollars, and the vessel was turned over to Fletcher. It came out in subsequent investigations by Fletcher's successor, Lord Bellomont, that in the end Nicoll received a total of 800 silver dollars and Fletcher, in addition to the ship (worth £800), received unspecified Asian gifts for his wife and daughters from the crew.[36] Although Fletcher later claimed to the Lords of Trade that the *Jacob*'s crew, "hearing that Leisler was dead, threw a great deal of East India goods overboard," this was certainly a smokescreen.[37]

Where the *Jacob*'s crew members went from Gardiner's Island and New York Harbor, what they did on their first days and nights back on home turf, and, most significantly for this study, what goods they carried with them, are all questions left unanswered in the documentary record. But one can be sure that Fletcher's wife and daughters were not the only women to receive gifts that week. In deposition after deposition made in the 1690s to admiralty officials, former privateers describe this very same sequence of events. Red Sea men return to an island or remote beach, a collection is made, many crew members flee with their goods, and the captain and a few others remain behind to obtain legitimacy and protection from colonial officials and leading merchants, always in exchange for gold, silver, and East India goods. In his deposition before the East India Company in 1696, mariner John Dann named the American vessels he had encountered in the Indian Ocean in 1693 alone.[38] There had been a Captain Want in a "Spanish bottom" fitted out near Philadelphia; Captains Joseph Faro and William Mayes with vessels fitted out in Rhode Island; a Captain Thomas Wake sailing a brigantine from Boston; and a Captain Thomas Tew commanding a Rhode Island sloop with a New York commission. In each case the vessels were manned with seventy to eighty men. Captain Want returned to Pennsylvania, offering gifts to Governor William Markham.[39] Tew allegedly returned to Rhode Island in 1694 with cargo valued at £100,000, and gifts were offered to Governor Caleb Carr.[40] Some of the remaining crew and cargo from these four vessels ended up on the ship of Captain Every, which put in at the Bahamas. There a collection of twenty dollars per man was made and gifts offered to Governor Nicholas Trott. Deponent Dann returned on this vessel and stated that, in addition to coins, Trott received "Elephants Teeth" and "some other things to the value of about £1000."[41] Unfortunately, here as in most cases the "other things" are left unspecified in official English records. By the 1690s, elite London was simply too heavily invested in the East Indies commerce to look lightly on such competition so far outside its ranks.

Asian Trade Circuits and New European Companies

The power and wealth of the English East India Company, based in London, swelled during the last decades of the seventeenth century as it became in-

creasingly tied to the government.[42] In 1683 Sir Josiah Child, a director of
the East India Company, repaid his loyal bookkeeper Mr. Vaux with a plum
job. "For his good Services and Behaviour, [Vaux] was preferred by his Master
to a Supercargo's Post in a ship to *China*, which Trade in those Times, was
the most profitable of any within the Limits of the Company's Charter."[43] A
hundred years earlier when the English had first sailed into Asian waters on
Sir Francis Drake's *Golden Hind*, they were merely rough-hewn adventurers
tramping after Spanish wealth.[44] In their unsophisticated ignorance of global
refinements, the idea of precious metals and jewels shone brighter than Chinese silks or porcelain. The "china mania" that gripped all of Europe by the
eighteenth century was only emerging. The rest of Asia, however, had been
under China's spell for at least a millennium. In about the year 980 an Arab
geographer named Al-Muqadassi described the Arabian Peninsula as being
surrounded by the waters of the "China Sea."[45] Such geographical slippage
does not indicate that Al-Muqaddasi was ignorant of all the sovereign territories between the Near and the Far East; he was simply less interested in them.
"The Indian Ocean derived its identity from an unspoken role assigned to the
Celestial Empire," historian K. N. Chaudhuri has pointed out. "They [Mus-
lim geographers] could see, as we can, that the sea that washed the desolate
beaches of the Suez or the marshes around Basra provided an unbroken means
of travel all the way to China."[46]

Knowledge of China's technical superiority and refined manufactures came
very early through the transcontinental trade known today as the "Silk Roads,"
a series of trans-Asiatic trading centers extending all the way to the Mediterranean and held together by ponderous camel caravans.[47] During the Song
dynasty (960–1279), control over the Silk Roads slipped away from China.
Chinese maritime trade came to supersede overland trade, shifting the major production centers southward while the wealthier patrons of the arts remained in the north. By the twelfth and thirteenth centuries, Mongol rulers
from the north governed China. With a population of 100 million, economically integrated over a vast territory, the Celestial Empire exerted an enormous
economic advantage.[48] The Chinese claimed to sail the world's largest ocean-
going vessels until the fifteenth century, when a Ming emperor, suspicious of
the growing power of coastal merchants and pirates—often considered one
and the same group—issued statutes outlawing a Chinese maritime fleet. But
these oft-cited government edicts were evaded, and thousands of Chinese
based in and out of China continued to trade by sea.[49] By the fifteenth century
Quanzhou and Canton were the two greatest mercantile cities in East Asia,
supporting large communities of Arab and Persian merchants.[50] This exten-

sive commercial network spanning outward from the China coast remained inured to political strife, civil wars, and foreign invasions. Foreign interest in Chinese goods sustained over centuries gave long-distance commercial routes time to become deeply entrenched at every waypoint, even to the degree that the Chinese origin of certain objects was superseded by the names of their transshipment centers: consider the Chinese porcelain called "Batavia ware" or the Chinese lacquered "Coromandel screens," examined in the next chapter.

Just as the traders defied political strife and edicts in continuing commerce, the rulers often ignored the traders and their oceanic realm, allowing commercial relations to thrive. "Wars by sea are merchants' affairs, and of no concern to the prestige of kings," Sultan Bahadur of Gujarat is alleged to have said when confronting the Portuguese for the first time.[51] A very different mentality was introduced by the Europeans, succinctly expressed by the English governor of Bombay in 1718. He said, "if no Naval Force no Trade, if no Fear no Friendship."[52] Certainly the rapid onslaught of armed European vessels, flying various flags from a continually warring, highly competitive, materially ambitious and jealous group of states altered the character of centuries-old, inter-Asian trade patterns. By the sixteenth century in Europe, state politics and oceanic commerce were inextricably entangled. As much as territory, monarchs and court patrons vied for the imported material prestige that garnered power, and there was no better *sign* of prestige than seaborne cargoes of mystifying and rare Chinese commodities, refined products beyond the scope of any European manufacturer's ability and knowledge.

Porcelain had been admired and imitated (unsuccessfully) outside China for hundreds of years before Europeans entered the Asiatic trade arena, and it provides an excellent example of the cultural exchanges occurring there. Blessed with an abundance of both china stone and kaolin, Chinese kilns produced porcelaneous wares as early as the eighth century in the Tang dynasty. No other ceramic could be fired to such a high temperature or yield a body so impermeable, white, and translucent. An export market for Chinese ceramics already existed, but with the development of this beautiful, vitreous pottery, demand increased. Some of the earliest specimens of Chinese porcelaneous wares have been found outside China, such as a tenth-century phoenix-head ewer made in a kiln at Chi-chou, about three hundred miles inland from Canton, found in the Philippines.[53] The impact of the development of an entirely unique and superior ceramic type had far-reaching consequences, not only within China but in all the far-flung potteries to the west.

The history of porcelain and the history of maritime trade in China go hand in hand. Heavy, fragile china dishes, difficult to carry overland, were easily packed by the thousands in the damp cargo holds of ships. Crated dishes were nested one within the other, providing marketable ballast and a boon to maritime commerce.[54] Ships crowded the harbor of Canton during the Southern Song dynasty (1128–1279), and as one merchant in the city remarked, "the greater part of the cargo consists of pottery, the small pieces packed in the larger, till there is not a crevice left."[55] The discovery and excavation in recent years of shipwrecked vessels dating from the ninth through the eighteenth centuries in the China Sea reveal the vast quantities of porcelain exported from the earliest days of its development.[56] An eighteen-meter, fourteenth-century Chinese ship found off the Malaysian coast, for example, carried about 10,000 pieces of ceramic, mostly the prized pale green celadon porcelain. A twenty-eight-meter, fifteenth-century wreck, also in Malaysian waters, carried 100,000 individual ceramics.[57] These ships were both sailing in the vicinity of the Straits of Malacca, a central exchange point for Arab and Indian traders taking Chinese goods to other parts of Asia[58]—and, not coincidentally, a popular destination for Anglo-American mariner-privateers in the seventeenth century.

The flourishing Muslim community in Canton and Quanzhou facilitated transoceanic exchanges of taste, design, and technology as well as goods. Metalwork, glass, crystal, and textiles flowed east from Persia and Syria, and silk and ceramics left China, all leaving their mark on local traditions. The pan-Asian market for porcelain expanded exponentially, and Chinese potters drew on Near Eastern forms and colors. The underglazed cobalt blue, soon to become the single most pronounced aesthetic component of Chinese porcelain in the West, was introduced to the Chinese by Persian merchants in the fourteenth century.[59] Porcelain by the boatload also reached the eastern ports of Africa, and shards have been found on archaeological sites hundreds of miles inland dating back to the Tang dynasty. Somalia was a major importer of porcelain, and some historians believe contact between Africans and Chinese extends back two thousand years.[60] As early as the ninth century Islamic communities had sprung up on the northern coast of Madagascar. By the fifteenth century in the northern towns of Madagascar, Islamic ceramics constituted only 10 to 20 percent of imported wares; Chinese celadons and Ming and Qing blue-and-whites and polychromes dominate ceramic assemblages from archaeological sites in the western Indian Ocean. They were regularly in use by Asian elites in this region at the time Europeans first arrived.[61] The Island of St. Mary's (also Ste. Marie; see Fig. 1.1), the late seventeenth-century provisioning station for so many mariners from North America, including

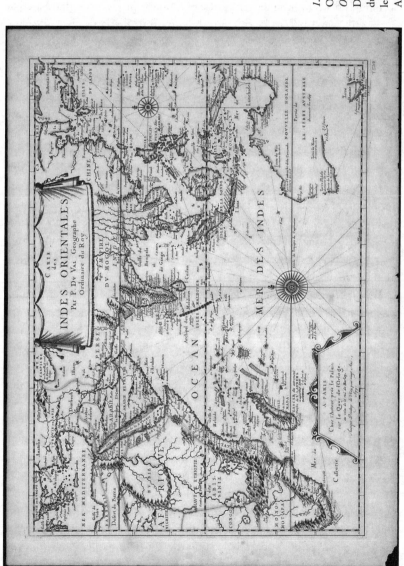

1.1. Map of the Indian Ocean, 1677. *Cartes des Indes Orientales*. Drawn by Pierre Du Val, Geographe Ordinaire du Roy. Rex Nan Kivell Collection, National Library of Australia (MAP NK 1532)

William Mason of the *Jacob*, is situated right alongside this northern coast and
would have a similar ceramic profile.

Getting Out of the Atlantic

It was into this Indian Ocean—an ancient and relatively apolitical oceanic
trading zone, integrating the majority of the world's most sophisticated em-
poriums and all throbbing to the pulse of Chinese producers—that Vasco de
Gama sailed in 1498, to be followed by a train of Iberian ships and subsequently ships of all European countries. The Spanish came from the Pacific
and never traveled further than the eastern Indian Ocean, finding a market for New World silver and many Chinese commodities readily available
among Chinese traders in Southeast Asia. The Portuguese, followed closely
by the Dutch, sailed across the Arabian Sea, across the Bay of Bengal, until
they reached the entrepôt of Malacca and the China Sea, carving out a place
for themselves in the complex inter-Asian trade circuits as they moved ever
eastward. The Portuguese established a presence in Canton by 1517 and were
most responsible for the steady flow of Chinese porcelains and lacquers into
Europe in the sixteenth century. In the seventeenth century, however, it was arguably the Dutch who made the deepest impact in Asian trade by moving into
the Pacific, setting up trade depots in Taiwan and Nagasaki, and ultimately
inserting a strong European presence in ancient inter-Asian commercial routes
from Persia to Japan.[62]

Despite Drake's precocious Pacific crossing, the English also preferred the
western approach to Asian trade.[63] But it was not until 110 years after the English East India Company was chartered in 1600 that it finally gained access
to the Chinese coast and was permitted by the Chinese to build a factory in
Canton. The delay was not for lack of trying, as seen in the 1637 attempt of
Captain Weddell, nor for lack of interest, as seen in Child's 1683 promotion
of a valued servant to the "China trade." Even without access to China—until
a mere seventy years before US ships arrived in China—England still had a
thriving China trade. A market and taste for porcelain and other Chinese
products had caught fire in England decades before the English traded directly on the Chinese coast. Nearby Holland offered a ready market for prized
Eastern commodities, as did seaports in India and the western Indian Ocean,
regularly frequented by the English East India Company and English "interlopers" throughout the seventeenth century. When James I granted the East
India Company a "perpetual renewed charter" in 1610, a celebration followed

on board the largest ship in the realm, where "the whole party was served entirely upon Chinaware, then a most elegant rarity."[64]

The North American colonies were affected by the magnetic economic pull of the Far East as much as every other shipbuilding region in the Atlantic, despite their official absence from the China coast. Unlike the southern plantations, residents in the northern plantations owned the vast majority of their own shipping, giving them a vested interest in general maritime commerce (as opposed to a specific staple crop or resource that was then transported by others). Between 1666 and 1714, 70 percent of Massachusetts shipping was owned by locals as opposed to European residents. This number was ever on the rise, increasing to 87 percent by the revolution, exerting competitive pressure on local shipowners to find marketable commodities—wares that would sell, wares that would appeal to local buyers.[65] Americans, like everyone else around the Atlantic, were great admirers of refined Asian products and willing to pay more for them. In 1686 over half of the exports from England to the North American colonies were textiles, and nearly half of those textiles were Asian silks.[66] It is impossible to reconstruct an "Atlantic World," as so many historians have done, apart from the centripetal economic force of the trading world of the Indian Ocean;[67] and this would be especially true for regions heavily invested in the shipping trades such as Massachusetts, Rhode Island, New York, and Pennsylvania.

Regulating Irrepressible American Consumers

Despite the broad-based cultural interest in the East across the European Atlantic, any concrete attempt by Anglo-American traders to tangibly link themselves to Asia threatened to decentralize England—its economic, political, and ideological centrality within an emerging Whig conception of its imperial body. Shortly after arriving in New York in 1698, the new governor, Richard Coote, Earl of Bellomont, wrote anxiously to the Lords of Trade in London that the colony's former governor had been transacting business with Madagascar without consent "in a matter so highly relating to His Maj'ties Crown and dignity and of so great consequence to the East India Trade of Engld."[68] Few issues were as significant to the dignity of the Crown—and more to the point, the power base of Parliament—than the so-called East India trade. Any independent attempts at trade in the Indian Ocean brought on, therefore, an immediate retaliatory and regulatory response. Adolph Philipse, son of New York merchant Frederick Philipse, the foremost initiator of nonmilitarized trade to Madagascar, bemoaned this situation in a 1698 letter to an English colleague:

> We had a ship come in Lately from the East Indies, that brought home several of that Country comodities. And they are so Extream Severe & Strict at N. York that wee are Lost to Import them there. And tho that trade be as free as any other (the Company not having Such authority and privilidges as formerly).[69]

Statutes put forth by King William and his parliament a few months later reinstated the East India Company's monopoly, legally closing the Indian Ocean for the next three-quarters of a century to American traders.[70]

Meanwhile young American-born Adolph Philipse had an order for porcelain and lacquer outstanding. Before his father's vessel, the *Margaret*, had set sail, he had entrusted its captain, Samuel Burgess, with a few valuable items to barter "at St. Mary's, Maskarin, Madagascar, or elsewhere" for "a verry good Cabinet . . . Costs what it wil" and "So much good China Ware (of the best) as wil fit a Mantel peice."[71] "Maskarin," or the Mascarene Islands, was situated to the east of Madagascar and, like that island, was a centuries-old waypoint in the east-west trading world of the Indian Ocean. The special-order porcelain and lacquered cabinet would have originated in China. As we have seen, Chinese products had circulated in the western Indian Ocean for centuries by this time, and distinctly Far Eastern goods were typically prefaced in Europe with the adjective "India," such as "India china." Thomas Roe, for example, states in his seventeenth-century publication, "I thought all India a China shop, and that I should furnish all my Frendes with rarietyes."[72] In 1697 Josiah Child, who had over thirty years' experience in the Indian Ocean, published a pamphlet arguing that India was valuable to England for its textiles and "China-ware."[73] But porcelain was not manufactured in India. The important point here is that, while Americans often did not sail further than the coast of India, this did not hinder their access to prized goods from China, as seen in Philipse's special order. Neither had it hindered English access to Chinese commodities throughout the seventeenth century. Chinese products remained the most highly valued of all Asian products, and they were readily available across the Indian Ocean. Going all the way to China was not necessary to obtain Chinese wares, although it was a mark of manly pride (evident in Child's 1683 promotion of Vaux and, a hundred years later, the many boastful accounts of Americans sailing east in the American China trade).

By the time ships based in the North American colonies entered the Indian Ocean in the late seventeenth century, the exchange of goods occurring there was extremely sophisticated, with products from all over the East circulating on all sorts of different carriers to and from any number of diverse geographic locations, covering distances much greater than most in the Atlantic. Americans, like the northern Europeans generally, simplified their discourse about the East, calling this vast, complex region "India" or "the East Indies." This geographic imprecision and vagueness continued until the nineteenth century. In stark contrast to the Eurocentric bent of most historiography about seventeenth-century maritime trade, over 80 percent of Chinese ceramics were exported to other Asian countries in the late Ming period (ca. 1620–43), with only 16 percent traveling to Europe.[74] Inter-Asian trade networks were extremely dense. Despite a certain level of intellectual fascination with the places of the East, and a fairly large number of English-language travel narratives and Jesuit accounts on the distinct regions of that part of the world, Americans were overwhelmingly focused on trade in commodities and the need to take advantage of cheap labor, price discrepancies, and materials and manufactures not available in Europe. In a word, they were interested in exploitation. The incompatibility of economic opportunism and a heightened humanist interest in the geographic places and people making the luxury wares so valued in the North Atlantic was discussed in the previous chapter. It may have been the case that a certain ambiguity about cultural origins was perhaps necessary to keep Eastern peoples and their wares exotic on a Western market.[75] As a leading historian today of Asian export art has said, "Chinese ceramics, furnishings, wallpapers and furniture are sometimes treated as honorary British objects, with little consciousness of the cultural context from which they sprang."[76]

We do not know if young Philipse ever managed to sneak his desired Chinese luxuries into New York under the new climate of British jealousy regarding East India goods. But we do have his estate inventory, taken fifty years later, which contains an enormous holding of china as well as lacquered furniture spread over several Hudson Valley properties.[77] Perhaps more significant for gleaning the types of Asian objects brought into America in the 1690s are the surviving estate inventories for two of the sea captains who sailed to the Indian Ocean. Cornelius Jacobs (d. 1700) and Giles Shelley (d. 1718) both commanded vessels for Philipse's father, Frederick. They were also called "pirates" by Bellomont, although they were well regarded within their communities. Whatever the label, Shelley and Jacobs were spared the gallows and lived to enjoy the fruits of their "private adventures" of East India goods. It was standard practice for the East India Company as well as independent merchants to allow their captains and other officers a certain amount of private trade, called "adventure," which they purchased on their own account for their own profit.

It was this private trade that was always responsible for the highest quality Asian products in Western markets, the products that "created a revolution in perception, affecting all fields of art and design."[78] It is also this trade that makes it difficult to find documentation for incoming porcelain and lacquer, as private adventure cargo was largely undocumented. Jacobs's probate inventory lists the following tantalizing commodities: "1 Chyne Lacked Bole," "a parcel Chyne ware," "3 Eastindia Small Trunks," a page listing bolts of Asian textiles, including "striped Bengal," "Persian Silke," "flower'd Silke," muslins and calicoes, and many finished silk and muslin clothes and tapestries.[79] His inventory also contained various types of Spanish and Arabian coins and a gold-chained pearl. Shelley's inventory of eighteen years later is five times as long and worth that much more, probably because he lived longer. Although it does not specifically mention china in any of its orthographic incarnations in the West (*cheney, chainie, chinaia*), the twenty-one cups, chocolate cups, a teapot, and many "punch boles" are all probably porcelain. The absence of the word may be due more to the political culture surrounding China and Chinese goods than to a genuine absence of porcelain in his household. But there is an abundance of muslin and silk clothing and textiles, an "East India sash," "India carpets," and many maps, "Landskips," and pictures, indicating his worldly interests. Also listed are "images." These were typically small, pure white statues made from a soft-paste porcelain from Dehua, located in Fujian Province about seventy miles from the port of Xiamen (today called "blanc-de-chine"). They were popular mantelpiece objects found in many American estate inventories at this time. Many represented the Chinese goddess of mercy, Guanyin, who was often sculpted holding a child in response to Portuguese and Spanish demands for images of the Virgin and Babe, but hundreds of other little figures from popular Chinese and Buddhist culture are found, such as the Buddha himself, scholars by rocks, small beasts, and boys on buffaloes (see fig. I-1). Many of the same themes from Chinese religions and popular culture were presented on the face of porcelain dishes as well.

Regulating Eastern and Western Bodies

Red Sea men returning to the northern plantations in the 1690s generally seem to have received a welcome reception by the inhabitants. There was a readiness with which their goods and their persons were absorbed, quickly becoming part of the colonial landscape. Setting aside for the moment the legal, political, and ideological status London ascribed to Americans voyaging to the East Indies, let us try to recover the status these individuals and their wares had within the northern colonies. When interrogated about his dealings with the crew of the *Jacob*, New York merchant and town councillor William Nicolls acknowledged that he had indeed received money for his services, but he knew no pirates.[80] While this may seem like the obvious self-serving response during an inquisition on piracy, other testimony during this same meeting indicates that Nicolls was not the only New Yorker having difficulty defining piracy at that time. A Captain Evans of the *H.M.S. Richmond* had told Lord Bellomont that he could fulfill his crew quota for a voyage to London with privateers from Captain Alleson's vessel, which had just returned from Madagascar. When Bellomont later raided the *Richmond*, accusing Evans of using "pirates" to man his ship, Evans protested that he "knew of no pirates on board his ship ... and would not suffer them."[81] Although successfully villified by Bellomont, former governor Fletcher's impression of one of the most notorious Indian Ocean pirates, Thomas Tew of Rhode Island, may approximate colonial attitudes toward the Red Sea men. Fletcher said of Tew:

> This Tew appeared to me not only a man of courage and activity, but of the greatest sence and remembrance of what he had seen, of any seaman I had mett. He was allso what they call a very pleasant man; soe that at times when the labours of my day were over it was some divertisement as well as information to me, to heare him talke. I wish'd in my mind to make him a sober man, and in particular to reclaime him from that vile habit of swearing. I gave him a booke to that purpose.[82]

Fletcher was probably not the only colonial resident privy to Tew's stories and impressed by his worldliness, nor the only one to discount his coarse seafaring ways. In a New York council meeting with Lord Bellomont, clerk Chidley Brooke observed that protecting pirates had never been much cause for concern and that "all the neighboring Governments had done it commonly." Bellomont abruptly informed him that from now on the King and his ministers regarded it as a high crime, to which Brooke responded that he was not defending piracy, rather merely telling the governor what had always been accepted practice.[83]

By 1699 Governor Bellomont was aggressively pursuing the colonial "pirates" and their sumptuous treasures, leaving historians a valuable, albeit one-sided, record of their activities. In his correspondence, and that of a handful of dutiful colonial agents, there is a constant refrain that calls forth images of uncouth, unworthy colonial upstarts sneaking off with piles of unspecified "East India commodities." Edward Randolph complained to the Lords of Trade in

May of 1698, for example, that eight "pirates" had just arrived in Rhode Island from Fisher's Island with a "great deal of money and East India commodities." They fled to Boston when his ship arrived, he alleged, "with a great quantity of goods and money."[84] In his letters, Randolph described the native-born colonial governors presiding over this influx of Asian commodities variously as "illiterate," "infirm," and "ignorant."[85] He urged the king to take strong control of "all these petty independent Plantations," pointing out "should a hundred Acts be made for their regulation, they will never be Obeyed."[86] The king responded, not by altering the charters of Rhode Island and Connecticut, which he viewed as not worth the political battle, nor by offering royal cruisers to police the coast, but by uniting New York and New England into the Dominion of New England and leaving the policing to their newly appointed governor.

Randolph had been in the colonies as a royal agent, and anti-Puritan, for over twenty years, residing in Boston and steadfastly defending Crown prerogatives against wayward colonial traders and seafarers. Coote, or Lord Bellomont, was certainly a positive addition to his unwavering cause. But Bellomont, unlike Randolph, had landed in New York in 1698 in a desperate attempt to restore his waning place in the royal retinue rather than due to any experience or interest in the American colonies. The status and security of the Coote family in English aristocracy derived from a peerage in ever-unstable western Ireland, and Bellomont had a long history of straitened personal finances. Like his father, grandfather, and great-grandfather before him, Bellomont displayed staunch loyalty to reigning monarchs in return for a livelihood. He had little regard for colonials or commerce. His game was entirely made of land, titles, and royal favor. His overriding objective in governing New York and Massachusetts was to *appear* to promote the monarch's interest so as to bask in royal favor and remuneration—the only way he knew how to survive.[87] That any coins, jewels, or precious Asian status objects might flow into private hands was contrary to Bellomont's thoroughly hierarchical worldview, in which such things were only permissible as gifted or granted *within* court privilege, not *outside* it.

Bellomont and his small corps of loyal officials faced a number of genuine and pressing political concerns in 1698, in addition to port corruption and smuggled East India goods. These included settling land and border disputes between the colonies, Native American claims and hostility, and raising and paying for defense. It is not the intention of this chapter to rehash the administrative and juridical growing pains of the British Empire in North America at this critical juncture. Historians continue to give these important late seventeenth-century issues the attention they deserve.[88] The goal here is rather to call attention to one smaller aspect of this imperial crisis that has received less attention or been treated as unrelated to the issues mentioned above, issues that are presumed to be—and therefore become—more salient. The "Red Sea men," as they were called in the colonies, or "pirates," as English officials labeled them, were so successfully villainized that their activities have been marginalized as a side story of American history.

When William Kidd sent Lady Bellomont a Chinese lacquered box containing four jewels, the tainted merchandise was promptly returned. Bellomont alleged the jewels were meretricious, berating New Yorkers by saying, "there is nobody here that understands Jewels."[89] Bellomont raised his nose where other governors had given in to temptation, allowing alluring Eastern commodities to enter circulation in the colonies. In this epoch of witch-hunting par excellence, Bellomont proceeded to lead a veritable witch hunt for anyone with East India goods. Just as the mole served as a sign of communing with the devil in New England, a porcelain pot or lacquered box became a sign of communing with pirates—and, unlike the former example, history has let stand the ideological fabrication of the latter. As in the contemporaneous witch panics, the paranoia surrounding East India goods stemmed from elite, male power brokers who feared an evil that lay out of sight, deep within a society's most intimate or female realms. In his witch hunt for East India goods, Bellomont searched the homes of Jonathan Selleck of Connecticut, Duncan Campbell and Andrew Knott of Boston, Thomas Paine of Conanicut Island, John Gardiner of Gardiner's Island, Francis Dowell of Charlestown, and a large number of New York homes.

Bellomont went even further than searching within the intimate spaces of colonial homes to searching the very body of American suspects for evidence of East India contact. In 1696, following brutal treatment by their captain, James Gillam and his crewmates mutinied on board an East India Company ship near the Straits of Malacca and killed the captain. After spending time in India, Gillam returned to America on board William Kidd's ship in 1699. On a tip from an admiralty court judge in Rhode Island that Gillam had moved on to Boston, Bellomont sought help in tracking the seaman down but got no local cooperation; nevertheless he managed to locate Gillam. Bellomont had heard from an acquaintance in the East India Company that Gillam had not only killed the captain, but worse, had "served the Mogul, turned Mahometan and was Circumcised." He promptly had Gillam strip-searched by "a surgeon and also a Jew in this Town, to know if he were Circumcised." Both witnesses declared on oath that Gillam was indeed circumcised. Bellomont had his hands full with pirates, but he gave Gillam the honor of being "the most impudent hardened Villain I ever saw in my whole life." He was certainly not a kindred soul in any case.

The independent-minded Quakers in Pennsylvania had their own approach to gift-bearing sea marauders as well. Randolph called William Markham, governor of Pennsylvania, the pirates' "steady friend." Former Red Sea men settled down in Philadelphia and took up businesses in town, as did for example Danish sailor Peter Claus, who opened a shop there. Many married local women, and even the governor's daughter accepted a proposal from Red Sea man James Brown. Under examination by Randolph, both Claus and Brown acknowledged having taken prizes off the coast of Persia and stopping in Madagascar, but they claimed not to realize they were on piratical voyages.[90] Governor Markham, meanwhile, staunchly defended them and other accused pirates. A Robert Snead was sent to Pennsylvania by Crown officials to deal with Markham. This emissary visited Markham, informing the governor that he (Snead) was under oath as a magistrate to bring in the pirates. Markham countered saying the Red Sea men were civil to him and had brought many advantages to his colony. The theater of resistance that Snead then describes to the Lords of Trade is quite interesting. He reports,

> [Markham's] wife and daughter (as I was afterward told) heard what passed between us, and warned Robert Clinton of it, who immediately told the rest of the pirates. They were so impudent as to call me informer as I passed in the streets. I went again to the Governor.... His wife and daughter, who were in the room, then said that they did hear our discourse, and that I deserved to be called an informer.

Snead sought out the help of "fellow-justices" in town, who feigned willingness to assist, but were somehow impeded by Justice Maurice's wife who was related to the wife of one of the accused pirates. As Snead labored to arrest several men, Governor Markham thwarted his every move, telling him he had no jurisdiction in Pennsylvania. Snead complained, "He ordered the constables not to serve any more of my warrants ... [and] the under-sheriff accordingly took my sword and pistols from me in Philadelphia, leaving me to ride home unarmed." Needless to say, Snead's erstwhile pirates escaped, but his reports leave impressive evidence of the grassroots support given to Red Sea men by elite women, judges, sheriffs, and people in the streets.[91]

The lines of kin and friendship in the northern plantations ran so deep that Bellomont moaned in a pessimistic moment, "The people there [New York] are so in abetting and sheltering pirates ... that I can never expect to check that vile practice of theirs." Many of those labeled pirates in the northern colonies married well, settled down, and led respectable lives, contributing not only financially but also civically to their communities. An old Rhode Island pirate, Thomas Paine, was one of the founders of Trinity Church in Newport, an institution that epitomized the English Establishment. In addition Paine was a tax collector and relative by marriage to a Rhode Island governor. He was also a friend of Bellomont's nemesis, the privateer William Kidd, as were many other freemen in northeast colonial towns. Kidd had married Sarah Bradley several years before sailing to the Indian Ocean, and they had two daughters and a house on Water Street in New York. Paine corresponded with Sarah on Kidd's return to America from the Indian Ocean; allegedly Paine kept some East India goods for her during the cat-and-mouse game that Kidd eventually lost to Bellomont. Captured and sent to England, Kidd was convicted on trumped-up charges, hung and fed to the birds in England in 1702—as an example to all Americans with designs on Eastern trade and commodities. The Kidd home was then sold to New York merchant Robert Livingston, an associate of Bellomont.[92]

These ambitious and thwarted American mariners, as an identifiable regional or political entity, aided and abetted by their New World communities, came late to the Indian Ocean. The English had been there, with their guns, bravado, and transnational sailors, for a century already, even though in the European parade of sail eastward, they were among the last. As an established state power, however, with court connections across Europe, healthy textile and shipping industries, and, most important, some very healthy consumers with lots of money to spend, the English government had certain advantages. In 1680 the state-supported English East India Company paid out an impressive 20 percent return to shareholders and was responsible for 14 percent of the total value of all English imports.[93] But the gradual building up of land-based commercial posts in Asia, beginning with Surat in 1612, slowly altered the way the English acquired goods in the East—and their renegade comportment off shore.[94] In 1670 King Charles II retroactively granted the Company the right to territorial acquisitions, to mint money, to make war and peace, and to exercise both civil and criminal jurisdiction over its acquired territories. The Company, in turn, concentrated its rising revenues in investments in fortified settlements in India. With an extensive presence on Asian land by the 1690s, Asians became more than inconsequential "infidels"; they were politically infused bodies on a geoeconomic game board, increasingly empowered to hold the English accountable for acts of lawlessness. If the English East India Company wished to maintain the commercial viability and security of its valuable commerce around the Indian Ocean, it needed to press the home government to prosecute—for the first time—ill-behaved privateers waving the English flag.

When pillaging Catholics and "infidels" at sea, so recently the nursery for English lords and knights, lost the wink of the Crown, it lost its heroic aspect.[95] Over the course of the seventeenth century the East India Company, and its highly placed, propertied directors, became integral to the political economy of London, replacing marauders such as Sir Francis Drake and Captain Henry Morgan as a source of exotic wealth for the English court. Few chartered commercial enterprises could hold a candle to the power and influence achieved by the English East India Company by the opening of the eighteenth century. Out of the imperial crisis of the 1690s, this chartered enterprise would emerge victorious, while the chartered American colonies generated little interest and would continue to struggle. At the same time that King Charles II granted increased autonomy and privilege to the East India Company, he further constrained the colonial traders with yet another navigation act. He imposed severe restrictions on colonial trade, banning all foreign shipping and forbidding Anglo-Americans from directly exporting their most important staples to non-English consumers. Only trade with England, in English goods, was permissible for Americans.[96] At stake for American colonists was access to foreign textiles, sugars, and other staple commodities that made up the bulk of the colonial carrying trade. But they also lost a precious piece of the wealth of the East, which served as an important mercantile symbol of commercial mastery and independence, punctuating other more ordinary forms of commerce. When the English East India Company temporarily lost its monopoly and faltered in the 1690s following the political upheaval of the Glorious Revolution, it was kept afloat by English consumers and their vigorous demand for "East India goods"—the very same goods that American mariners and merchants were then trying to bring to American consumers as evidence of their commercial prowess.[97]

While Randolph's derogatory representations of the colonists were clearly politically motivated—forming part of his advocacy for a stronger imperial presence in the charter colonies—his and Bellomont's numerous references to, specifically, "East India goods" in their discourse about governing base colonials should not get lost in the historiographical shuffle. Government placemen repeatedly singled out East India goods for notice, so we should take notice too. Even though the historian's job is made difficult by the general lack of specificity in their communications about exactly what goods the Red Sea men brought in, the picture becomes clearer when we move beyond official correspondence to examine the goods themselves, recovered from colonial estate inventories and archaeology.

The Fine Line between Lawful and Unlawful Trade

My goal here is certainly not a defense of sea robbers and murderers, although probably very few of Bellomont's "pirates" were hardened criminals, at least by the naval standards of their time.[98] It is rather, first, to point out how close to *normalized* the Indian Ocean escapades of these mariners were for most Americans, having been committed across heathen seas and having such *interesting* outcomes for the recipients—and being very much part of an Atlantic culture that had looked to the East for two centuries. All seafaring European polities had accumulated wealth and Asian luxury goods in similar ways since first breaching the perimeters of the Indian Ocean. Indeed, the first large quantities of Chinese porcelain to come into northern Europe resulted from Dutch attacks on Portuguese vessels in 1602 and 1604, not from any direct trade within Asia.[99] With all these polities desperately competing, as they were, for the upper hand in Far Eastern trade, each called the other "pirate." The designation is semantically justified by the violence, since they all carried guns and they all stole from each other, but rarely by contemporary legal codes at home. Stealing and shooting were permissible, not criminal, if directed against enemies and outsiders. The problem lay, therefore, in defining *who* was inside and *who* outside. Insider-outsider distinctions at sea were governed by personal interest conceived and justified along lines of ethnic, religious, and class affinities. A sea captain generally did not see his crew members as part of his interest group, and he beat them.[100] A sea captain placed himself in the same socioeconomic class as merchants in mercantile centers, sharing both their concerns and their wealth. The state and religious affiliations of the merchant-owners were displayed as ensigns strung up in the rigging of ships, serving as a provocation to the nonaligned just as tattoos and clothing do for today's urban gangs. Pirate captains, however, forfeited allegiance to land-based merchants and their state affiliations, and, as Rediker has described, shared a community of interest only with fellow seamen. Only a relatively small proportion of European and American seamen in the Indian Ocean professed this degree of alienation. While called a "pirate," Henry Every declared himself a "privateer"; he sailed under the flag of St. George and made his fortune explicitly at the expense of Catholics and non-Christians. Similarly, in forging alliances with colonial government officials, the vast majority of American "pirates" saw themselves as privateers, and so did their landlubber neighbors, regardless of the violence associated with a profitable seafaring enterprise. In accepting their wares, Americans were merely following time-honored practice, as the puzzled Chidley Brooke made plain when confronted with the entirely new terms of English imperial commerce manifest in Bellomont's witch hunt.

This unsuccessful decade-long battle for an American commercial mooring in the Indian Ocean, which resulted in a statutory blockade erected by the British Parliament between Americans and East India goods obtained outside London, was fundamental to the form American trade and decorative arts took in the eighteenth century. While commerce in Chinese commodities was small by comparison to trade in bulk goods with the West Indies, it was no less significant to questions of political identity and the symbols of material wealth that could be used to define that identity. Bellomont's pirate hunt and the subsequent arrest and execution of Captain Kidd as a pirate mark a pivotal change in the structure and philosophical basis of the relationship between the British government and its overseas settlements.[101] No longer do we see a single powerful monarch befriending and accepting gifts from independent sea rovers, mariners whose conduct outside the British Isles could be overlooked as long as the Crown received a handsome share of the exotic material and monetary wealth brought back into the kingdom. After the Glorious Revolution in 1688, Crown power was redistributed over several bodies located in the metropolis of London, and this composite body—this *state*—implanted itself around the world, in a global arena of states. The English *imperial* state could be and was held accountable by other states for its ganglike behavior. While Kidd, like thirty-odd "pirates" before him, dutifully returned to New York with fabulous treasures for his benefactors, never having violated the cross of St. George, these gifts, which would have formerly brought rewards and recognition—knighthood even—were of less consequence to the home government than the disdain of another state, represented in Kidd's case by the Indian Mughal court whose ships had been robbed.[102]

It is not a mere coincidence that this great imperial misunderstanding arose over access to Eastern goods. As noted above, trade in the Indian Ocean was the arena of highest stakes for any Atlantic polity, and certainly for the emerging British Empire at the end of the seventeenth century. At this time several highly placed London-based mercantilists vested in the West Indian and East Indian trades, including Josiah Child, began to hint at the idea that the northeast American colonies were, in the end, less valuable than the other colonies, and, moreover, they might be viewed as competitors in the more important—*Asian*—arenas of trade.[103] English foreign and imperial policies in the seventeenth and eighteenth centuries were guided almost entirely by commercial interest, and in their conflict with interloping American mariners, one sees the kernels of the British *familial* breakdown that would resurface three-quarters of a century later, not surprisingly over a Chinese commodity.[104]

While the drive to establish a firmer direct trade relationship with the East Indies was not fulfilled by Americans in this decade, many other important cultural consequences of their Indian Ocean voyages can be observed. First and foremost, a large number of American mariners and merchants acquired direct experience navigating to and around the Indian Ocean. Unlike their English counterparts, American craftsmen and workers rarely reproduced their technical knowledge and skills in print. This was certainly the case in the maritime trades. Scholars researching American shipbuilding techniques today, for example, need an actual vessel to learn the various highly distinctive tricks of the trade developed by shipbuilders on the western side of the Atlantic.[105] The technical knowledge acquired in the 1690s about navigating and trading around the Indian Ocean would have been only two or three generations old by the opening of the US China trade in the 1780s, and most likely formed the basis of the oral knowledge that would later guide US ships east of the Cape of Good Hope. The existence of this body of knowledge, constantly being augmented and perfected as sailors from the European East Indies companies migrated to American ships, served as a constant lure to American merchants and captains, who pushed the watery limits of mercantile profit.[106] The pent-up frustration at not being able to exploit this well-known Asian outlet for American capital exploded the moment the Peace of Paris was signed in 1783, under names such as *Empress of China, Hope, Experiment, Harriet,* and *Grand Turk.*

In addition to acquired firsthand knowledge of navigating eastern seas, American interest in China was sustained throughout the eighteenth century by colonial consumers. Many more Americans came into contact with the commodities of Asia than would have if American commerce had been truly confined to England alone, as the Navigation Acts dictated. The cargo holds of at least thirty-four Red Sea vessels were unloaded on North American shores, and practically none of this commercial activity was documented. Our best evidence today for the objects contained in these cargoes comes from a careful reading of estate inventories along with archaeology and collected objects. This evidence is piecemeal, and more archaeology on late seventeenth-century sites is necessary at this point to fully understand the estate inventories. The near hysteria aroused in Lord Bellomont, Edward Randolph, and other English officials over what seems from their descriptions to have been a veritable flood of East India goods into North America suggests the availability of such

China in 18th-century Inventories

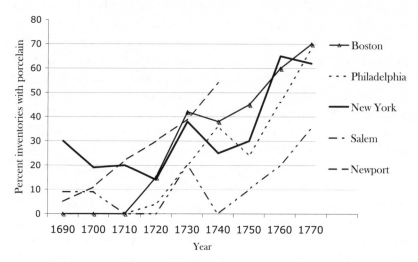

1.2. Chinese porcelain in eighteenth-century estate inventories. Percentage figures are based on a sample of the first twenty to twenty-five complete household estate inventories at the beginning of each decade, 1690–1770, from each of the five seaports and their immediate environs.

goods at this time. The court depositions of Americans also refer repeatedly to unspecified East India goods. Thirty-five percent of New York estate inventories, 9 percent from Marblehead, and 5 percent from Newport from the 1690s contain Chinese porcelain. This porcelain practically disappears in the next two decades (see fig. 1.2). By the 1730s we see the number of inventories containing porcelain on the rise again. These data will be evaluated in chapters 3 and 4 below, but we might ask at this point whether or not the disappearance of export porcelain in inventories from 1700 to 1720 was real—or merely political subterfuge.

Finally, no less important than the political context, which outlawed Asian trade to Americans, and no less important than the firsthand experience gained in Asia and the influx of Asian wares, is one other outcome. Local systems of resistance to English controls, laws, and officials were forged over the question of access to the Indian Ocean and Eastern goods. Once in place these systems of resistance could be elaborated, and they were. A large number of individuals—cutting across class lines, because mariners and their friends and families cut across class lines—came to an unwritten, unarticulated, "quiet" (as Governor Beeston noted) agreement, that they would support each other's desire for

Eastern trade; they would work together to deflect English control over their access to Eastern wealth and commodities. They would definitely participate in the China-mania afflicting Europe, but they would have to work quietly together to do it—differently than if they were living in London. Two chartered colonial enterprises within the English Empire butted heads at the end of the seventeenth century over access to Asian goods, and the East India Company emerged victorious over the North American plantations—this time.

2

Imagining China at Home

Architectural Japanning in Early Newport

If Americans could not travel to China directly, they would go indirectly. With the consolidation of the East India Company's hold on Asian sea-lanes and the positioning of Britain in the South China Sea and on the Chinese coast, a flood of Chinese commodities poured into British space. A fascination for the Far East only intensified in the early eighteenth-century North Atlantic, and despite vigorous attempts by the Crown to discourage worldly pretensions in ambitious colonials, Americans fully participated in the China-mania.[1] As the improved skills and technologies of Atlantic seamen greatly diminished the distance and dangers posed by the ocean, colonial American culture began to converge with that of England.[2] Americans were now excluded from the Indian Ocean in no uncertain terms, but the allure of the East was greater than ever, especially if we consider the number of booty-toting Anglo-American mariners at the opening of the eighteenth century who *had* been there. Ultimately, Americans participated in the

China craze in a way that was distinctive both to their place in the British Empire *and* in the world. Asian commodities were readily available in colonial American seaports and some rural areas in the early decades of the eighteenth century. In the previous chapter we saw how, through ordinary mariners and their close ties with local merchants and governing elite, many such goods trickled into a wide spectrum of American homes and resale markets. In the next chapter we will more closely examine the legal and illegal channels—and creative loopholes—through which Chinese porcelain entered the country.

In a somewhat different vein, this chapter examines a purely Anglo-American work of art, produced in interaction with Chinese commodities and strongly influenced by deeply embedded, early modern European perspectives on China. This European baggage, carried with the colonists to America, becomes part of the referential content of this artwork specific to early American culture. Sometime in the first quarter of the eighteenth century, a Newport sign painter splashed a sequence of Chinese scenes in oils all over the parlor walls of his home. They were rediscovered in 1936 when a leak sprang up behind the wood paneling in the northwest corner of this still-standing Georgian home. Located in the center of town on Clarke Street, the house was then being used by the charitable Family Service Society, but it boasted a more illustrious past. During the revolution, a lieutenant-general of the French army, Comte de Rochambeau, had resided there for a year before his famous march to Yorktown. Prior to that the erudite merchant and speaker of the Rhode Island Assembly, Metcalf Bowler, owned the house. Today it is called the Vernon House after the wealthy Patriot William Vernon, who purchased it from Bowler in May of 1774.[3] Removal of the room's wood paneling in search of the leak revealed sixteen astounding faux-lacquer Chinese scenes framed within trompe l'oeil bolection molding and marbled woodwork, all covered with a thin, peeling coat of whitewash that evidently had been applied before the painted walls were paneled over. A decorative arts curator from Boston's Museum of Fine Arts immediately examined the murals and declared, "this unique example of mural decoration is more interesting and more skillfully done than any that has appeared in New England, or in Colonial America for the matter." He judged the work to be from the hands of a skilled painter, executed in the first half of the eighteenth century and painted directly on the walls of the original two-cell seventeenth-century house.[4]

Remedial restoration was undertaken right away, and an associate curator for the Metropolitan Museum of Art's American Wing was also called in.[5] Although a comprehensive study was never completed, she judged the technique used to paint the murals to be akin to eighteenth-century furniture japanning, without the characteristic gesso relief or gilding. The murals had a pink undercoat over which a pigment mixed with varnish was applied. Within each framed panel, the first paint layer was a very thick, shiny black, and on this background decorative scenes were etched and then filled in with colored pigments, also mixed with varnish. Fine black lines were used to define details such as faces and bird feathers. Of the eight longer panels, each placed directly over a smaller one, three are scenes that use human figures to depict a violent or confrontational event (figs. 2.1, 2.2, and 2.3). All remaining thirteen large and small panels depict birds, beasts, rocks, and flowers that are stylistically Chinese and similar to patterns seen on porcelain and lacquered objects circulating in the West throughout the seventeenth century (fig. 2.4; note the birds, rocks, and beasts). As for the flush, wainscotted wood paneling later mounted over the paintings, architectural historian Antoinette Downing notes that it is similar to paneling in other Newport homes finished in the second half of the eighteenth century.[6]

Vernon descendants sold the house to the charity organization in 1913. It was returned to private hands in 1964 and designated a National Historic Landmark a few years later, in part because of its revolutionary role as Rochambeau's headquarters. (In 1908, a bronze plaque had been placed on the exterior of the house noting the site's association with Rochambeau and George Washington.) The new owner undertook a more complete restoration of the murals, using paint analysis to return the scenes to their original hues. The wood paneling that had covered the paintings was either removed or hinged, in order to view the now brilliantly painted, fanciful Chinese-style scenes beneath. Although these paintings have been returned to their early eighteenth-century glory as the centerpiece of the parlor decor, seventy years after their discovery and forty years after their complete restoration several important questions remain unresolved, and little historic research has been done to address the problems raised by these paintings. Who painted them? What was their source and aesthetic context? Did they once represent the height of Newport parlor art or were they unusual? A close reading of their content can tell us about the colonist's attitudes toward China.

A Veil of Colonial Innocence

At first glance these murals and their historical context in Newport demonstrate that Americans were actively and independently engaging with a Far Eastern aesthetic at an early date and that they understood China and Chinese art with much the same level of sophisticated prejudice as any Londoner.

2.1. Center panel of a triptych of trompe l'oeil panels. Wall murals, ca. 1720, Vernon House, Newport, RI, owned by the Newport Restoration Foundation. Photo: Warren Jagger.

2.2. Painted panel left of window, Vernon House wall murals, ca. 1720.
Photo: Warren Jagger.

2.3. Painted panel left of north-west corner of parlor, Vernon House wall murals, ca. 1720. (Startled figure is out of picture to left.) Photo: Warren Jagger.

None of this is surprising if we consider the significance of Asian trade to early modern Atlantic seamen, but curators and scholars are, nevertheless, dumb-struck by these murals and have left them virtually unstudied. They are indeed a fortuitous survival of an overlooked element of colonial American culture, of American engagement with the Far East and its material culture from a very

2.4. Triptych, Vernon House wall murals, ca. 1720 (see 2.1). Photo: Warren Jagger.

early date. The paintings are comprised of sixteen different scenes covering the north and west parlor walls of a colonial home built before 1708. Having been carefully restored and preserved by the present owners, they look today as they did three hundred years ago. But they are certainly more astounding to today's viewer than they would have been to a viewer in the early eighteenth century.

Paintings that were confidently stylish then appear today as conspicuously awkward and strange because they are incongruent with the arts and crafts normally associated with colonial America and found in recent compendiums of colonial material culture.[7] They beg the question of what other tangible evidence of early American engagement with the Far East might be found if one began, in earnest, to look for it.

The problem is not that the evidence does not exist, but that we have been handicapped by a powerful colonialist paradigm handed down through successive generations—an ideology, in effect, that belittles early American ambition and cultural sophistication. Colonial Americans absolutely *could not* have had a relationship with a place as important as China, by all means could not have had the means to trade for Chinese commodities, and could not have possessed the cultural experience necessary to comprehend the East or appreciate Eastern styles. On the heels of being barred from one foreign market after another in a series of imperial navigation acts, colonial Americans took on a new identity, not of competitor to London-based capitalists but of obedient children. Like winning the girl, succeeding in the China trade was a mark of masculinity in seventeenth-century Europe, and in this contest American merchants backed down, feigning obedience—for the moment. A discursive veil of innocence, of simplicity and underdevelopment, has cloaked colonial Americans in one historical narrative after another ever since. It even permeated their own view of themselves, to the very core of their collective identity. Responding, for example, to the English perception that the religion of New England was less developed than that of England, Cotton Mather did not disagree, but he added a new spin in asserting that American churches were "very like unto those that were in the first ages of Christianity."[8] They were not simply immature, but in their youthfulness they were pure and uncorrupted by worldliness. Eighty years later Thomas Jefferson responded to queries by French intellectuals who observed that "America has not yet produced one good poet" and speculated that the American climate may inhibit healthy development. Jefferson said, "America, though a child of yesterday, has already given hopeful proofs of genius." Ingenuity and initiative were but a *hope* for the future, according to Jefferson, as they were for a promising child. But he also countered that in Europe, unlike America, there was too much legislation, and too much urbanization and industrial development, "submit[ting] men to the greatest evil." While Europe had grown old and corrupt, "those who labour the earth," he pointed out defensively, "are the chosen people of God."[9] The typecast of colonial Americans as simple, childlike people lagging far behind Europeans has dominated historiography through the ages. In a Pulitzer Prize–winning history of the revolution written in our own generation, an eminent early Americanist echoes the colonialist narrative of humility and naïveté: "In 1760 America was only a collection of disparate colonies huddled along a narrow strip of the Atlantic coast—economically underdeveloped outposts existing on the very edges of the civilized world."[10]

As we are considering a painter in this chapter, let us see how one accomplished colonial artist humbly described his situation in the 1760s before his awesome European colleagues. Boston portraitist John Singleton Copley wrote to Jean Etienne Liotard in 1762 to request some Swiss crayons, saying,

> You may perhaps be surprised that so remote a corner of the Globe as New England should have d[e]mand for the necessary eutensils for practiceing the fine Arts, but I assure you Sir however feeble our efforts may be, it is not for want of inclination that they are not better, but the want of oppertunity to improve ourselves.

Copley pays respect to the colonialist ideology that America could not possibly be a seat of fine arts; America was, he parrots, "remote" and the efforts of its artists "feeble." But nevertheless, in his next phrase, he carefully asserts his ambition for his country:

> however America which has been the seat of war and desolation, I would fain hope will one Day become the School of fine Arts and Monsieur Liotard Drawings with Justice be set as patterns for our imitation.[11]

Following the great success of some of Copley's paintings in London, he was pressured to relocate there by English artists, as if such talent in the colonies was unseemly. He was told by one European patron, "If you have been able to attain this unassisted in Boston, what might you not achieve in Europe? Your coming *home* as an Artist travelling for Improvement will cost you very little" (emphasis added).[12] London suddenly becomes "home" for this American-born artist, and his skill is appropriated for the mother country. All this indicates the way in which the skilled brushwork of an American working forty to fifty years earlier in the even more remote colonial location of Newport might exist outside scrutiny and might even cause discomfort. The deftly painted Chinese scenes in the Newport parlor were exposed to view for most of the eighteenth and twentieth centuries but yet were unknown. We have lacked the framework for understanding them, having only a framework for disregarding early American art that blatantly refers to a world beyond the North Atlantic.

Citizens of the World

Despite living on "the very edges of the civilized world," Americans were as motivated as any European to learn more about the empire on the other side of the globe that held such a powerful economic grip on the seafaring countries of Europe. As early modern Europe emerged from the plagues and hunger of earlier centuries, individual material comforts and wealth increased substantially.[13] Fernand Braudel has pointed out that no single sector of pre-industrial Europe offered enough economic possibilities for the growing corps of wealthy merchants.[14] Thus nearly all the European countries promoted an oceanic Age of Exploration out of an intensified desire for more and better objects of capital investment. Spurred on by the voracious consumer demand for Chinese commodities, merchants allocated a tremendous amount of wealth and intellectual energy to developing fruitful sea routes to the Far East. With Dutch and English traders heating up East-West trade in a space once dominated only by the Portuguese, Chinese commodities poured into seventeenth-century northern Europe, moving them from the curiosity cabinet to the dining table.[15] By the opening of the eighteenth century, Chinese trade goods such as silk, sugar, spices, porcelain, and tea had become entrenched as Europe's most highly valued quotidian consumables. Rebounding from the disappointment that Asia did not, in fact, lie in the western Atlantic, European capitalists had sought to use New World resources to balance their trade with China. Far Eastern demands and Far Eastern material standards dictated the terms of trade in the Atlantic throughout the early modern period.[16] Even with the additional input of American resources, there was a net drain of specie from the West to the East, with European nations running a constant deficit vis-à-vis China.[17] In this cultural context, America was not only valued as a source of precious metals but as a possible source of Asian substitutes—exotic woods, exotic foods, even silk—that would satisfy voracious consumers and enhance the position of European state-based capitalists *always* somehow in reference to Asia.[18] Of course America was also associated with a never-ending search for a faster—hence commercially more competitive—passage to the East. What is important to understand in this gloss of early modern economic history is, simply, that the search for China lingered under the cultural and economic surface of growing New World colonies. The northern plantations, as small, predominantly maritime Atlantic settlements dependent on a diversified trade, were profoundly impacted by the European China trades, by the various government-chartered East India Companies, and, above all, by the vigorous consumer demand for Chinese commodities. Literary scholar David

Porter compares China's place in the early modern world to that of the United States today: "If any one distant place could be said to have exercised a comparable grip on the collective self-consciousness of Western Europeans in the seventeenth and eighteenth centuries [as the United States does today], that place, without a doubt, would be China."[19]

Colonial Americans, even in the year 1700, had access to a wide range of visual and textual sources reflecting the Celestial Empire. Some of these came directly from the Far East as scenes painted on porcelain or engraved in lacquer (fig. 2.5). As it is unlikely that any Americans had been to China at this early date, these objects represent an important reference point for how Americans imagined the East. In both the Atlantic and the Indian Ocean, American mariners were caught up in circuits of trade that looked eastward and that were, ultimately, gravitating farther and farther east.[20] But the Chinese people remained subsumed by Chinese objects, with the face on the vase—and the hackneyed chinoiserie take-offs—taking precedence over any effort to imagine real people. Meanwhile, the Chinese developed an Atlantic-wide reputation for being proud and haughty. Even Roger Williams in late

2.5. Chinese porcelain. Partial tea service, with label noting it had been bought in Surinam, 1757. From Jean McClure Mudge, *Chinese Export Porcelain in North America*, p. 160. Photo: John Harkey.

seventeenth-century Providence drew on the stereotype of Chinese aloofness to describe the ruling theocracy in Boston. He said the close-minded are "like the men of China, [who] judge all the World to have no eyes but themselves."[21] Some Americans, either native-born or immigrant, served in the English East India Company—a well-known case being Nathaniel Higginson of Salem— but again they were rarely in China before 1711, when the English were finally permitted to build a "factory" in Canton. Higginson was the son of the Reverend John Higginson, who wrote a number of letters pointedly questioning his son, stationed in Madras, about the pagan practices of the East Indians and the nature of their interactions with Europeans.[22] The elder Higginson's questions indicate not only an unsatisfied thirst for knowledge about Asian peoples that Americans had difficulty quenching more directly but also the importance of preconceived notions based on religious stereotypes.

Many representations of China in colonial America came through a European filter. At the end of the seventeenth century, Marblehead was a small face-to-face community of fishermen, even smaller than Newport. But in the 1695 inventory of Captain Andrew Craty of Marblehead, we find inlaid, "japanned," and "lacker'd" furniture and screens and a "p'cell Cheny ware." Japanning was a European method of imitating Far Eastern lacquerwares, but authentic Asian lacquer was often also labeled "japanned." Amid Craty's collection of Far Eastern imports were also listed numerous pictures and books. Published accounts and illustrations by European travelers or missionaries in the Far East were popular throughout the seventeenth and eighteenth centuries. These publications often included illustrations of exoticized places. Engravings from Johannes Nieuhoff's lavishly illustrated 1665 publication, *An Embassy from the East-India Company of the United Provinces, to the Grand Tartar Cham Emperor of China*, were available for all to see as similar illustrations were mounted, framed and unframed, on colonial walls from Philadelphia to Marblehead (fig. 2.6).[23] The 1685 inventory of New York merchant Jacob de Lange, for example, lists "Five East Indian Pictures" and "thirteen East India prints pastd upon paper," which may well have been Nieuhoff's engravings.[24] A free black woman in Philadelphia had an inventory containing "1 pair India pictures," which gives some idea of how widespread their circulation was in the colonies.[25] Books about China are regularly found in early New England and mid-Atlantic libraries. The preeminent colonial bookworm, James Logan of Philadelphia, had a library that contained many seventeenth-century descriptions of China, including Arnold Montanus's *Atlas Chinesi*, a 1671 sequel to Nieuhoff's book.[26] Books on China are found in smaller libraries as well. A 1693 auction of books belonging to Boston resident Samuel Lee, for

2.6. Title page of the 1673 English edition of Johannes Nieuhoff's *An Embassy from the East-India Company of the United Provinces to the Grand Tartar Cham Emperour of China*, first published in Dutch in 1665.

example, included a "Samdy's History of China," which is probably F. Alvarez
Semmedo's *History of the Great and Renowned Monarchy of China*, published
in London in 1655. The 1717 estate inventory of a Mr. Ebenezer Pemberton,
also of Boston, listed a book entitled "Memoirs of Chinese People," probably
Memoirs and Observations . . . [of a] Journey through the Empire of China by
Jesuit Louis le Compte and published in English in 1697.[27] Published collections of Jesuit letters from China appear as early as the late seventeenth
century in French and English translations, and the 1735 English edition of
Jesuit Jean Baptiste Du Halde's *History of China* quickly became a best seller in
America, judging from its frequent appearance in newspaper advertisements.[28]
It was even chosen by Newport minister Ezra Stiles to prominently represent
his intellect in his 1770 portrait, in which he stands in front of a bookshelf
with three volumes apparent directly adjacent his head: Du Halde's *History of
China* joins works by the Roman historian Livy and church historian Eusebias
de Caesaria.[29]

Indeed, the activities of the Jesuits in China aroused great interest in the
West, not the least excluding America. Between 1711 and 1719 a number
of articles appeared in the weekly newspaper *Boston News-Letter* concerning
Jesuits who had allegedly integrated Confucian practices into their worship
and the papal response to these innovations. The Jesuit missions, certainly not
the first emissaries of Christianity to proselytize in China but the most significant of the early modern period, had been in the Far East since the end of
the sixteenth century. During the reign of Kangxi (1662–1722) they achieved
great favor in the Chinese court and the number of their converts grew dramatically.[30] In 1692 Kangxi issued an imperial decree praising the missionaries' contributions to China and gave them extensive freedom to practice and
proselytize within China. This was partly because the Jesuits paid respect to
Confucian and Taoist traditions, even those considered sacrilegious in Rome,
such as overt veneration of ancestors (viewed by Christians as idol worship).
Finally in 1715, Pope Clement XI issued a papal bull explicitly disallowing a
host of Chinese practices previously tolerated by the Jesuit preachers. The Boston paper reported these controversies within the Catholic Church in detail,
and not always with the dispassionate journalistic distance considered appropriate today. In the November 17, 1712, edition, the practices of the Jesuits
were labeled "scandalous" and the job of overseeing worship in China called
"so dangerous an Employment." These remarks show complete disregard for
the goodwill of the Chinese emperor and the positive relations that had been
established between the Chinese people and Europeans. It is not surprising

that a few years later, after the hard line taken by the pope and years of derogatory accounts, Anglo-American reporting documented a complete collapse of
those good relations. An article in the April 20, 1719, edition of the *News-
Letter* read:

> We have a dismal Account from China, of the violent Persecution of the Chris-
> tians in that Country of whom a great many, have been burnt on the Forehead,
> as a token of their professing the Christian Faith; and many of the Natives who
> had embraced the same, have been Murdered by the Populace, and others are
> Imprisoned and laid in Irons.

As portrayed in newspapers circulating the North Atlantic, Christians in
China were being tortured. A month later in the same paper, a conversation
between a "Mandarin" and the Chinese emperor is reported (by somebody
who evidently had inside sources) in which European missionaries are accused
of political ambition. The mandarin allegedly warned the otherwise friendly
ruler, "under Pretence of Propagating Christianity, they aim at worldly Power,
and that China may expect one Day or other from their Hands, the same Fate
as has fallen great Part of the East Indies & the Phillipine Islands." The Boston
paper reported that Christians consequently received even more persecution.
But meanwhile, the article continues, the Jesuits had gone totally native, and
they "even hinder the Christians who do not side with them to receive the
Sacraments from the other Missionaries, who differ from their Opinion about
introducing of Pagan Ceremonies into the Publick Worship of the Christian
Religion."[31] Not surprisingly, in the Protestant heartland of Boston, the *News-
Letter* blamed the Catholics for all the political tension and all the gruesome
acts of persecution. Indeed, by 1721 the modus vivendi between resident
Christians and their Chinese hosts had dissolved. Kangxi issued the following
proclamation:

> Reading this proclamation [the 1715 papal bull], I have concluded that the
> Westerners are petty indeed. It is impossible to reason with them because they
> do not understand larger issues as we understand them in China. There is not a
> single Westerner versed in Chinese works, and their remarks are often incred-
> ible and ridiculous. To judge from this proclamation, their religion is no differ-
> ent from other small, bigoted sects of Buddhism or Taoism. I have never seen a
> document which contains so much nonsense. From now on, Westerners should
> not be allowed to preach in China, to avoid further trouble.[32]

This was a pivotal moment in relations between Europe and China, and Westerners would henceforth be lodged exclusively behind walls in Canton. But the important point for our purposes is that Americans actively observed this profound transcontinental struggle over spiritual and political authority. With their own newspapers reporting the Chinese emperor's whispered conversations and the Jesuits' papal correspondence, Americans were hardly out of touch with the ideas bred by European commercial ambitions in the Far East.

The very next mention of China in a Boston paper was a year later, in 1720. Thomas Selby at the Crown Coffee-House offered "China Ware, good Bohea Tea and Tea Tables" for sale in the *Boston Gazette*—the first instance of a porcelain advertisement in an American paper.[33] From about this point forward, American perceptions of China seem to be crowded out by another, more powerful visual representation of the East that loosely reflected not the engravings of travelers or the accounts of missionaries but the scenes depicted on objects, especially European objects. While an intellectual interest in China and Chinese philosophies continued in the colonies, as manifest in the number of travel books and histories that circulated in personal libraries and book shops, scholars today overwhelmingly acknowledge another source of cultural information about the East as dominant, that is, the visual pastiche of French and English "chinoiseries." This term denotes a European art style dominated by pseudo-Chinese ornamental motifs evoking a romanticized or fairy-tale East. The popular engravings of the French artist François Boucher from the 1740s (fig. 2.7, *Le Mariage chinois*) offer a typical example. Art historical research has shown them to be built from a variety of existing Far Eastern, Near Eastern, and Western visual sources.[34] Boucher borrowed costumes, poses, and architectural details from Chinese woodblock prints, from a Turkish designer, and from Montanus's 1671 *Atlas Chinesi*, exaggerating tropical exoticism and opulence to suit new rococo tastes. From the late seventeenth through the nineteenth centuries, such chinoiserie decorations were applied in Europe to tin-glazed earthenware pottery, metalwork, textiles, and pseudo-lacquered furniture called "japan work." Their style exudes a longing for a newly romanticized medieval "Cathay."

Chinoiserie, especially on japanned furniture, is the first thing that comes to mind when viewing the Newport wall murals.[35] This European art style offers the best study—often the only study—of the slim trails of evidence linking colonial America with the Far East. In the first half of the eighteenth century, Boston artisans excelled in furniture japanning. As Europe and America lacked the raw materials necessary to produce true Asian lacquerwork, tech-

2.7. Le Mariage chinois (Chinese wedding), by François Boucher, 1742. Design for a tapestry.
Photo: G. Dagli Orti, Musee des Beaux-Arts, Besançon, France.
Photo © DeA Picture Library / Art Resource.

nically elaborate imitations were developed in Holland and England during
the seventeenth century. American artisans simplified the European process,
applying ordinary oil paints directly to maple and pine rather than painting
over oak with a whiting base using a complex mixture of pigment and seed-
lac varnish. Eventually even the English adopted the less complicated Bostonian process.[36] Curators today outbid each other vying for works of Boston
japanners. A 1730s japanned high chest signed "Rob Davis" (similar to Josiah
Quincy's in fig. I.6), put up by Skinner in a 2004 Americana auction, sold for
a record $1.8 million[37] even though, with more than a dozen known Boston
painters working in this field before the revolution—and certainly many more
unknown artists such as our Newport painter—there are many works that survive. The aesthetic aspects of Boston japanwork, in comparison to the murals,
will be discussed in more detail below. The proliferation of this furniture style
throughout the colonies indicates, without doubt, colonial American engagement with an imaginary China, both in the content of the designs and in the

overall style of lacquered furniture itself. But whose imagined China was it? American japanners have long been viewed as borrowing lock, stock, and barrel from European global experience and imaginary repertoire. The unusual Newport wall murals can help us address this question.

A Newport Japanner

Who painted these unsigned murals? Not long after William Kidd was strung from the gallows for disrupting Eastern trade routes, a Boston sign painter named William Gibbs moved to Newport with his new wife and baby daughter. He was probably the same "Willyam Gibbs" who had been baptized on January 28, 1669, in the First Church of Boston, and he was definitely the same William Gibbs who married Elizabeth Robbins in Boston's South Congregational Church in March of 1701.[38] Their daughter Elizabeth was born exactly nine months later in Boston.[39] The Gibbses first appear in Newport records in 1708 as already owning the Clarke Street house.[40] So sometime between 1701 and 1708, the Gibbses moved to Newport and took up residence in this desirable part of town just across the way from Trinity Church, probably purchasing an existing two-cell, central chimney home from the Clarke family.[41] Gibbs apparently pursued his profession as a painter, decorating coaches and overmantels with European heraldry and the like. In 1711 the colony treasurer paid him £6 for painting the staffs used by bailiffs when opening court, and in 1725 he was paid £5 for painting the king's arms in the Colony House.[42] Gibbs was also a house painter, as he shows up in Newport court records suing a blacksmith for payment for painting the outside of his house in 1725.[43]

Gibbs died in 1729, and his house passed to his daughter Elizabeth and son-in-law William Gardner, a mariner who was lost at sea. Gibbs's estate inventory contains all the tools of his trade. Fine paintbrushes and paints were found in every room of the house. The paint colors closely match those found in the murals, as evident in one section of the inventory:

> In ye cellar Barrells of lamblack, 1 small cas redd oadker, 1 cask red lead, 1 small case and paper of umber, 3 papers of yellow, a broken cask of English Oaker, 1 broken d° of spanish Brown, half a hhd of Spanish white a tubb & broken cask Venision Redd 1c w^{gt} of white lead 5 galls of oyl of turpentine.[44]

Both the colors and materials itemized are precisely those recommended by contemporary advice texts on oil painting and japanning. "Venice-Turpentine,"

"Red Oaker," "White lead," and "Lamp-Black" top the list of supplies recommended in John Stalker and George Parker's popular 1688 publication, *Treatise of Japaning and Varnishing*, which was used by amateurs and professional japanners alike throughout the eighteenth-century English-speaking world.

While Gibbs's inventory does not name any items of japanned furniture, that taken two years later for his live-in, drowned son-in-law does.[45] This 1731 inventory is much more extensive than Gibbs's as the claims on the estate of his son-in-law, William Gardner, were contested. The household goods listed in 1731 are clearly those of the former Gibbs household of which Gardner was a part. Here we find in the "Great Chamber" a "case of japand drawers" and "a japand table and looking glass." In the "Great Room," probably that with Gibbs's Chinese wall murals, we find a dozen china plates, three dozen tea cups and saucers, a tea set, and two china punch bowls. The estate also included numerous tea trays and eight tea tables, which may well have been decorated in an Asian lacquer style. There are no surviving pieces of japanned furniture attributable to Gibbs's hand that might help us identify, beyond his wall murals, such skills and interests on his part, but then very few early American japanners signed their work.[46] Given Gibbs's connection to Boston, this skilled painter may well have worked as a japanner in addition to his other work. Indeed, eight tea tables is a surprising number for any early eighteenth-century household, and they were all located along with brushes, picture frames, and small containers in "the porch chamber," which perhaps served as a studio.

Japanned furniture is commonly associated with New England households from the second quarter of the eighteenth century, but no other examples of such extensive "architectural japanning" have survived.[47] A late eighteenth-century notebook of New Yorker John Cruger does indicate, however, that such a technique existed. Much of Cruger's jottings deal with furnishing and decorating his house at 87 Greenwich Street, and in August of 1803 he records a receipt of $58.54 for "Japaning 2 Rooms."[48] Painted walls were a common decorative treatment throughout the colonial period, especially in the late seventeenth and early eighteenth centuries, but only one other case has come to light where a faux lacquering technique similar to japanning was applied. A Dutch colonial home in Belle Mead, New Jersey, had trompe l'oeil panels, as does our house in Newport, but only the darkly painted rails and stiles with faded yellow decorations were suggestive of Chinese lacquer, whereas their central motif of flower baskets and vases was entirely European.[49]

If Gibbs worked as a japanner, it is possible that this elaborately painted front room served to showcase his work to potential clients.[50] He chose, therefore, painted design motifs that not only expressed his own imagined China but a China that would, of necessity, be recognized by and appeal to other members of his Anglo-American community. Although oversized cranes, little beasts, and diagonal fencing are found on his walls and on American japanwork, a close examination of Gibbs's three figural panels reveals little resemblance to the lighthearted Chinese figures typically painted on Boston furniture. When human figures do show up on Boston japanwork, they are often playful, leading an oversized beast on a leash, wearing oversized pointed hats, or casting a fishing line under a cocked palm frond. These people are scattered across the surface of the furniture willy-nilly, arbitrarily placed alongside larger-than-life garden vases, stylized pagodas, and huge birds, with little attention to proportion or perspective and no serious effort to convey narrative meaning.

Gibbs's wall murals, on the contrary, are not at all playful, and even the symbols considered auspicious to the Chinese artist, such as scholar's rocks and little beasts, here come across as quite sinister. The elements of Gibbs's three figural scenes (figs. 2.1–3) exude narrativity, and the tale in each case is a dark one. While the methods used to paint these murals may owe something to furniture japanning techniques known in America in the first quarter of the eighteenth century as well as to the enduring medieval fashion of wall painting, the aesthetic inspiration for the murals certainly lies elsewhere. Ultimately they draw from a variety of sources that are most remarkable in their global scope. European chinoiserie artists combined artistic expressions from the Near and Far Easts, blurring geographic distinctions east of the Danube, using the imagined East constructed in European travel accounts and atlases. American artists, however, have never been credited with this same degree of cultural sophistication. The work of Boston japanners has been mainly viewed as imitative of European chinoiseries, and one degree further removed from the East. Gibbs's murals indicate that Americans fully participated in a Western perception of the East, built on centuries of remote contacts. Gibbs employed Eastern design motifs as well as medieval European depictions of a geographically imprecise East to make an original contribution to Western chinoiserie styles, giving chinoiserie a transatlantic dimension, not just a European locus. They are unlike any other imaginary scenes engraved or painted in Europe about China, chinoiserie or otherwise. They are not purely imitative of European responses to the East. They should be viewed, rather, as representing an American response to China as it was then imagined in the northern plantations.

Design Sources

At the end of the seventeenth century, two authentic Chinese commodities used in wall decoration appeared in England for the first time, wallpaper and Coromandel screens. The practice of lining walls with hand-painted Indian chintzes preceded the earliest imports of Chinese papers into Europe, and, indeed, the lush and sinewy gardens of the Chinese papers may reflect the earlier tree-of-life patterns found on Indian cottons. As the paper trade heated up in the eighteenth century, the Chinese artist interspersed vignettes of daily life and industry in China, such as those found in woodblock illustrations, with these lush landscape scenes.[51] Small doll-like figures set within lush tropical landscapes were characteristic of European chinoiseries of the eighteenth century, and one might ask if the Chinese did not, in fact, borrow this style from the West in catering to that particular export market. But whether for reasons of taste or availability, Chinese papers only became popular in American interior decorating in the second half of the eighteenth century.

Unlike the later wall papers and European-style chinoiseries on American furniture, Gibbs's wall paintings separate the figural and garden scenes into panels and are much more reminiscent of, if not directly copied from, Chinese Coromandel folding screens. Despite the European name taken from their transshipment location on the Coromandel coast of India, these screens were first produced in southern China in the sixteenth century. The technique, considered the last lacquering method developed in China, is a combination of carving, lacquering, and polychrome painting. They were first exported west in the Kangxi period of the Qing dynasty (1661–1722) in response to strong European demand for Japanese lacquer screens.[52] A 1702 East India Company fleet returning from the China coast, for example, is recorded to have carried thirteen chests of lacquer, fourteen chests of scrivetoires, and seventy chests of screens.[53] In China, screens bearing propitious scenes were generally made as gifts for distinguished individuals, often presented by merchants trying to advance their social status. Expressing good wishes was taken as a form of respect among the Chinese, and a gift of a Coromandel screen constituted the most valued, and most expensive, way a Chinese merchant could bestow this respect on a government official.[54] Generally they depict a continuous scene that spreads angularly across an even number of panels, usually in six or twelve folds held together by diagonal fencing. On the reverse side, panels function individually, portraying long-necked birds, floral splashes, and inscriptions. Very often these individual motifs are also repeated around the border of the front of the screen or in smaller panels beneath the longer pictorial ones. An early eighteenth-century example (fig. 2.8) is covered with trees, flowers, and animals (pine, bamboo, prunus, pheasants, parrots, mandarin ducks, deer, the mythical dragon-headed horse, and the divine tortoise) which all have symbolic meaning in Taoism.

Gibbs's painted wall panels are a slight modification of this ideal form, presenting individual flora and fauna alongside figural scenes, without any attempt to connect the images. But their palette and overall form—long panels atop smaller ones—closely match a Coromandel screen. During the seventeenth century, imported lacquer and porcelain were used as integral elements of room decoration in elite European country homes and palaces. We know that between 1700 and 1704 fifty-four "lacquered room screens" were shipped to London for use in wall covering.[55] By that time, with the boat loads of Asian commodities arriving in Europe, this room decorating trend was spreading to an ever-wider group that included Dutch burghers, British sea captains, East India Company officials, and many others outside court society.[56] In his circa 1700 *Nouvelles Cheminées faittes en plusieurs en droits de la Hollande*, Huguenot court artisan Daniel Marot depicted a room lined with the panels resembling those of a Coromandel screen.[57] In some cases, wood panels were japanned in the West, in imitation of a Coromandel screen, and then mounted on the walls. This process is described in chapter 13 of John Stalker and George Parker's 1688 *Treatise of Japanning and Varnishing*. Very few of these rooms have survived, and then only those in the most elaborate estates, such as the "Princess's Lacquered Chamber" dating to 1665 in the royal Danish Rosenberg Castle.[58] As surprising as it may seem, even a middling sign painter in colonial Newport, a small town on the western shores of the Atlantic, was aware of and an active participant in this multifaceted, cross-cultural trend in interior design. The Coromandel screen itself was an amalgam of Chinese and Japanese design motifs and techniques.[59] The screen's use and imitation in wall decorating was a European innovation, and the japanning techniques Gibbs used to participate in that trend represent a specifically New England improvement.

The artistic details within Gibbs's murals are, overall, quite close to authentic Chinese designs. The fingerlike clouds, the scholar's rocks, and the little auspicious beasts repeated across his parlor walls are singularly Chinese. Also the dotted relief of some of the trees and flowers as well as the striped and dotted patterns on the clothing and other textiles are so close to original Chinese designs that it is difficult to imagine a colonial American, far from the lacquer-paneled rooms of Europe, remembering such details without the aid of an authentic model. When Gibbs first appears in the record in 1701 in Boston,

2.8. Coromandel lacquer screen. China, Qing dynasty. Early eighteenth century. 269 × 640 cm. Inv.: FE.130–1885/7496. Victoria and Albert Museum, London. Photo: V&A Images, London / Art Resource.

rococo style, with its affinity to Chinese art, was not yet in full bloom in Europe, and certainly not in the American colonies. But by the end of the seventeenth century, the Chinese artistic idiom was available all over Europe on porcelain pots, on lacquer trays and boxes, or dancing across silk embroideries and paper hangings. Moreover, the rich design source of Chinese woodblock prints was available to European artists in a number of illustrated Chinese books imported privately by employees of the Dutch East India Company as curiosities, or perhaps even with the explicit intent to serve as models for the emergent japanning trades.[60]

It is entirely possible that Gibbs had a Coromandel screen at his disposal when painting his murals. As we have seen, a number of New England seamen traveled to the Indian Ocean in the decade preceding the arrival of the Gibbs family in Newport, and by 1700, New Englanders were sailing all over the Atlantic. In the first decade of the eighteenth century, Newport boasted twenty-nine registered ships and, in the year 1700 alone, recorded three slave voyages to Africa.[61] Lacquer boxes specifically appear in the records of this time as gifts given to women by returning mariners. Even Lord Bellomont's wife was one of the recipients.[62] Moreover, many Newport estate inventories from the first decade of the eighteenth century contain a costly "screen."[63] John Holmes's inventory taken on October 13, 1712, included a "screen" in the kitchen chamber valued at 15 shillings—and he lived directly across the street from William Gibbs. Both Jedidiah Howland (December 1711) and William Collins (January 1712) have screens in their inventories worth £1.10 each, as well as Asian silks and muslins. While it is impossible to say with certainty that these screens are lacquered Asian screens without any further description, given the certain presence of lacquer boxes and porcelain in New England as well as the large number of lacquer screens in England, they very well may have been. It is significant that many of the artistic details in Gibbs's murals are specifically characteristic of Coromandel screens, such as the oversized birds and the diagonal fencing.[64]

The China of Gibbs's Imagination

Examining the narrative content of two of the three long wall panels with figures, however, complicates the academic exercise of identifying artistic borrowing. As we have seen, Coromandel screens in China were specifically designed to express positive ideas and good wishes. They usually depict palace scenes with families gracefully moving between gardens and buildings, or officials celebrating propitious events like the Tang hero's birthday, scenes often taken from popular literary traditions.[65] Unlike the standard thematic content of most surviving Coromandel screens, Gibbs's images are explicitly agitated and violent. Two are perfect examples of Chinese punishment scenes, which were quite popular in Europe from the earliest days of maritime contact with China. Directly opposite the room's entrance, in the center panel of the triptych of panels, is a man impaled on a very tall pole with a spearhead. Above him, the Chinese-style fingerlike clouds actually take the form of enormous hands reaching out toward him. Below four men use spears and bows and arrows, while another with a large cutlass strapped to his belt stands with his back to the punishment, arms folded. On the same wall in the double set of panels to the left, we see a crowned, seated official presiding over a kneeling and naked man about to be decapitated by another raising a large cutlass over his head. Several other men stand by with long spears. In the third scene on the adjacent wall, a woman holds a fan out at what appear to be attackers, approaching her by boat and waving spears, bows, and arrows at her.

That Chinese punishment scenes were in popular demand at this time, as integral to the oriental aesthetic, is evident in some of Stalker and Parker's "Japan-patterns," attached in the back of their 1688 *Treatise*. One pattern recommended for a lady's "Comb Box," for example, depicts an official with a wand overseeing a man who appeals to him while a third is prostrate in stocks (fig. 2.9)—curious motif for the boudoir! A fascination with Chinese forms of brutal punishment extended deep into Europe's medieval period, carrying us as far back even as Marco Polo. Christopher Columbus read Polo's account closely before setting out across the western sea in search of Cathay. He noted in the margin of his 1485 edition of Polo's manuscript the precious commodities that could be found there, and also the dangers to Western traders, including an assassin's garden of sensual delights in addition to run-of-the-mill pirates and cannibals.[66] To the early modern European mind, shaped by centuries of literal biblical interpretation, Chinese commodities presented themselves in the same light as the tempting apple in the Garden of Eden—objects of desire that were inherently objects of destruction. Stories of actual torture of Europeans within China filtered back to Europe following an incident in 1549 in which an impatient Portuguese sea captain let greed get the better of him while trading along the Fujian coast. He attacked a Chinese official and, in reprisal, members of the Portuguese embassy were imprisoned and tortured. An account by one of the prisoners, Galeote Pereira, described skin-tight cages and bamboo whips that became an important source for later European de-

2.9. Japanning pattern from John Stalker and George Parker, *A Treatise of Japanning and Varnishing*, London, 1688.

pictions of Chinese cruelty.[67] Of the ten illustrations of China engraved by German artist Theodor de Bry in the best-selling Asian travelogue *Petit Voyage* (1599), two depict gruesome scenes of torture, two are scenes of death, and two scenes of idol worship. Whipping and encaged people figure prominently, while executed figures attached to high poles serve as background to one of the torture scenes. De Bry had never traveled to China, but descriptions of Chinese torture circulated so widely in Europe by that point that de Bry probably had no difficulty visualizing the scene, although the buildings and perspective in his illustrations are entirely European (fig. 2.10).[68] European and American fascination with imagined Chinese forms of punishment has persisted into present times and stands as a pervasive, age-old backdrop to the Western longing for Chinese commodities and East-West commerce in general.[69]

With this cultural background, it is not surprising that Gibbs turned to scenes of punishment when depicting the Chinese, especially given the growing discord between the Qing emperor and resident Jesuits so faithfully recorded in Boston newspapers. But if it can be argued that Gibbs was copying directly from a Chinese lacquer screen in putting together these painted panels, can the source for the punishment he depicts be laid at the feet of a Chinese artist? In the case of the panel with a seated king presiding over the

execution of a half-naked, kneeling man (see fig. 2.2), such imagery was found
in China. In her 1952 *Architectural Heritage of Newport*, Antoinette Downing
notes in passing that these wall murals are extremely unusual and demonstrate
familiarity with scenes of the Buddhist Hell or "Chinese courts of punishment." She speculates that someone who had actually visited China must have
painted them.[70] Downing did not take into account the prevalence of Chinese design motifs circulating in the West, including the British colonies, in
the seventeenth and eighteenth centuries, but her suggestion that the scenes
might represent Chinese images of hell is of interest. The concept of numerous hells, often numbering eighteen, dates back fifteen hundred years in Buddhist texts and has had a place in Chinese popular culture and folk religion
into the twentieth century.[71] The hells are depicted on temple walls and on
scrolls, and after 1600 in woodblock-illustrated books as well. Buddhist hell
relief sculptures were also carved into a mountainside in Sichuan Province by
a Chinese monk in the thirteenth century. This spot was an active religious site
in the late Ming period (1570–1644) and was probably familiar to Europeans

2.10. Theodor de Bry, copperplate engraving number 30 from *Pars Indiae*
(known also as *Petit Voyages*), Frankfurt, 1599. Courtesy of the John Carter Brown Library.

as well as many Chinese artists.[72] Gibbs's depiction in this scene is archetypal of Chinese images of Buddhist hells, which are very bureaucratic places with the various punishments of sinners always meted out by an appropriate presiding judge. The punishments are often very specific and quite gruesome, such as being tied to a flaming copper pillar or rolled in boiling human excrement. The punishment being meted out to the sinner in Gibbs's scene, if it is in fact a hell depiction, is nondescript.

There are a number of factors to consider in asking whether Gibbs constructed this scene or copied it directly from a Chinese source. First of all, while court scenes and military officials are often seen on Coromandel screens of the Kangxi period (1654–1722), I have found no cases of hell scenes depicted on such screens. Such images would indeed be contrary to the very reason the screens were produced, that is, to express good wishes. A seventeenth-century screen now in the Lilly Library at Duke University offers a typical court scene found on Coromandel lacquer (fig. 2.11). Represented in the center is depiction of the daily life of a district magistrate. Government workers, identified by their dark gray hats with flaps, and soldiers, identified by their boots and weapons, are engaged in various activities. A magistrate seated in the middle attends to a person who is perhaps making an appeal. Framing the screen are individual depictions of ceremonial vessels, objects symbolic of scholarly or artistic work, and flowers representing the four seasons. A presiding seated official is a motif commonly seen in seventeenth and eighteenth-century Chinese artwork, but here, unlike in Gibbs's scene, the overall atmosphere is auspicious and tranquil. The figures in Gibbs's depiction, however, are stomping about waving spears, and one even raises a cutlass over the head of someone clearly about to be executed. Moreover, the cutlass may even be modeled after a Turkish scimitar rather than a Chinese weapon.[73] The most blatant irregularity is the British crown on the official's head (fig. 2.2). No Buddhist judge presiding over hell or any Chinese magistrate is known to have worn such a headpiece. While this detail does not necessarily throw out the potential authenticity of the whole scene, it does indicate that the artist was willing to take imaginative liberties. The crown is not a surprising addition from somebody earning his living painting European coats of arms.

The impalement scene in the center of the triptych of panels is much more difficult to match up with a Chinese original. Sinners in hell are often depicted in temple art, scrolls, and woodblock prints as being poked by long spears or crushed by a wall of swords. In the spectacular Baodingshan rock carvings, executed on the Sichuan mountainside, a kneeling figure is pierced through by a spear (fig. 2.12).[74] But he is not mounted high up on a pole. Impaling, as

2.11. Typical court scene on a seventeenth-century Coromandel lacquer screen. Collection of
the Lilly Library, Duke University. Photo: Lee Sorenson.

painted by Gibbs (see fig. 2.1), never appears in traditional Chinese sources as
one of the standard Buddhist hells or in any other context.[75] Gibbs's depiction
can be viewed as a direct descendant of medieval European illustrations of impalement, and in particular those related to Vlad Tepes, or Dracula (d. 1476),
the fifteenth-century Romanian prince who impaled thousands of invading

2.12. Baodingshan rock carvings, Dazu, Sichuan Province, China. Carved in the mountains primarily during the Southern Song dynasty, under the direction of monk Zhao Zhifeng, between 1179 and 1249 AD. Photo: Piero Scaruffi, www.scaruffi.com.

Ottoman Turks.[76] The impalement painted by Gibbs closely resembles medieval German woodblock illustrations of Vlad Tepes's victims, which, given the early modern taste for spectacles of torture (as described, e.g., by Michel Foucault[77]), were no doubt still widely circulating and being reproduced in Europe in the seventeenth and eighteenth centuries (fig. 2.13).[78] Evidence for impalement is found in both the Middle East and Europe, and it is often associated with religious friction or holy wars. The Greek historian Herodotus describes how the Persian King Darius I impaled thousands of Babylonians, and a neo-Syrian rock relief depicts the impalement of Judeans.[79] The Ottomans used impalement against Christians in its occupied European territories. Vlad Tepes had originally been a puppet of the Ottoman sultan and was alleged to have acquired his taste for impaling victims as a child in the Turkish court. On returning to Romania, he became a Christian again and vowed to undo the sultan's hold on his kingdom. The battle he subsequently fought against the Turks has often been interpreted as yet another holy crusade against Muslim oppressors.[80] By the late fifteenth century, an explosion of printed pamphlets depicting the extreme cruelty of Vlad Tepes flew off newly established print-

2.13. The Forest of the Impaled, woodcut from the German pamphlet *Dracole Wayda*, published by Matthias Hupfuff, Strassburg, 1599. Mary Evans Picture Library.

ing presses around central Europe, and a taste developed for illustrated tales of bloody tortures by an orientalized Vlad Tepes. In these pamphlets, readers experience the exotic and fascinating regions east of Europe as threatening and Vlad as a European prince who crossed the line dividing the cruel East from the civilized West.[81] Less than fifty years after Vlad Tepes's death, Pope Leo X issued a papal bull (1514) authorizing Hungarian rebels to promote a Christian crusade against the Ottomans, and when the rebellion went out of control, the rioters impaled members of the Hungarian landed gentry.[82]

It is likely that by the end of the seventeenth century, given the nature of these impalement stories and the illustrations accompanying them, this form of torture came to be associated in the Anglo-American imagination with a generalized East, blurring distinctions between Eastern Europe, the Ottoman Empire, and Persia, implicating China by virtue of its cardinal orientation. Based on this popular understanding, an Anglo-American could easily have imaginatively invoked impalement in response to situations of religious tension between a Christian West and a non-Christian East. Gibbs, a transplanted Bostonian in nearby Newport, was certainly aware of the religious tensions—and even tortures—alleged in the *Boston News-Letter* to be taking place between the Jesuits and their Chinese hosts. That Gibbs erroneously ascribed impalement to the Chinese is explicable within the transatlantic cultural context of the early eighteenth century. These murals demonstrate above all how bound early Americans were by early modern European popular culture, even while, at least in Gibbs's case, giving an original performance in the theater of avant-garde interior decorating.

As we have seen with Stalker and Parker's "punishment" pattern for japanning a comb box (fig. 2.9), there is a precedent for the use of scenes of Chinese torture in English decorative arts. Gibbs, therefore, can be seen as working within an English cultural paradigm, indeed as making an active contribution to the staying power of that paradigm. His enthrallment with the Chinese commodity is conspicuously painted in powerful colors and dimensions all over the walls of the principal room of his home. The aura of Asian lacquer is almost overpowering when applied floor-to-ceiling on his walls, so much so that it is hard to imagine that a middle-class, church-going, husband/father/sign painter in Newport would have done this without having already experienced its effect in another much-admired room. But we have no evidence that Gibbs traveled farther than New England. His detailed attention to Chinese—not European—design motifs, such as the oversized cranes, the birds flying beak-to-beak (fig. 2.4), the grinning wiry beasts, and the circular scholar's rocks indicates the impact Chinese commodities had made on him.

Yet at the same time that his murals demonstrate a longing for the Chinese object and Chinese aesthetic, Gibbs conveys a concomitant antagonism. This is patently evident in the impaling scene. But also we see it in the Chinese magistrate to whom he has given an English crown, expressing a wry sense of

2.14. Japanning pattern from John Stalker and George Parker, *A Treatise of Japanning and Varnishing*, London, 1688.

hierarchy in which England, despite its relatively impoverished material aesthetic, dominates the great Celestial Empire. Stalker and Parker offer another pattern in their *Treatise of Japanning*, this time suggested for drawer fronts, that makes this hierarchical West-over-East statement much more blatantly (fig. 2.14). Here a man in Western clothing uses a bamboo pole to flog a half-naked Chinese man lying on the ground tied to a spear-like stake. Indeed, by comparison, Gibbs's discreet placement of the English crown in an otherwise seemingly Chinese context benefits from greater subtlety.

It should be noted that Chinese and Japanese artists did, in fact, depict European people and European design motifs on both lacquer and porcelain objects, especially after the late seventeenth century when a bona fide export market catering to Western tastes heated up in China.[83] European-subject figural designs were sometimes original. Scenes of the Portuguese "black ships" arriving on the shores of Japan in the late sixteenth century and memorialized on Namban screens by fascinated artists convey real events in an original visual record. But more often the Western designs were take-offs of a European original. Scenes on porcelain vases of Dutchmen in hunting regalia complete with dogs and blunderbusses were probably not viewed firsthand by Chinese artists, and may even have come to China thirdhand by way of Japanese artists who had viewed Dutch drawings and paintings.[84] By the early eighteenth century an entire industry of imitating European pictorial models on porcelain emerged in China, promoted by the consolidation of East-West commerce in the urban port of Canton. Special orders for porcelain services adorned with European family coats of arms were shipped en masse to the workshops of Canton—so British crowns like that on Daniel Updike's porcelain coffee pot (Rhode Island; fig. 2.15) were certainly not unknown to Chinese artists.[85]

But all sorts of European design sources show up on porcelain, from Greek gods to Hogarth drawings. Considering the widespread circulation within Europe of popular depictions of Dracula and the centuries-long battles against the Turks, one might think that impaling, as depicted within this tradition by Gibbs, might also have been reproduced on a Chinese object. Yet, given the Chinese artistic tradition of depicting scenes that promote good fortune or recall morally uplifting heroes, using such dark imagery as impaling on a Coromandel screen or any Chinese export commodity is extremely unlikely. Indeed, today only a handful of European-subject Coromandel screens are known, and all these depict ships and Dutchmen, either hunting or bearing

2.15. Monogrammed, special order Chinese porcelain coffee pot belonging to Daniel Updike (d. 1757) of Wickford, RI. Museum of Art, Rhode Island School of Design, Providence. Photo: Erik Gould, courtesy of the Museum of Art, Rhode Island School of Design.

gifts.[86] Chinese export artists were known for some satirical play with the images in their artwork, and while the Dutchmen in these scenes might be viewed as loading cargo, the inscription reveals that they are actually paying tribute to the Chinese emperor. Moreover, not only did export art have a "low art" status in China, but late Ming tastes that held the genre of figural art in low esteem endured into the Qing dynasty.[87] The Coromandel screens and porcelain dishes so admired in Europe were probably considered tacky, throwaway works of art in China, especially those objects with European-subject motifs. Nevertheless, the Chinese artist adhered to certain dicta. Such scenes as Gibbs splashed all over his walls would have been abhorrent to the Chinese. But Gibbs did not know that. Ironically, he chose the fashionable, much-admired Chinese artistic idiom in order to energetically express a complex response to Chinese-European relations—a response built from immediate newspaper accounts of Jesuit activities in China as well as centuries of European experience with the Ottoman Empire. It is not the least bit probable that these images came from a Chinese artist.

Matteo Ricci, the first Jesuit to live in China and the first Westerner to have extended, intimate contact with the Chinese people (1583–1610), struggled to find something from his part of the world that could possibly impress those he sought to convert to Christianity. The best he could offer, in an account that was known and repeated throughout Europe, was a global map.[88] The moral of this much-loved story is that Westerners were accomplished first and foremost through their knowledge and experience of the scope and limits of the world. Americans were great map lovers, as evident in booksellers' advertisements. In 1720, for example, the *American Weekly Mercury* advertised "Usefull and cheap ornaments for Rooms being 6 Beautifull Mapps each on two large sheets of Royal Paper."[89] World maps are regularly found in estate inventories, regardless of class, across the northeastern colonies. By demonstrating knowledge of China and the Chinese aesthetic, Gibbs was likewise communicating his worldly wherewithall to any fellow New Englander who might visit his home. But Gibbs also engaged in satire because while vaunting the Chinese aesthetic, he deprecated the Chinese people by portraying them as armed and dangerous, and moreover, discreetly set beneath a *superior* English crown.

In the first decades of the eighteenth century, almost all knowledge in America of the Chinese came from reports by and about the Catholic missionaries. Americans were not privy to the experiences of members of the English and Dutch East India companies, even though they did see the European engravings by non-Catholics who voyaged there, as well as the chinoiserie imitations. While Americans shared an attraction to the Chinese aesthetic with the English, the commercial aspect of their imagined relation to the Far East was not as prominent. Instead, New Englanders in particular, who were more impacted by the austere culture of reformed Protestantism, were more likely to react squeamishly to the non-Christian beliefs and practices of the Chinese than would have the English. While embracing the English fascination with the Chinese aesthetic in creating his wall murals, Gibbs could not help expressing his prejudices at the same time by depicting the Chinese as brutal and indistinguishable from the hated Turks. Moreover, the Chinese interactions with the Catholic Jesuits would not appease a church-going New England man, who had been married in a Congregational church and was also a pewholder and pallbearer in Newport's Anglican Trinity Church.[90] In fact, the idolatry of the Catholics was revealed in the *Boston News-Letter* reports that the Jesuits in China were going native.[91] This all confirmed that if one let oneself get too close to "infidels," an expression used by Rhode Island mariners setting out to the Indian Ocean in the 1690s, especially such cultured and alluring infidels, one might end up ruled by despotism or perhaps even impaled! It is hard not to wonder if, after painting his umpteenth japanned tea table, William Gibbs, a devout Protestant, needed a creative release to the emotions aroused by engaging with this heathen art form. He expressed the imagined violence he associated with the Chinese on his walls, feelings he successfully contained while painting fairy-tale Chinamen on his customer's tables.

At some point during the eighteenth century the creative fusion represented in Gibbs's artistic contribution to the nascent Sino-Anglo relationship was abruptly covered over. Downing gives the wooden paneling a mid-eighteenth-century vintage.[92] Metcalf Bowler, whose father purchased the house in 1744, enlarged and refurbished it in 1759 (using money earned the good-old-fashioned American way, privateering against popish states). In 1768, Bowler invited all of Newport to his beautiful home to celebrate the repeal of the Stamp Act. Bowler was a Sinophile with a large porcelain collection, and he authored a treatise on agriculture in 1786 that opens with praise for Chinese practices. Might he have found the torture scenes distasteful for his semi-public salon? Or did reveling Newporters sip tea from Bowler's porcelain while gazing on Gibbs's heavily prejudiced artwork? At the outbreak of the revolution, the house passed to William Vernon, a passionate Patriot who hosted Count Rochambeau and his suite of officers. The courtly guests were hard on the house, and Vernon was obliged to sue for damages at the close of the war.[93] With this compensation, the house was again refurbished. Vernon had amassed many paintings while traveling in France during the war, including a copy of the Mona Lisa.[94] Perhaps he covered over the japanned walls in favor of his collection of European "high art"? As we see in Cruger's 1803 invoice for japanning two rooms, this style remained current throughout the eighteenth century, and Chinese wall papers were very popular during both Bowler's and Vernon's tenures. Knowing at exactly what point these paintings were covered over, and why, would make an important contribution to our understanding of the direct march colonial Americans made into the China trade following their independence from England, but these are questions that cannot be answered here.

The wall murals do provide, however, important insight into the active engagement and vivid attitudes of Americans toward China in the 1720s. They allow us to see the degree of exposure Americans at this early date had to the arts of China and to the sophisticated, cosmopolitan styles provoked in Europe by contact with Asia, contrary to conventional historical accounts of a marginalized colonial North American. Gibbs's murals offer the wonderful advantage of carrying observers today directly into the imaginary world of a New England artisan. We glimpse the fantastical but nevertheless foundational, prejudicial vision of China that Gibbs most likely shared with other members of his Anglo-American community, given the public nature of his commercial japanning business. The experiences Americans had in the East and in contact with Asian material culture in the 1690s were not isolated, fleeting experiences but part of the ongoing, larger place they shared with other Euro-Atlantic peoples in interaction with Asia. Their relationship to an imagined China changed over the course of the eighteenth century, evidenced by the covering up of Gibbs's murals, but the fact of a regular and intensifying contact with the arts and material world of Asia long before the opening of the US China trade cannot be doubted.

3

Islands of Illicit Refinement

Bohia and Chaney for the Northern Plantations

> I long to see you here for I am now getting worse and the more so because I don't have any bohee tee.
> —Alida Livingston in Albany, October 12, 1717

> I am credibly informed, that Tea and China Ware cost the Province yearly near the sum of Ten Thousand Pounds; and People that are the least able to go to the expence, must have their Tea tho' their Families go hungry.
> —*New York Weekly Journal*, April 22, 1734

In 1717 the wealthy Dutch-American Alida Livingston, then sixty-one years old, wrote to her husband Robert, who was residing down the Hudson River at their New York City home. She begged him to send up some tea, telling him, as well as us, that consumption of this Chinese beverage was necessary to her well-being. But it was not the tea alone she craved. Six years earlier she had written several letters to her husband insisting that he send up the river "cups and saucers to drink the tea," meaning Chinese porcelain.[1] Warm beverages had been drunk for centuries in northern Europe in stout earthenware and stoneware mugs. Some of these vessels were quite decorative (fig. 3.1), in shape often styled after silver forms. For the wealthy, such as Livingston, tea could have been drunk from silver-trimmed mugs or fancy European pottery. But for Livingston, Chinese porcelain cups and saucers, not earthenware, were the necessary vessels for drinking tea. At this time Chinese cups did not have handles, so, if Livingston did not want to use a mug, why couldn't she drink tea in small delicate bowls made of delftware, which were easier and cheaper to obtain? This tin-glazed, buff-colored earthenware pottery had been developed in direct imitation of Chinese

3.1. Lead-glazed English earthenware "tyg," with slip-trailed decoration and stamped pads of white clay, dated 1649, with initials J[ohn] L[ivermore] of Wrotham, England. Courtesy of Victoria & Albert Museum.

porcelain in Persia and the Mediterranean. First introduced in Italy and Spain in the fourteenth century as majolica, its enamel glaze yielded brilliant whites and colors similar to porcelain. By the early seventeenth century the town of Delft in Holland had become a center for ceramics, and potters there were able to produce tin-glazed earthenware dishes that copied the look of Chinese blue-and-white porcelain to perfection (figs. 3.2 and 3.3).[2] Yet, in every early modern and colonial American description of pottery handed down to us today in estate inventories and ship manifests, delftware and china are distinguished. Nobody was fooled by the cruder European imitation.

Perhaps Livingston preferred real china cups and saucers because high-fired porcelain better retained heat and did not chip as easily as the low-fired body of European earthenwares, which were heavier, more fragile, and more porous than porcelain, even though the two wares looked alike on first glance. Did Livingston request china cups for these practical reasons, or was she interested in the social status porcelain conferred, or any other cultural subtext implied in using an authentic Chinese dish? In order to answer these questions, it is first necessary to have a more precise picture of how porcelain arrived in the colonies in the first place and its extent and distribution in colonial households. This chapter examines trade for Chinese porcelain in colonial American households from 1700 to 1770. It is the necessary background to better interpreting the cultural work of Chinese objects in the northern colonial context, the topic of the next chapter.

As seen in the previous chapter, by the second decade of the eighteenth century, colonial Americans residing in the northeast had a much richer exposure to the material arts of Asia than historians or curators have traditionally acknowledged.[3] Colonial seaports welcomed a continual stream of immigrants and visitors from European cities, where orientalism in all its finest Eastern trappings was moving to the forefront of popular fashion.[4] A deluge of Chinese objects poured into the North Atlantic basin in the seventeenth and eighteenth centuries, including some 70 million pieces of porcelain.[5] With the growing popularity of tea and punch drinking, as well as formal dining, the odd pieces of Chinese porcelain expanded into larger services, moving from the curio cabinet and the manteltree to architecturally standardized china closets, tea tables, and dining tables.

Consumption—the ownership of particular possessions—is preceded by culturally complex economic activities. Anthropologists and material culture historians have made important contributions in recent years toward elucidating the meaning of consumption patterns within early modern cultural

3.2. Tin-glazed earthenware plate, ca. 1760, Liverpool, England. Gift of Barbara Chase Mayer, 1984, E81506. Peabody Essex Museum, Salem, MA. Photo courtesy of the Peabody Essex Museum.

3.3. Chinese porcelain plate, eighteenth century. Gift of Mrs. Weston P. Figgins, 1980, E81159.21. Peabody Essex Museum, Salem, MA. Photo courtesy of the Peabody Essex Museum.

contexts.[6] Many of these studies begin with the type of information provided by estate inventories; in other words, they begin by examining the specific things already owned by a regional or politically defined group of people and then develop theories about their socioeconomic status and cosmology using an analysis of those things. While this study of Chinese objects in the Anglo-American colonies is situated within their methodological historical frameworks, historians of consumption need a more dynamic starting point for analysis. Objects were not simply willed into a household. The political and social pressures surrounding a point-of-purchase moment engender a cultural momentum that continues once objects are in a household. The colonial American owner of porcelain did not forget all the angst, capital, and labor involved in bringing that object into the household once it was on the mantel. Trade had an impact on taste just as taste formed domestic markets that impacted trade. We must therefore begin with an analysis of trade and strive to integrate an inventory-based cultural history of the "meaning of things" with an examination of real economic practices and constraints—with the mechanics and politics of trade and the commercial marketplace.[7]

In "good hope" all of Europe had sent vessels beyond the Cape of Good Hope by the eighteenth century, into maritime Asia, which comprised both the Indian and Pacific oceans and where Chinese goods had circulated widely for centuries.[8] Far from oblivious to European attempts to enter the Asian China trades, people who called America home in the eighteenth century fully participated as integral members of the commercial Atlantic. Within living memory in eighteenth-century British America, local mariners had sailed to Indian Ocean ports, at least as far east as the Straits of Malacca, bringing back both oral accounts and commodities. With the Crown's renewed enforcement of the English East India Company's monopoly in Eastern waters and its turn toward prosecuting Indian Ocean interlopers as pirates, many of these far-ranging sailors sank quietly into the colonial landscape, leaving their stories and trinkets to future generations. While the stories may be lost to us today, estate inventories offer a valuable resource for positively identifying not only a taste for china but also a China trade in young colonial seaports.

The first part of this chapter relies on business documents, newspaper articles, and personal letters to sketch out how Chinese porcelain probably arrived in Atlantic colonies. There were basically five important circuits of trade, often overlapping, that allowed colonial Americans broad access to the European East Indies trades and commodities. First, there was the legal, highly regulated, and taxed London-based trade with the English East India Company; second, piracy and privateering in the Indian Ocean and the Caribbean; third, the Dutch global network that connected New York to Amsterdam and the Dutch Caribbean; fourth, legal and smuggling trades in the Spanish, English, and French Caribbean; and fifth, the fish and grain trade to southern Europe, giving Americans access to Iberian East Indies commodities. All of these arenas proved to be copious but often undocumented sources of Asian commodities, including Chinese porcelain—what we might call a shadow economy for porcelain. After an examination of these trade arenas, the second part of this chapter looks at the circulation of Asian commodities within the northern colonies of America, relying on supporting material-culture evidence from a survey of over a thousand estate inventories in the principal northern seaports. Looking at the various overseas circuits of East-West trade alongside internal informal and commercial circuits allows us to more concretely determine how many and which colonial households contained Chinese porcelain. More important, we can begin to understand the cultural baggage a porcelain pot accumulated on the long road from a kiln in central China to Alida Livingston's parlor. All these elements—refined manufacturing processes, Buddhist-laden design motifs, mutually suspicious sales contracts between strangers speaking different languages, piracy and shipwrecks, a Company culture invested with aristocratic pretensions and greed—were refracted in one form or another in the object's final landing place. Out of them Americans constructed their own interpretations, vesting each little Chinese pot with a new social heritage.

Chinese Porcelain Trade to the Northern British Colonies

The Nature of Chinaware as a Commodity

Finding evidence for Chinese porcelain in colonial homes is a less difficult task than figuring out how it got there to begin with. A simple commodity paper trail that allows historians and economists to work out trade routes and quantitative snapshots for imports is almost impossible for American consumption of Chinese objects in the eighteenth century. Even in England, documenting the importation of porcelain is difficult. In 1704, two years after the English East India Company solidified its monopoly, it brought home the largest shipment of porcelain into England yet, and the Crown laid its first tax on chinawares, duties that continued throughout the century on both sides of the Atlantic. Chests of porcelain proved an ideal companion cargo to delicate, easily spoiled chests of tea. Spices, camphor oils, and other odorous East Asian products had to be carried separately from tea, which would absorb other scents like a sponge. Porcelain had no smell at all. A single chest could hold about six hundred nested dishes, weighing over five hundred pounds, providing both excellent ballast and a dry platform on which to place the more important and fragile commodities of tea and raw silk.[9] The fetid saltwater pools of a ship's bottom hold had no impact on porcelain (as proven by recent auction sales of unspoiled chinaware recovered after several centuries on the sea floor[10]). But unlike tea and silk, porcelain stowed away in the deepest hold of the ship often traveled *unrecorded* as "private adventure"—a crew member's personal cargo—and was subsequently sold privately or given as gifts.[11]

From its earliest days in the West, extending back to the Crusades, Chinese porcelain functioned as a potent gift rather than as a marketable commodity.[12] The Portuguese, the first to sail to Chinese waters, called these porcelain gifts "pilgrim art," denoting an object associated with a voyage to a sacred place.[13] Dazzling and exotic, irreproducible in the West, porcelain was a central symbol used by merchants in offering gratitude and compensation, or *splendidum furtum*, to their royal and aristocratic patrons.[14] Even after trade in porcelain became an integral part of commerce (after the formation of the various state-sponsored East Indies enterprises), it never shed its tributary status as a precious gift, proffered as a token of a kingdom's far-reaching territorial influence, valued more for the politically charged statement it made about the worldly status of the gift-giver and receiver than for its market price. This cultural background is necessary to understanding why British mercantile restrictions were much more relaxed for the porcelain carried by ship's officers than for staple commodities such as tea or textiles. Large-scale commercial vending and consumption of fine porcelain was unseemly, and a distinction developed early in the China trade between special order dishes that were elaborately emblazoned with armorial insignia and lowly general market, utilitarian wares.[15] English captains were known to bring in over a hundred chests of porcelain, most of it special order, and they did so on their own private accounts, not on Company accounts.[16] Company records for porcelain, therefore, are much less complete than for tea and silk.

After about 1720 the East India Company gave up any attempt at itemization in its invoices for porcelain, and instructions to supercargoes from London were equally vague, such as "chinaware must be of all useful sorts."[17] Private orders may have been very specific, but preservation of these documents is, of course, haphazard in Europe and almost nonexistent in America. The East India Company explicitly discouraged importation of nonuseful, decorative ceramics like large monteiths and garden jars, perhaps considered suited only for kings but which were nevertheless found throughout Britain and the British colonies.[18] All of this nonuseful, prestige-oriented, or purely decorative porcelain points to the extent of the underground commerce, especially when it is found in the colonies. Mid-eighteenth-century Newport merchant Metcalf Bowler was said to have planted his best apple trees in large porcelain pots, and as a West Indies trader and privateer extraordinaire, his source was undoubtedly not a London-based china vendor.[19] Bowler was a new breed, a man of commerce not lineage, residing on the edge of the empire, "trading" outside the empire, and styling himself in the manner of British aristocrats.[20]

If documenting incoming porcelain is difficult in England, the situation is even more obscure in the colonies. While the three principal Chinese imports of tea, silk, and porcelain were highly regulated in law,[21] American captains, like English ones, also carried individual chests of luxury items such as porcelain as unrecorded adventure cargo. Some of this china was sold and some given away as gifts. But whatever its route once in the colonies, most of this porcelain—like so much else—slipped in despite the watchful Crown customs apparatus. It is a mistake to look for porcelain in colonial shipping records or business accounts. Beginning in the 1720s china shows up regularly in retailers' daybooks and colonial newspaper ads placed by local merchants, but almost never in customs records or shipping records. One example from a 1720 *Boston Gazette* advertisement reads, "Just arrived from London in Capt. Martin, several Setts of fine China Ware, with good Bohea Tea and Tea-Tables, and choice Florence Oyl. Sold by Thomas Selby at the Crown Coffee-House in Boston."[22] Just because "Capt. Martin" arrived from London does not mean the china advertised came from a legitimate dealer, or even from London. The ship may have touched in London to clear a load of alcohol or sugar without ever declaring a few chests of porcelain picked up outside imperial channels along the way and stowed with the officers' adventures.[23]

The American Mariner and Spanish Silver

In the colonies, porcelain, or "Chaney," does show up with the most frequency in the estate inventories of those with seafaring connections—sea captains, mariners, and merchants—but unlike the claim made in the *Gazette* for "Capt. Martin," only a small percentage of these men carried on direct trade in London. The vast majority of American merchants and mariners worked the coastal trade, sailing to ports that lay in the western Atlantic between the West Indies and Canada. Of 139 recorded entrances for the port of Salem, Massachusetts, in 1751, for example, a mere two returned from Britain while sixty-six came from the British and French West Indies, forty-six from the Iberian Peninsula, and sixteen from Canada.[24] Clearly the vast majority of imports into the colonial northeast, including European and Asian finished products, came from the Caribbean and southern Europe. As early as the last quarter of the seventeenth century, mariner-merchants in New England were routinely carrying fish and lumber products to the Iberian Peninsula—a region then engaged in regularized commerce with the Far East—and returning to the West Indies with goods to exchange for sugar products. These colonial merchants were active agents in the transatlantic transport of these goods, often bypassing London altogether.[25]

Most conventional narratives of colonial North American material life stop short of acknowledging the wide geographic penetration of northern mariners and its corollary, the great quantity of global commodities circulating in the western Atlantic. These narratives overlook the entire Spanish Empire with its brisk transpacific Chinese–American trade routes and, arguably more important, its wellspring of silver necessary for the purchase of Chinese products. Research that compares *registered* silver production in Peru to *estimated* production has shown that, beginning in the mid-seventeenth century and continuing through the eighteenth century, *real* production often ran 50 to 100 percent greater than what was registered on the books, leaving millions of silver pesos unaccounted for.[26] "Unregistered and/or contraband bullion has long been the bane of modern historians seeking to unravel the history of colonial [New World] mining," states one economic historian who also notes that Mexico and Peru accounted for more than 80 percent of silver worldwide from 1550 to 1800.[27] From the seventeenth century on, northern colonial sailors were quite familiar with the Gulf coasts of Mexico and Central and South America. Economic historian Alejandra Irigoin has argued that after 1750 the primary centers of Spanish silver were not the mining and producing areas of Peru and Mexico but outposts set up by the Spanish Crown for the maintenance of its empire, such as Havana.[28] From the earliest days of settlement, North Americans were well aware that there was more to be found in the West Indies than agricultural produce.[29] Bullion flowed out of the Spanish imperial mainland, through Caribbean island entrepôts, into a hospitable sea basin shared by the Dutch, French, English, and Spanish. Silver was the lone commodity that attracted the interest of the Chinese—the engine of global trade—and its presence in the Caribbean where foreign interests mingled so closely made illicit commerce all too easy.[30]

This silver made its way to wily American mariners working the coastal trades, mariners who, by the mid-eighteenth century, were running a deficit with England.[31] With so much of English mercantile capital tied up in the East Indies trade, and specifically trade for Chinese commodities, preserving an American debt that could be paid off in silver was clearly advantageous to English merchants. As one illustration of the access North Americans had to silver, the Jamaican governor Charles Knowles reported that over the years between 1735 and 1752 vessels from North America carried away from his island about £71,000 of sterling silver a year.[32] Little of this silver shows up on incoming cargo manifests,[33] nor do the smuggled chests of luxury wares buried within the vessels returning north from the islands and southern Europe.

There were some holes in the colonial subterfuge, however, and especially in the former Dutch colony of New York we find evidence for the extent of northern involvement in the West Indies commodities mart. The 1732 invoice for the ship *Catharine*—owned by Alida Livingston's son Robert Livingston— which entered New York from Kingston, Jamaica, openly declared 160 ounces of Spanish silver and a box of china, "viz 3 large burnt China dishes, 6 ditto, 1 doz. Plates."[34] Both silver and Asian luxury items made their way into the hands of customs officials in all the northern seaports in compensation for not noticing that the principal commercial cargo, sugar and molasses, had not been cleared in England.[35] Little had changed, evidently, since Governor Bellomont, fearing the seepage of foreign goods into the American colonies, had tried to close the American coastline to global trade. That silver and Asian luxury wares continued to characterize this extra-imperial trade remained a brazen affront to the pretenses of British officialdom, yet few officials cared. In 1738 Boston merchant Benjamin Greene sent a vessel to Surinam and returned with a cargo of bohea tea, coffee, cocoa, and molasses—and very likely some Chinese porcelain and Spanish silver dollars as well.[36] He sold his goods to an eager market in Massachusetts. The colonists' allegiance to England was, at least in most instances of commerce, purely a question of affect, not interest.

Imperial Interest versus Ambitious Traders in Outer Entrepôts

Increased British customs surveillance after midcentury became a thorn in the sides of colonial merchants, who constantly complained and warned each other about the lurking presence of Union Jack vessels, sometimes offering specific instructions to captains on how to avoid them. American vessels regularly sailed with several flags ("flags of convenience") to slip by English patrol ships and carried foreign speakers who could sign papers in banned ports.[37] In 1764, with the renewal of the Sugar Act, Nicholas Brown would give his captain two sets of orders: one fictitious, directing him to sail to Barbados, and the other genuine, dispatching him to Surinam.[38] In 1758, Francis Higginson in Salem wrote to a business partner complaining about "ye Engl[ish] Men-of-War" taking "all Dutch vessels that shall be found trading from ye Dutch Plantations in ye West Indies to any French Port / The consequence of wch will be ye ruin of the Trade in this Towne to St. Eustacia." What is as interesting as the conflict of commercial interest between England and its colonies in global arenas is the conflict of identity it engendered in colonials. In complaining about "ye English," Higginson apparently thought twice about the expression, crossing it out and changing it to "*our* Men-of War."[39]

Despite the naval artillery, controlling thousands of miles of coastline, island entrepôts at the threshold to the Spanish Main, and hundreds of European and American merchants outside London was simply impossible. There was an upsurge in European traders in Asia after about 1717,[40] so that even with its heavy-handed tactics (such as stringing interlopers to poles as pirates), England simply could not control the flow of Asian commodities into the colonies in the eighteenth century. Parliament promulgated laws prohibiting direct commerce between Asia and western Atlantic ports and declared war on the "interlopers," but there was little it could do against other European states. In 1718, confronted with the mounting strength of the English East India Company, the French king reorganized his Compagnie Perpétuelle des Indes. He placed both the East and West Indies routes under the same company, within one trade system, unlike that of the English.[41] French East India ships regularly stopped in the Caribbean for an escort, and of course to trade their valuable Asian goods.

English control over Asian commodities in Atlantic waters, however, was plagued by more players than just the French. A host of minor East India enterprises sprang up, most of which functioned as cover for British interlopers outlawed from trading in the East.[42] In 1721, news that the Flemish Ostender ship *St. Francis* had landed a large quantity of Asian goods in Barbados provoked an immediate response from the English Parliament. The trade ministers explained that the reason they did not let East India Company vessels send slaves to America was precisely "for fear of filling the plantations with India goods."[43] The Privy Council followed up a few months later with an order outlawing trade between the Indian Ocean and the West Indies in any and all commodities, including slaves and china pots.[44] In addition to the Ostend enterprise, other small companies over the century included the Scottish Darien Company, the Danish East India Company, the Swedish East India Company (initially made up of pardoned English pirates), the Prussian Bengal Company, and the Imperial East India Company of Trieste. European mariners wishing to circumvent the large company monopolies also resorted to "flags of convenience," sailing in the East under Polish or Holy Roman Empire colors, for example.[45] Moreover, within the growing body of Company men residing in Asia were those who could not resist using their local connections to carry on private trading ventures.[46] These multinational, renegade operators internationalized trade in the Indian Ocean and the Pacific, and nothing stopped them from extending their commercial ventures into the booming market for luxuries in the western Atlantic.

England's efforts to control the East Indies trade were only moderately successful, but they nevertheless fostered a powerful ideology of imperial control and domination that in itself did more work than fifty men-of-war. By 1776 Adam Smith could write in *The Wealth of Nations* that the discovery of America and a passage to the East Indies were the two greatest events in the history of mankind, but he stopped short of placing them in an unbroken trading sphere. "By uniting, *in some measure*, the most distant parts of the world, by enabling them to relieve one another's wants, to increase one another's enjoyments, and to encourage one another's industry, their general tendency would seem to be beneficial."[47] Even Smith, the strongest proponent of free trade the world had ever known, was unable to envision global commerce without England at the center, to "measure" all exchanges between the distinct trade spheres of Asia and America. But continental European merchants, confronting unprecedented demand around the Atlantic for Asian commodities, were no more likely to follow orders set down by British imperialdom than were resistant Americans, and the Caribbean Islands and French Canada continued to offer accessible markets for Asian commodities.

American merchants as well as Parliament were very aware of the potential magnitude of a direct trade that bypassed England. Colonial newspapers were filled with commentary on the comings and goings of the various statesponsored East Indies vessels, to and from all Atlantic ports. Northern papers often carried news of the presence of French East India ships, "loaded richly with China goods," in nearby Canadian waters.[48] Philadelphia's *American Weekly Mercury* carried several articles in 1722 and 1723 closely following the formation of the Ostend Company. One of these articles reads "we understand that the Priviledge is granted them exclusive of all other his Imperial Majesty's Subjects, of trading not only in the East Indies, on the Coasts of Africa and Asia, as far as Japan, and even as far as their Commerce can be extended that way; but likewise in the West Indies."[49] American merchants would be ready for them when they arrived in the western Atlantic, or would even head out to intercept them.

In 1777 Benjamin Franklin received a letter from a veteran captain of the French Compagnie des Indes. The captain was looking for a Philadelphia merchant who had once given him a bad bill of exchange during a "private" business transaction in, of all places, Ascension Island, an isolated spot in the south Atlantic and a watering hole, apparently, for French ships coming from Asia. Returning from China, he said, he put into Ascension Island for turtles and encountered a Benjamin Salter out of St. Eustatius, "waiting to make purchases from passing vessels." The French captain sought Franklin's help in recovering the American debt, and he cautiously added, "Please do not let the ship's owners [Compagnie des Indes] hear of my misadventure; they do not like such private business, although it is the only way that the underpaid can survive."[50] We see plainly the pressure felt by company traders to support themselves with off-the-books transactions, and what better business partner than an out-of-the-way Philadelphia ship on an isolated island. We also see how colonial merchants exploited American maritime capital and expertise to connect with Indiamen, obtaining chests of porcelain along with profitable cargoes of tea and silk, perhaps laying over in the Caribbean until winter, when they could more easily smuggle the goods into the northern colonies unnoticed.

Franklin, a man privy to inside knowledge of colonial commerce and so skilled in bluntly articulating the social and political realities of his time, pseudonymously wrote a series of articles from London in early 1770 entitled the "Colonist's Advocate." Americans were then smarting under a renewal of revenue acts that severely threatened the sort of free circulation of their ships described above, oppressing trade to an extent unmatched since the time of Lord Bellomont. Under such pressure, Franklin, their mouthpiece, was forced to broach the unspeakable idea that Americans might sail to the East themselves, returning loaded with "East India Goods":

What will they [Grenvillians] say when they find, that Ships are actually fitted out from the Colonies (they cannot, I suppose hinder their fitting out ships) for all Parts of the World; for China, by Cape Horn; for instance, to sail under Prussian, or other Colours, with Cargoes of various Kinds, and so return loaded with Tea, and other East India Goods. . . . The whole Navy of England, if stationed ever so judiciously, cannot prevent smuggling on a Coast of 1500 Miles in Length. Such Steps as these will soon be taken by the Americans.[51]

Franklin singles out China from a world of possible ports as that most likely to raise the ire of the English. He was certainly not the only colonist or the first to envision such a scenario, but as long as tea, chinaware, and Asian textiles were readily available on islands to the south, why wound the vanity of England and risk a confrontation with a self-consciously mighty sea power? In the same article Franklin boldly describes exactly how American masters might (and certainly *did*) charter a vessel in France, sail to Eustatia, load foreign goods, and wait until winter "to smuggle them into all Parts of North America in small Vessels."

Once we take into account the illusory, ideological character of eighteenth-century European monopolistic empires, especially the Spanish and the English, and the reality of overlapping circuits of trade—the Spanish American–West Indian circuit, the European–West Indian/Canadian circuit, the East Indian–West Indian/Canadian circuit, and the northeast American–West Indian/Canadian circuit—it is no longer possible to assert that because so few American merchants were in London, Asian commodities were less accessible to them. In the 1721 *Boston Gazette* ad, "All Sorts of European and West India Goods, and Fine China Ware lately Imported," we see a mixing of worldly goods at *one* Boston warehouse, whose source—based on American port records—was probably *one* incoming vessel from the Caribbean.[52] The Caribbean was a central, common location to almost all global trade networks in the eighteenth century, not a peripheral location, and Americans from the northern plantations—as a distinct (although not yet unified) interest group—had been there since the mid-seventeenth century.

In the *Universal Dictionary of Trade and Commerce* published in London after the Seven Years' War, an English author comments, "There is no port in the world out of Europe, where all sorts of European goods are to be seen in greater plenty than there, in Curacao."[53] The Dutch Caribbean was especially well linked to Spanish America (and its silver) by its large Spanish-speaking Sephardic Jewish population, which made up about a third of Curaçao's population throughout the eighteenth century. The Spanish Main dominated Curaçao's trade, but about 11 percent of the island's shipping went consistently to North America.[54] It is not surprising that New York merchants, many of whom were tied by kinship and business to long-standing Dutch and Jewish communities around the globe, were more closely connected to the Dutch West Indies than to London.[55] Examples of their trade outside the British Empire are easy to find in their business correspondence, they being perhaps less awed by English Crown officialdom. In 1740 Philip Livingston, oldest son of Alida, wrote from his manor in Albany to his brother Robert in New York, "I wish you could ingage some trusty Capt. who goes to Curacao to bring some tea." Curious place to look for Chinese tea! A few months later he complained to Robert about a missing set of china he had ordered. "Among the goods from

Curacao are 6 doz. Chanee tea cups and dishes which are not come. Inform me whether they be with you."[56]

Livingston's orders were not only for his own elite manor household. In a 1735 account book entitled "Store at the Manner," articles sold to local farmers on the vast Livingston patroonship are itemized, and here we see listed "48 Chine Cups & Sucers."[57] Livingston, like his mother, liked his tea in china cups, but he clearly had no compunction about promoting the spread of Chinese porcelain to lower-class farmers, many of who were peasants from the Palatine. Tea drinking was big business in the colonies, both in towns and countryside, and even hard-working farmers needed Chinese cups for their Chinese tea.

Anglo-Americans from the other northern colonies were also present in significant numbers in the Dutch West Indies. In 1756 Philadelphia merchant Thomas Willing directed his young partner, Robert Morris (later to send the United States' first ship to China), to head to Curaçao from Jamaica as he heard "they are in want of provisions there."[58] In the lively 1755 painting "Sea Captains Carousing in Surinam" (fig. 3.4) we get a peek at this history of northern British Americans trading in Dutch colonies. Artist John Greenwood, also seen in the painting, depicts a roomful of Rhode Island merchants in this Dutch colony drinking punch from large Chinese porcelain bowls served by black servants, while their sloop holds were being filled, no doubt, with Chinese teas and tea services for their more abstemious wives. A collection of Chinese porcelain bequeathed to the Rhode Island School of Design Museum by a descendant of the Providence merchant families Brown, Ives, and Dorr contains several pieces labeled "from Surinam" dating to the 1750s (one such example is pictured in fig. 2.5).[59]

The Browns of Providence began trading in the West Indies in the 1720s with a voyage to "some of the Leeward Islands in the West Indies," as James Brown imprecisely recorded the destination in his notebook. The Leeward Islands included English, Dutch, and French colonies. On his next voyage south a few years later, James headed straight to the French island "Martinecco" (Martinique), carrying horses and tobacco and returning with a cargo of molasses and rum. We will never know what smaller, unrecorded novelties and luxury commodities he certainly brought home for his family and close friends, but Greenwood's painting twenty-five years later allows us to see the rich material culture colonial Rhode Islanders were exposed to in the West Indies. Within a few years the Browns were regularly sending sloops to Dutch Surinam, further south than Martinique, loaded primarily with horses and barrels of meat (and also occasionally enslaved children born on local farms).

3.4. *Sea Captains Carousing in Surinam*, by John Greenwood (1727–92), oil on bed ticking, 95.9 × 191.2 cm, ca. 1755. St. Louis Museum of Art, St. Louis, MO.

Before his death in 1739, Captain James Brown was running a distillery and a shop. Rum was an important source of income for the Browns, but tea begins to show up increasingly in their accounts as well.[60] Rhode Islanders were hooked on tea, like everyone else around the Atlantic, so it is notable how few orders for chinaware are found in their accounts. But if one looks a little below the surface the evidence is there. Onto the leather back cover of an account book dating to 1747 kept by James's son Nicholas, for example, we do see an order for chinaware cryptically scratched and then crossed out (perhaps meaning that it had been fulfilled): "27 lbs Coffee @ 5/ 3 brls mols 90 @ 6 / 4 Cups & Sussers / 12 Chany Plates @ [?] / 1 Coffee pot / 9 Su[?] / 1 set of Chany / 9 Bols."[61] In the 1740s James Brown Jr., Nicholas's older brother, made several trips to the Caribbean, including to the Dutch island "Sant Eustata," and by 1750 silver-rich destinations such as Cuba and the Bay of Honduras show up regularly in Brown records.[62]

Illicit importation was, of course, significant in the British Isles as well. Taxes on tea in continental Europe were much lower, or even nonexistent, compared to those in Britain, creating a magnetic northern pull on European teas. In fact, the continent came to depend on the smuggling trade into Britain as a dumping ground for its Asian commodities.[63] Nevertheless, until about 1765 the English East India Company managed to maintain its hegemony in its home ports, with taxed commodities and legal Company traders holding strong over the tax-free, low-cost, low-volume—and often low-quality—contraband of the continental traders.[64] The only reason smuggling figured more prominently on the colonial side of the Atlantic was because it was not counterbalanced by a booming legal East Indies trade as in England. In Philadelphia in 1757, for example, merchant John Kidd estimated, "not more than 16 chests of tea legally imported from England have been consumed in Pennsylvania in two previous years, although total yearly consumption must have been ca. 200 chests."[65] Kidd was in a position to comment as he struggled to maintain a legitimate trade importing tea from London. Even historians who argue that smuggling was insignificant to the colonial economy agree that tea was well worth the risk. The savings afforded by avoiding duties was always more than a shilling per pound and sometimes as great as three shillings.[66] In his study of the colonial British customs service, Thomas Barrow noted that tea was found in the cargo of almost every ship searched or seized.[67] In both the legal and illegal tea trades, smaller quantities of porcelain tended to inconspicuously follow tea. But it is likely that rather than recording seized chinaware, customs inspectors took it home for their own use. In his study of smuggling in prerevolutionary Boston, John Tyler found written evidence of outright smuggling for only 7 percent of his sample of 392 merchants, but he noted that this figure grossly understates the true extent of the contraband trade. Tyler points out that, under the stress of the 1764 Revenue Act, Boston merchants were forced to acknowledge "the extent to which their trading interests outside the empire had grown during the long years of salutary neglect."[68]

Kidd in Philadelphia was well aware that the entire colonial coastline served as an open door to global markets, something British port officials in the colonies ignored or, more often, participated in and benefited from, even while compiling their incomplete—albeit detailed—import lists. In 1750 a Crown official in Virginia wrote to the Philadelphia collector William Peters, urging him to send to Parliament missing port records for the years 1739–42. He gave an indication of exactly why the missing records were of concern: "Upon information that great Quantities of European & East Indian Commodities, particularly Linnen & Tea, are run into his Majesty's Plantations in America by the French, Dutch and others, the Commissioners have directed me to use my utmost Endeavours, to prevent these Frauds for the Future . . . be particularly carefull, that no foreign Vessel touching in your District, land any Tea, Linnen or any other European or Asiatick Commodities." The Virginia collector added haughtily that he had "Great Reason to believe that Philadelphia and the other Northern Colonies are principally aimed at" in this accusation, because he knew of no such illicit trade at his port in Virginia.[69]

In the Coves and Little Islands

Each colony and each colonial governor played the smuggling game differently, which is why mariners away for more than a year or two—such as the Indian Ocean privateers discussed in chapter 1—regularly stopped at an outer port first to assess the political situation in the main port before sailing in (or not). Smuggling, or as American merchants called it, "free trade," occurred throughout the colonial period, although today we are most aware of it as a prerevolutionary phenomenon.[70] While the British imperial crackdown on colonial trade and revenue sources in the 1760s is common knowledge to all Americans today, the infrastructure for illegal trade on the American coast had been built up for decades. Exact numbers for the extent of the contraband trade have never been calculated and could be very difficult to judge, but there is plenty of evidence that it formed a fundamental part of the colonial economies.[71] An eyewitness account of colonial smuggling by a Crown official in 1768 is useful for our understanding of how northern contraband trade had probably operated since at least the time of Lord Bellomont's death in 1701. In a "memorial" entitled "Observations on the Illicit Trade of Connecticut, New England, and New York," Andrew Brown writes to the king's treasury,

> On the North Side of Long Island as well as upon the Connecticut opposite, there are a great many good Bayes & Harbours for Shipping to run into and safe to lye for the Discharge of their Cargoes and where there are no Customs House Officers. A great many Vessels do actually arrive from Holland and the West Indies with commodities that are subject to Duties and in these Havens unload their cargoes into the Holds of small Sloops and filling their decks with Fire Wood run up to New York even, the Centre of their Traffick, and are not suspected to have any Customable Goods on board. . . . Vessels that go directly from these parts . . . return from Holland with rich Cargoes of all Spices, Teas, and other East India Piece Goods. . . . I am very certain that the Return made for East India Piece Goods, Tea, Etc. brought from Holland to these Places is in Dollars [Spanish silver currency], which must be a great loss to the Government.[72]

Brown concludes by calling the northern colonies a "Nursery for Smugglers." His anxiety about valuable Asian commodities slipping into the colonies and silver slipping out, all despite British control, recalls almost word for word Bellomont's and Randolph's hysteria about East India goods and free traders three-quarters of a century earlier. The difference is that in the interim, during a relaxation of official port surveillance and a dramatic rise in the number of Europeans in Asia, many more Americans had made "Asiatick Commodities" an integral part of their households. The demand for such Asian wares had exploded, and once tea and china occupied a permanent place in domestic life, it could not be reversed.

Running along the mid-Atlantic and New England coastlines, in the "Good Bayes & Harbours" referred to by Brown, are hundreds of small islands. In the survey of colonial inventories discussed next, I focused on identifying and quantifying ownership of porcelain over the eighteenth century. But in this research I was surprised to find another, entirely different sort of possession occurring regularly, one that is related to porcelain ownership. This is an island. Islands were often highly valued parts of estates, carefully identified and passed on from generation to generation. They were ideal locations to put livestock out to graze without having to go to the expense of building fences or worry about mainland predators. But they also served other functions. Maritime trade impacted everyone living in the coastal northeast in the eighteenth century, if not as a source of employment then as a source of almost all household possessions, a certain portion of which came in surreptitiously. It is therefore easy to see the advantages of owning a small island near a principal seaport. A merchant vessel might simply anchor itself offshore at dusk, quietly run illicit goods to an island during the night in lighters or canoes, and sail into port for clearance in the morning. Indeed, in individual estate inventories dating back to the seventeenth century, there is a co-occurrence of islands, scales, maps, small boats, and exotic imports such as china. The meaning of this coincidence of possessions will be discussed in the next chapter, but it is of interest to point out here a colonial trend of island ownership and remark on its probable utility to both smugglers and householders wanting affordable access to goods that carried high taxes.

Owning an island gave coastal dwellers a vested stake in smuggling, even if they did not own ships, and gave them direct access to contraband "Asiatick Commodities" without leaving home. In 1736 James Brown sent a letter to the captain of one of his returning West Indies vessels instructing him "to bring too [stop] down the river and send your cargo some to Road Island and some up here in boats, so as not to bring but a few hhds [hogsheads] up to my wharf."[73] Narragansett Bay had many little islands that would serve well for keeping "boats" and stashing contraband. One of these was owned by the Greenes in Warwick, the family of the first colonial official to issue privateering licenses—unlawfully according to Bellomont—and who at the time of Brown's letter were illegally manufacturing iron on their property. The Browns were well aware of the Greenes' island. In 1772 James Brown's brother John ran the *Gaspee*, a customs ship, aground there and in 1782 he bought the property.[74] Meanwhile, the 1762 estate inventory of John Greene Jr. notably contained "China" and several yards of East Indian textiles ("piece goods"), and in his will he bequeathed all his property, including explicitly "my little Island," to his sons.[75]

Legal Trade

Clearly we have much hard and soft evidence for the arrival of Chinese porcelain in the northern colonies as an accompaniment to contraband Asian tea, textiles, and other staples from the West Indian and Canadian smuggling trades. Significantly the value of British imports remained below rising population growth during the first half of the eighteenth century, even while the ownership of porcelain grew dramatically after about 1715 (see fig. 1.2).[76] Chinese porcelain imported to Atlantic destinations tended to imperceptibly follow shipments of tea for a variety of reasons, including their common source (China), their compatibility as cargo items, and their complementary use in consumption. Porcelain is almost totally invisible in the record when tea was smuggled, but it is also barely glimpsed in the surviving accounts of legal tea traders, who by all indications were outnumbered by the illegal tea traders.[77] Philadelphia merchant John Kidd maintained a lawful trade in tea, and his business records are among the few in pre-1760 America where we see actual orders for chinawares placed in London—and of course he needed to pay for his goods in Spanish silver. In a 1750 letter to the London firm Neate & Neave, he complained that the Spanish market for American grain had dried up, saying "We begin to feel very sensibly the effects of a want of Cash since our Trade with the Spanards [sic] has been knocked up." He then concludes this letter with a china order: "You'll please to observe this small order for China and please to put up nothing but what is ordered."[78] Unfortunately, the original itemized order has not survived. Similar orders for china and other Asian products occur about once every year in Kidd's brisk grain-for-tea trade. But in these few instances we see quite tangibly the link between American access to Spanish silver, through sales of North American staples, and their trade in East India Company merchandise. In this triangular transatlantic trade, American grain was sold to Spain or Spanish colonies for silver, which was then sent to England for tea. How much easier it would have been for Kidd to do all of his business in one place, by smuggling! Going to London added an expensive additional voyage. Silver, tea, Asian luxury goods, and a ready market for staples were all available much closer, in the tax-free Caribbean islands.

The Boylston family in Boston also traded in London for tea and other European commodities, maintaining close ties with certain mercantile houses in England. The business ledgers of Thomas and Sarah Boylston and their son Thomas span almost the entire colonial part of the century (1704–74), and tea and ceramics made up an important part of their sales from the outset.[79] "Chaney" begins to show up periodically in the 1730s, after the East India Company had gained a solid foothold in Canton. China was almost always accompanied by tea purchases. But the Boylstons' business was diversified, like all colonial trading enterprises. While they vended many luxury foreign goods, such as champagne, spices, gold rings, and silver swords, they also sold a full range of textiles, including "homespun," barrels of potatoes and tallow, and pigeons and pork. The tea and china are obscured amid a large range of commodities. By the revolution, written evidence exists for the involvement of son Thomas in smuggling, yet his family had long-standing trade connections in London and a history of extensive legal commerce.[80] Diversification in a colonial business was defined not only by the range of commodities sold but also by the wide range of business ethics and methods practiced. The Boylstons, like many, if not most, aggressive colonial merchant houses, mixed legal and illegal trades.

It is very difficult to quantify the extent of legal china imports into the colonies over the colonial eighteenth century. Chinese porcelain was not a trade staple for American merchants, and consequently there was no comprehensive effort to record all entrances. We only begin to see it listed in customs house records after 1760. This is probably due to increased scrutiny on the part of customs officials at that time but also to the greater number of English officials in the colonies ordering china the way they always had, from East India Company auctions and vendors in London. One such official was William Tryon, who first served as governor in North Carolina from 1764 to 1771 and then took over the governorship of New York, holding commanding positions in British forces throughout the war. An inventory taken in 1775 of the damage sustained at Tryon's house at Fort George, New York, reveals an enormous holding of Chinese porcelain itemized on eighteen lines in a separate section entitled "China." Tryon was part of a growing upper-crust community of English placemen along the colonial seaboard who all owned copious china collections.[81] Their lifestyles ran in excess of anything yet seen in the northern British colonies. Much of their porcelain was ordered from merchants specializing in china and glass, located primarily in New York, Boston, and Philadelphia. These merchants were in a distinct and highly lucrative sphere of transatlantic trade, beyond the smaller seaport chinaware dealers who included middling widows and grocers and who dealt in smaller parcels from a range of sources.[82]

It is not surprising that customs house records for Chinese porcelain become more complete in these years. In a document entitled "Imports from Great Britain and Ireland, 5 January, 1772 to 5 January, 1773," porcelain is listed under "Foreign Goods" and further itemized into decorative types. Under "Ware China" a total 200,000 pieces, 4,200 parcels, and 3 cases were reported, primarily for New York and Philadelphia.[83] It is therefore also not surprising, given this surge of china imports, that in 1766 British chancellor of the exchequer Charles Townshend had revived a plan to raise revenues by *canceling* tax rebates on luxury items sent to the colonies, targeting East India Company chinawares at the very top of a list that also included fruits and oils from southern Europe. The London Customs House reported to Townshend that the East India Company had exported about 400,000 pieces a year from 1662 to 1664.[84] This is a huge quantity if one considers that in 1772, the total

Company order for china in Canton was the same amount (400,000), a reduction that probably reflects the Company's mounting inventory backlog.[85] We can see from the customs records cited above for the early 1770s that perhaps as much as a third to a half of this quantity went to the northern colonies. Townshend calculated in 1766 that the government would make good about £8,000 by canceling the china rebate for exports to America.[86] This points to a substantial trade in legal porcelain in the decade before the revolution.

Looking at American evidence, we see at least 1,514 advertisements for china in twenty-two newspapers north of Delaware from 1766 to 1768 (a few years later than Townshend's estimates). About a quarter of these ads ran twice, which leaves about 1,325 distinct ads for china. But we do not know the number of porcelain pieces each ad references, which could be anywhere from a few dozen to hundreds of pieces, or from 50,000 to over 800,000 total over the three years. An ad in the *New York Mercury* in 1767 reads: "China Bowls, Cups & Saucers, Fine Tureens and Dishes, Sm Enam'ld Fruit Plates."[87] It is impossible to know how many pieces this announcement comprises. One chest exported by the East India Company contained about six hundred pieces, but "chests" of chinaware are almost never found in American shipping invoices. Special order china, such as that found in Kidd's account books above, seems most often to arrive in America in boxes, which held only four or five dozen pieces. Custom orders for china placed in America—wares that would not be retailed—could take several years to fulfill and could run from fifty to three hundred pieces.[88] These private orders, which comprised the largest proportion of the legal trade from London, if not all of it, would not appear as merchantable stock in advertisements. Such trade from large, well-capitalized colonial china merchants emerged as a new phenomenon at this time.

James Beekman was one well-known "India" china dealer in New York who operated on a large scale from 1766 to 1799, trading in all sorts of goods from London but especially pottery. He had set up shop in 1750 with stock from his father's dry goods business and found his affairs increasingly including tea and its corollary, Chinese ceramics.[89] In April of 1767, Beekman placed an order with Francis Harris of London for over a thousand pieces of china, three-quarters of it "India china" and the remainder "English china." In an order six months later with Thomas Harris in London he included, among other nonceramics, over a thousand pieces "India blue & white china" and 150 pieces "India Enamelled China." But Beekman added a note on this last order that "if the Draw back is taken off the India China then you must send none, as you mention it will be 3 pds dear if taken off."[90] In other words, Townshend's plan to raise revenue in England directly impacted the cost of the East India

Company's Chinese porcelain, making a dent in the legal overseas commerce of London merchants. Colonial merchants must have gone elsewhere for their china, though, as there is no sign that consumption of porcelain dropped off by 1770 (see colonial probate information in fig. 1.2).

There was a surge in British imports to the American colonies, relative to population growth, after about 1755.[91] A handful of late-colonial china dealers, such as Beekman, and the governing elite that ordered from them participated in this surge, accounting for a sharp rise in porcelain imports and ownership in one sector of colonial society just before the revolution. Outside of this group, which is fairly transparent in colonial documents, it is harder to answer questions about quantities of china imported, especially as this commodity was so often reexported, sent as gifts, or secreted past customs officials as private adventure of one sort or another. We have no way of knowing if the china advertised in the newspapers was legally or illegally imported. Probably the best measure of the relative proportion of legal to illegal Chinese porcelain in colonial trade comes by looking at its travel companion, tea. Both historians today and contemporary participants in the tea trade note that legal tea accounted for only 10 to 20 percent of that consumed in British America in the decade leading up to the revolution, and in some colonies, notably New York and Rhode Island, no "English" tea was said to be imported.[92] Benjamin Labaree, historian of the Boston Tea Party, notes that tea smuggling reached its zenith in the 1750s, so we can assume that legal tea imports accounted for *less* than 10 to 20 percent in the earlier part of the century when enforcement of trade regulations was much more lax.[93] It was simply much easier and much less expensive to purchase tea and china illicitly.

An important factor influencing the way tea was purchased also influenced other East India Company imports, that is, the relatively small number of American merchants trading in London by comparison to other parts of the Atlantic. Although historian John Tyler notes that about two-thirds of Boston merchants were involved at some point in direct reciprocal trade with Great Britain, the vast majority of these merchants sent more of their ships elsewhere.[94] For many merchants, a transatlantic voyage was impossible given the small size or worn state of their vessels. This was especially true outside Boston. All other seaport towns, with the possible exception of Charleston, carried on *less* direct trade with London than did Boston. In nearby Salem, we saw earlier that in 1751 only two of 139 entrances came from London. The coastal and West Indian trades did not require an impressive shipping infrastructure. In Boston's case, even where a transatlantic voyage was possible, Holland remained an important lure for cheaper commodities.[95] There, and in Hamburg, Ostend, and other European ports, American merchants even dealt with English merchants who were working the margins of empire. Dutch sources are indeed evident in some popular styles found frequently in colonial porcelain collections, such as the row of five garniture vases, a decidedly Dutch arrangement.[96]

Chinese Porcelain as Booty

In the informal, diffuse colonial marketplace, contraband porcelain imperceptibly mingled with legitimately imported wares, but in both these cases we are theoretically talking about *new* china. There is another significant category of imported china complicating the colonial mix that was used and stolen. The fast road to riches in the northern colonies was not legal or illegal trade but privateering. Booty was easily procured during any of England's many eighteenth-century wars. From 1700 through 1775 England was at war more years than it was at peace.[97] The age-old antipathy between Anglo-Americans and the French in itself might offer a pretext for preying on France's colonial commerce, but such a pretext was unnecessary as Britain was at war with France for the better part of the century. In earlier years and into Queen Anne's War, many colonial privateers cruised shoulder to shoulder with named pirates, working in the ill-defined space between Crown defender and outlaw. Most all vessels, whether intending a privateering voyage or not, traveled armed and with official privateering papers at all times.[98] Commissions from colonial governors flowed freely under Bellomont's successors, especially Joseph Dudley in Massachusetts. In 1702, for example, Dudley issued commissions to the sloop *Charles* and the brigantine *Hannah and Mary*. Andrew Fanuiel and other Boston merchants were the owners. The vessels sailed to Cuba, taking the Spanish ship *Jesus de Nazareno* along with an itemized cargo of wine, dried fruit, silver plate, and silk. The crew divided the silk and silver among themselves, and certainly also other small, unrecorded spoils such as porcelain dishes. They condemned the ship in Rhode Island, no doubt trying to avoid claims by the Boston owners and governor. Dudley refused to recognize the actions of the Rhode Island Admiralty Court, and at least one vessel returned to Boston. Its master, Captain John Blue, retired on the booty extracted from his laundered cargo.[99]

Colonial maritime history is rife with similar examples, as the Scottish visitor Alexander Hamilton learned in touring the colonies during King George's War (1744–48). He attended a meeting of Newport's Philosophical Club but complained that "no matters of philosophy were brought upon the carpet.

They talked of privateering and building vessels." In New York Hamilton was bored by the dinner conversation of the town's ruling elite: "The table chat ran upon privateering and such discourse as has now become so common it is tiresome and flat."[100] Prizes came in all sizes and stripes. Big ones such as the Spanish *Jesus* were outnumbered by many small Canadian fishing shallops. Ultimately the act of pillaging itself was more important than the value of each individual plunder because every small act justified the larger ones and institutionalized a system of procurement on which great colonial fortunes were built.[101] The mix of possessions in the 1750 estate inventory of John Palmer of Marblehead typifies the leading edge of this colonial economic culture— not merely its wealth or *material* culture—a culture that apparently bored the erudite Dr. Hamilton. Palmer owned a silver-hilted sword, a mansion house, a pew in the meeting house, a schooner with two swivel guns, china tea sets and plates in the "Great Chamber," fifteen wine glasses, "3 Chana punch bols" in the "Clerk Room, and 137 ounces of silver."[102] The pew and mansion house tell us Palmer was an exemplar in his community; the schooner, guns, and sword tell us how he got his wealth; and the china and wine glasses say something about his taste. The circa 1760 overmantel painting of Moses Marcy seated amid his Connecticut River Valley estate allows us to visualize men like Palmer to a tee: we see a military man with his fine house, sailing vessel, and overseas luxuries, including a large Imari-style Chinese punch bowl placed in front of him in the center of the portrait (see fig. 3.5).

In a number of cases Chinese porcelain taken as booty has survived and is proudly displayed in family collections or museums today. Jonathan Sayward (fig. 3.6), a merchant mariner and later Loyalist, of York, Maine, accepted a commission in 1744 from the Massachusetts governor to lead an expedition against Cape Breton Island in Nova Scotia. His party captured the French fortress at Louisburg. A century later in 1841, when collecting Chinese export porcelain dishes as treasured *American* antiques and family heirlooms was supplanting the purchase of new china, Sayward's granddaughter Sally identified a set of Chinese Imari-style plates in the family china closet as booty taken by her grandfather in Louisburg (fig. 3.7).[103] Sayward was a proud man, able to hold steadfast in his loyalty to the King of England without leaving revolutionary New England, but he was not too proud to use and preserve as family keepsakes chinaware stolen from a French officer.

Displayed in a china closet in a period dining room of the Rhode Island School of Design's Pendleton House is a partial dinner service that, according to the label penned by a nineteenth-century collector, was "imported for

3.5. *Moses Marcy*, overmantel painting on wood by an anonymous artist, ca. 1760. Courtesy of Old Sturbridge Village, Sturbridge, MA.

3.6. Jonathan Sayward, portrait by unknown artist, ca. 1775, oil on canvas, 57 × 46 inches; hangs in the Sayward-Wheeler House in York Harbor, ME. Gift of the heirs of Elizabeth Cheever Wheeler, 1977.227. Photo: Peter Harholdt. Courtesy Historic New England (RS 32455).

3.7. China closet, or "bofat," of an 1884 inventory, with the middle shelves containing Chinese Imari-style plates brought back from the Louisburg expedition in 1745. Sayward-Wheeler House, York Harbor, ME. Courtesy Historic New England (RS 101974).

the Bowler family, 1759" and was "100 years old in 1842."[104] It includes two
sauceboats and trays, a scallop-shell dish, and two open salt dishes, decorated
with elaborate borders and chrysanthemums in a finely painted underglaze
blue.[105] The mid-eighteenth-century date is confirmed by similar pieces recovered from the wreck of the *Geldermalsen*, an unlucky vessel in a Dutch VOC
fleet of six that sank in the South China Sea in 1746 after loading a cargo of
porcelain in Batavia and Canton.[106] The forms and decorative motifs of the
porcelain pieces recovered from this wreck site closely match those attributed
to Bowler's dishes (fig. 3.8).

Bowler had immigrated to New England from London the year Sayward
raided French Canada. He settled in Newport and quickly became involved
in mercantile partnerships with other Newport merchants. During the French

3.8. Chinese porcelain "tray" with nineteenth-century label that reads "Imported for the
Bowler family 1759." Museum of Art, Rhode Island School of Design, Providence. Photo: Erik
Gould, courtesy of the Museum of Art, Rhode Island School of Design.

and Indian Wars (1757–63) he shows up in the record as sailing both privateers and "flags of truce."[107] His vessels were insured in New York and Amsterdam, and they traded principally between those ports and the West Indies.[108] His agents in New York were the Livingstons, who did business with the Dutch banking house Crommelin & Sons, and one of his captains appears to have been Dutch.[109] Bowler did quite well in his privateering ventures. A Captain John Ingles reported to Bowler that he had captured a French ship "with a few crates of Earthnware."[110] But then in 1758 John Livingston wrote to Bowler on the proceeds of an auction of the "take" of his brig *George*, "the goods sold so well that I did not purchase one article."[111] A few weeks later, Livingston wrote again to inform the Newport shippers that another of their vessels had captured a French ship and a Dutch ship.[112] The good news continued until February 1760, when Bowler's Dutch captain wrote that he had been captured by an English ship off the coast of Cuba and brought into Jamaica.[113] Why the British captured Bowler's supposedly British-American vessel is not hard to guess: it was most certainly waving a Dutch flag. With so many vessels of so many ports under his belt, he was clearly playing all sides for gain. It is also conceivable, however, that Bowler's captain was caught smuggling, that favorite North American pastime. In 1760 the British minister of trade, William Pitt, complained to the Rhode Island governor of the disloyal behavior of its merchants and decided to crack down on colonial vessels trading with the French. The response in Rhode Island was simply to fit out more privateers[114] and, perhaps, to wave another flag. In 1759 the Colony of Rhode Island alone granted forty-eight ships "flags of truce." These vessels were granted immunity from warlike behavior by virtue of waving a flag of neutrality, intended specifically to protect ships carrying prisoners of war. Eight of the flags issued by Rhode Island that year went to Bowler. Yet, this was a year in which the colony exchanged *not one* prisoner of war![115] Flying a flag of truce was a very convenient way of doing business, in other words, of sneaking up on unsuspecting vessels. In any event, we can assume that Bowler, in addition to acquiring the porcelain displayed today at the Pendleton House, made a substantial fortune in all of his privateering and neutral-flag ventures, because he falls out of the mercantile record by 1762.[116] He retired to the life of a wealthy plantation owner in Portsmouth, Rhode Island, where he was said to plant apple saplings in "porcelain tubs" acquired from foreign princes. He also wrote a treatise on agriculture that opened with a eulogy to the Chinese emperor.[117] A privateer's identity, apparently, served this enlightened transnational profiteer well.[118]

Obtaining Chinese Porcelain within the Northern British Colonies

Recycled China Acquisitions

Where did people look *within* the northern colonies for Chinese objects? While not considered "booty" in the eighteenth century, there is another category of *used* porcelain that today might actually be considered a form of plunder. This porcelain comes from estates within the community—not in French territory or on the high seas—that were repossessed by creditors, or otherwise taken over by influential town officials. This way of transferring china from one colonial owner to another represents one of the earliest forms of exchange or circulation of porcelain in the colonial north. It was extremely important, for it gave a cloak of legitimacy to the act of consuming Chinese dishes by a potential purchaser who might otherwise have been accused of extravagance, or worse.

Let's look at an example from Massachusetts. In the seventeenth and early eighteenth centuries, Marblehead was culturally distinct from nearby Salem and Boston. As a fishing community its population was more mobile and diverse. It exhibited higher instances of crime and less interest in established religion, but it also manifested a marked absence of witchcraft hysteria. Historian Christine Heyrman argues that Marblehead's townsmen openly repudiated Puritan visions of good order. A number of seemingly law-abiding Boston and Salem merchants took advantage of its open door to the Atlantic, and quietly operated through Marblehead, freeing their trade from London and giving them greater control over transoceanic commercial routes. Marblehead was, in a sense, yet another island of free trade—and free consumption—within the British Empire, similar to Gardner's Island in New York or the Isle of Shoals in New Hampshire or any number of Caribbean islands. In the 1680s its freewheeling atmosphere attracted Andrew Cratey, a sea captain who bought fish on consignment for British firms. He had sailed far and wide, but he settled down and married in Marblehead, building a house near the waterfront and furnishing it lavishly with all his accumulated worldly goods. At his death in 1695 his household contained a wealth of Asian furnishings, including "lackerd chears," a "Japan case of drawers," "1 screen cencerd with green bayes," "a pcell of Cheny Earthen ware," "7 India Callico quilts," as well as 350 ounces of silver plate.

One of the Cratey estate inventory takers, Nathaniel Norden, the son of a Boston merchant, served as town quartermaster and later a justice of the peace.[119] He was part of a merchant and civic elite dominated by monied men

from Boston and Salem who were taking control of Marblehead, consolidating
its wealth and economy in fewer hands. He oversaw the appraisal of several estates at the end of the seventeenth century, and he initiated many suits for debt
in subsequent years. In 1714, for example, when a storm at sea took the life
of a local fisherman, Norden took over half of his estate.[120] When he himself
died in 1728, he not surprisingly owned much of the real property and household possessions of those whose estates he had inventoried and insured, including Cratey's.[121] In Norden's house—the former Cratey household—we see
"23 Allabaster Images [small white porcelain statues; see fig. 3.9] & 2 Bowls,"
"a parcel of China," "1 Japand Cabinette," and of course 362 ounces of silver
plate, as well as an island off Gloucester.[122] He used Marblehead and his island
as convenient, out-of-view doorways to the world. Moreover, we can see how
his early work as a voyeuristic court clerk appraising estates, while insinuating
himself into this worldly domain of imported possessions by lending capital,
facilitated not only his accumulation of wealth but his engagement with an
Asian, or orientalist, aesthetic, something he might not otherwise have had
access to or even interest in. Norden's decision to decorate his home with Chi-

3.9. Soft-paste porcelain figurine brush holder. Dehua, Fujian Province, China, Ming dynasty.
8.4 × 15.5 cm, Inv. G 3119. Photo: Thierry Ollivier for Musee des Arts Asiatiques-Guimet,
Paris, France. Photo: Réunion des Musées Nationaux / Art Resource.

nese objects, the "23 Allabaster Images," was less a direct, active choice—less
a clear and unambivalent decision to seek out specifically Chinese goods and
engage an oriental style—than a matter of covetously and aggressively assum-
ing the material wealth of his neighbors. Whether or not this amounts to the
emulation described by Richard Bushman will be discussed in the next chapter. It is simply important, at this point, to acknowledge this common means
of obtaining high-status Chinese objects in the colonies—to acknowledge the
fairly common use of civic and political standing within a community to ac-
quire the prized personal possessions of one's neighbors.

In addition to the acquisition of estates, colonial Americans in less powerful positions also had access to the possessions of their fellow townspeople
through publicly advertised estate auctions. Newspapers from Philadelphia
to Boston were filled with auction announcements, for prize goods as well
as locally generated possessions. One advertisement in the *Boston Post-Boy*
in 1738 reads, "To be Sold by publick Vendue on Thursday next . . . at the
House where Mrs. Ruth Mills deceased, lately dwelt, all the household goods
of the said Mrs. Mills, consisting of Beds, Bedding, Looking Glasses, Tables,
Chairs, Chests of Drawers, a Clock, some China and Delph Ware, and a parcel of Books" (cf. fig. 3.10). Recycled china made available in estate auctions
had already been tried out and proven worthy, perhaps even by the purchaser
while taking tea at the home of the owner before death. In this way valuable
exotic commodities found in only a few corners of a community acquired an
air of comfortable familiarity. These routine public estate sales, today much
less often encountered, were a regular means to fitting out one's house. They
promoted the diffusion of new and daring tastes in the colonies, normalizing
once extravagant purchases.

Sometimes auction sales of a living person's personal possessions are found
in colonial newspapers. In 1732 Philadelphia's *American Weekly Mercury* ran
the ad, "To be Sold very Reasonable by Thomas Chase, in the Market Street . . .
most sorts of English Goods, Iron Ware, China Ware of sundry sorts, Green
Tea, Bohe Tea."[123] Chase adds a note that he needs to discharge his debts in
order to leave the country. It is quite conceivable that seeing this announcement, any local acquaintance who had ever been to Chase's house for tea and
admired his china might jump at the chance to purchase it. Public auction
ads do not always state the reason for the sale, which was presumably common knowledge to most people in town since deaths, bankruptcies, financial
setbacks, privateering successes, and other incoming overseas vessels were all
hot news in colonial seaports.

Advertisements.
To be Sold by AUCTION,
(By *William Nichols* and Company,)
THIS DAY, at the House in which the late Mr.
Pyam Blowers lived, (in the same Street, and just above
where Mr. *Bowdoin* lives) all the Houshold Furniture, &c,
belonging to the Estate of said *Blowers*, deceas'd, consisting of,
Fine Sconce Glasses, large Looking Glasses, Leather-Bot-
tom Chairs, sundry Mehogony and other Tables, a good
Couch Squab and Pillow, a very handsome yellow Damask
Bed, Chairs, an Easy Chair, a neat Case of Draws, Table,
sundry good Beds and Bedding, Pewter, Brass, all sorts of Kitchen Furniture, sundry Pieces of well wrought Plate, sundry
Suits of wearing Apparel, good Houshold Linnen, two Silver
Watches, sundry sorts of good China Ware, two Negro Men,
and one Negro Woman, &c. Together with a small Collection of valuable BOOKS.

3.10. Estate auction advertisement. *Boston News-Letter*, June 14, 1739.

Retailing China

Next to the ads for "publick vendues" in colonial newspapers were those for retail sales by merchants and shopkeepers (see fig. 3.11).[124] There one could initiate a *local* purchase of supposedly new china. The retail market for porcelain grew rapidly during the eighteenth century, fueled by the increases in porcelain coming in as prize booty or with either legal or smuggled tea. Actual china shops did not exist in the colonies as they did in London until the nineteenth century, even though proportionately as many people owned china.[125] It should be noted, however, that the distinction between "merchant" (a shipowner involved in overseas trade) and "shopkeeper" is a blurry one in this period.[126] A number of different types of people sold goods in a variety of ways depending on their personal and business connections to shipowners and masters. In addition to the few large "china & glass merchants" such as Beekman cited above, widows, innkeepers, and tradesmen of all classes, or "sorts," might keep a diversified stock of goods in their household or shop premises to sell more or less informally. Colonial seaports were saturated in a culture of retail and price margins on foreign commodities, a culture that depended on the capital and maritime investments of wealthier members of the community but ultimately included everyone from the seamstresses who clothed the sailors to the carters who stocked the stores, to the landlords who leased space to the shopkeepers. Without a doubt notions of gentility served the god of profit, and nearly everyone had access to the material objects, and material culture, of international trade.[127]

In estate inventories merchantable stock is identified by its location in an outer building, storehouse, shop, or attic. Richard Grafton of Newcastle (outside Philadelphia) sold all sorts of wares out of his "Joyners Shop," which served as a mercantile counting house and warehouse as well as a designated tradesman's shop. Listed in the "Back Room" of the shop in Grafton's 1743 estate inventory, one finds "1 half gallon Blew & White China Bowell, 2 qt. China Bowls, 2 pt. D[itto], 1 Doz. Burnten China Tea Cups & Sawsers, 1 Doz. Ditto Coffee Cups & Sawsers." It is likely these items are to sell, as one finds the family china, with pots "Tipt in Silver," in the "Front Room." Grafton also sold bulk goods such as textiles, brandy, and tobacco from the various rooms of this multipurpose building.[128]

Actual named shopkeepers shared the retail market with merchants and just about anyone else from any profession who could get his or her hands on a regular source of imports. Even when licensed to sell a particular commodity, such as china, all of these retailers stocked a broad inventory that reflected the diversified cargoes of the merchants that supplied them. The lack of china shops and china dealers, as in London, therefore, did not mean that china was not readily available to colonists, especially those in and around the major northern seaports of Boston, Newport, New York, and Philadelphia.

Prior to 1760 the most important sources of household wares within the northern colonies were gifts, auctions of plundered or recycled china, and sales from within transcolonial, transatlantic merchant networks. Before placing

To Be SOLD,

By THOMAS LLOYD, at the Sign of the Golden Mortar in Second-Street,

CALLICOES, Muslins and printed Linens, China Cups and Saucers, ditto Bowls from a Gallon to half Pint, Cutlery Ware, Combs, short and long Scythes, 8d. 10d, and 20d, Nails, Glass 8 by 10, Barbados & JamaicaRum, Mollasses, & sundry other sorts of Goods.

3.11. Merchant's retail advertisement, *American Weekly Mercury*, June 28, 1739.

goods in a shop on consignment, merchants preferred to advertise their wares themselves, selling them directly out of a wharfside warehouse or other waterfront location. In a 1754 letter to an agent in England, Philadelphia merchant Charles Willing wrote, "As to the Imports of the British manufactures, I am quite tired dealing in them. We can't sell them to any proffit for money & to trust them out amongst the Country retailers is like throwing your money on the surface of the water."[129] Under pressure to maximize returns, merchants like Willing were as reluctant to let others vend their imports as they were to pay high English prices. But Willing, one of the largest and best recognized merchants in town, did handle commission sales for other smaller or out-of-town merchants. A month after the above letter, Willing wrote to a Mr. Thomas Day about selling his "potts," stating also "Your Gloves are unsold . . . We can vend little but Rum Sugar & Wine." Two months later he wrote to John Perks saying, "We have a great quantity of goods by us—Don't send any manufactures on Comm."[130] Willing, even though one of the largest merchant houses in Philadelphia, felt obliged to involve his business in a wide range of bulk and dry goods from and to a variety of sources, and he struggled to keep ahead of the "Country retailers."

As noted above, chinaware began regularly appearing in colonial newspaper advertisements in the 1720s. At around the same time it also began showing up in the daybooks of large and small merchants. Here it is seen bartered or sold along with tea, coffee, sugar, household pots and pans, and textiles—in short, along with the whole range of goods a colonial merchant might sell. Typically the quantities were small, but sometimes surprisingly large sales show up. The daybook of Quaker merchant Samuel Powell Jr. in Philadelphia recorded sales for the period 1735 to 1739. His trade comprised both the West Indies and London. About 20 percent of his sales were tea, with textiles, chocolate, and spices also showing strong demand. Over this period he sold several sets of china to Clem Plumstead and William Morris, both wealthy, fashionable gentlemen who invested in Powell's ships and probably purchased the china for their own homes or for gifts. But on one instance he sold 396 cups and 396 saucers to an Ann Dudley, clearly not for this woman's personal consumption.[131] Powell was sending his vessels out during peacetime, so this quantity of china was not due to a privateering windfall, which in any event as a Quaker he probably would have refused.[132] Moreover, sailing instructions survive from the 1730s to one of his captains destined to Barbados in which he gave strict orders to clear goods in London and "Above all things be careful to observe the several acts of Trade and Study Frugality and dispatch only can make our ship Profitable to us and thee."[133] Powell's compunctions about the letter of the law were probably of little concern to his retailer Dudley, who would have been ready and willing to sell china at the best profit margin she could.

Powell was conducting a rather ample transatlantic trade in tea and china-wares, and he found a ready market in Philadelphia with the help of local shop-keeper Dudley. In Newport a few years earlier, middle-class widow Elizabeth Pratt also supported herself and her family by selling tea and porcelain. In fact women in all the major colonial seaports took advantage of the opportunity to profit in the tea and china trades. By 1755 in Boston, 171 people were li-censed by local officials to sell chinaware, and sixty-two, or 36 percent, were women.[134] This is an impressive figure, for in few other fields of mercantile retail were women counted as official players in such relatively high numbers. While many widows maintained a merchant husband's trade, the business continued in his name and was often transferred to a son once he became old enough. But women retained more publicly acknowledged independence where sales of china were concerned. In Portsmouth, New Hampshire, the first newspaper advertisement to appear for china in the *New Hampshire Gazette* was placed by a female shopkeeper, Elizabeth Pascall.[135] The strong association between women and china will be discussed in the next chapter, but it is important to note here the high incidence of professional, often middling-class women in the trade.

Chinese Porcelain in Colonial Homes: An Inventory Study

In arguing that Americans were awash in British imports in the mid-1700s and that this fostered a common consumer culture that ultimately allowed the colonies to unite, T. H. Breen identifies six distinct sources of informa-tion available to researchers today on those imports: accounts of travelers and government officials, customs officers' reports, colonial newspapers, museum collections, archaeological collections, and probate inventories.[136] To this list we might add wills, private family collections, recent auction sales, and, most important, business and personal correspondence. All of these sources are use-ful in reconstructing the place of Chinese porcelain in the northern colonies. Probate inventories, however, have a special utility for studies of material cul-ture as they are detailed legal documents with a specified domestic context and date.[137] They give us one of the most reliable descriptions available today of the objects found within colonial homes, and are, unlike artifacts in the ground or collectibles in museum storage, readily accessible to researchers at state and local archives. In addition to listing every object found within the deceased's possession, estate inventories give us other valuable contextual information.

As the purpose of the inventory is to assess the value of the deceased's estate so debts can be settled, each item is given a monetary value. These values, normally in pounds sterling, can be difficult to interpret as they vary widely from place to place, year to year, and from appraiser to appraiser.[138] They are best used for comparing values *within* one inventory or series of inventories done by the same appraisers. The values given Chinese porcelain, for example, run the gamut from £4 for one plate to a few shillings for an entire tea set. But looked at within the same inventory, china is always of greater value than earthenwares or an equivalent quantity of pewter, and it is always less than silver dishes. Where several china dishes or sets of dishes are listed, we observe differences in price that indicate a perceived difference in quality within the category of china, with "burnt" dishes usually getting a higher price than blue-and-white ones.[139] The given price of any one object in an inventory can also be related to the total value of the inventory. This point of comparison indicates that there was not a direct correlation between porcelain ownership and wealth, even though china more frequently appears in the estates of wealthier individuals. Looking at relative monetary values in this large collection of inventories, it becomes clear that the expense of china would not have been very burdensome for middle- and upper-class people, and a number of less expensive sorts were also affordable for tradesmen and fishermen. Slaves and silver are found in middling estates and were vastly more costly than porcelain. Individual china dishes or statues were a matter of shillings not pounds, becoming expensive only when collected in large sets.

In addition to itemizing objects and their values, appraisers often named the very room objects were found in and the profession of the deceased, allowing us to more clearly visualize the private spaces of different sorts of people and the place of china within those spaces. Except in the case of some early, wealthy Dutch New Yorkers,[140] Chinese porcelain is never found in the kitchen but in parlors and master bedrooms, places called "Front Room" or "Great Chamber." This location tells us that china was not viewed as utilitarian, despite being the most durable and least permeable of ceramic types. Kitchens were stocked with less healthy, lead-glazed, crumbly earthenwares. Over the course of the eighteenth century, pewter moved into the kitchen as well and was replaced in the more formal spaces of the home by china. Since the inventoried objects are generally listed in the order appraisers found them as they marched through the house, we are able to see with what other items any one object was associated. Porcelain is often listed on the same line as glassware but never with silver or pewter. This can reflect both the place of porcelain in the appraiser's mind—fragile and related to imported beverages—as well as its place within the home. Finally, the inventory identifies the appraiser by name, allowing us to better reconstruct social roles and relationships, as was the case with Captain Andrew Cratey and his appraiser Nathaniel Norden.

Re-creating the colonial past through inventories (tangibly in the case of museum period rooms), as with reliance on any documentary source, has its own set of caveats. Not everyone who died had his or her estate appraised, and the bias tends to fall toward the upper end of the wealth spectrum. Any uniform material picture that emerges from even a large body of estate inventories is, therefore, somewhat more comfortable and more urban than the average colonial household. We should not use inventories to posit an "average" colonial household nor to idealize a "simple" colonial farmer or a "genteel" colonial elite, nor to make any kind of two-dimensional generalization about colonial Americans as a whole, reifying distinctions that never existed.[141] With an understanding of how porcelain was imported and distributed once within North America, it is useful to see where pockets of ownership occur and how big or deep those pockets are. The estate inventories direct our attention primarily to the middle- and upper-class city and manor dwellers, among whom porcelain ownership varied greatly. Only archaeology and other documentary or visual sources can help researchers see where porcelain existed among the noninventoried lower-class, rural people who comprised a substantial part of the population. Arguably there is value in looking at this middle- to upper-class urban sector because they held the reins of political and economic power within their communities, and therefore their lifestyle choices had a powerful impact on society, if only to give less wealthy classes something to define themselves against. Such resistance and multivalent semiotic content, as we shall see in the next chapter, *always* complicated the place of Chinese porcelain in any given colonial American community. But the most important thing to keep in mind is that small, inexpensive porcelain objects did circulate within the seaports and were affordable novelties even to those on the meanest budget. This inventory survey reveals china in the estates of decidedly working-class sailors, carters, widows, and others in the seaport laboring groups.

In addition to the wealth bias, a number of other ambiguities emerge in looking at Chinese porcelain through probated inventories. Some researchers have posed the question of whether or not appraisers could or did distinguish between pottery types, especially in the early colonial years. Curator Elizabeth Pratt Fox believes that references to "cheney ware" in Connecticut River Valley inventories before 1720 "probably represent earthenware forms decorated in the Chinese fashion."[142] While that may be the case in that region, along the sea coast one finds distinct references to "Delft," "Earthen," "stone," "painted galley potts [earthenware]" and "cheney" from the seventeenth century forward, indicating that appraisers *did* know the difference. If appraisers knew the differences between them in Boston, they probably did also in Hartford. In any event, where the appraiser states "china," in any of its derivative spellings, we should take him at his word. But what if he only states the form of the pot and not its body type, as in "tea cups & sawsers"? Teacups and teapots were not made by European potters, at least in any quantities large enough to export, before the early eighteenth century. Generally one can assume that a "tea cup" at that time was of Chinese origin, especially if it is identified as being on the mantel, on a japanned table or tray, or with a saucer. This problem is especially apparent in early Newport inventories where one finds an abundance of other items from the East, such as nutmeg, silk, "Bengall remnants," "an East India sash," "Arabian pcs of Gold," along with "coffy cups" or "Earthen Ware on ye Mantel Shelf" or "little cups."[143] While these "cups" or "fine earthen dishes" were probably Chinese porcelain, I generally do not include them as such unless they are identified by the word "china." Therefore, porcelain is probably *understated* in the early years, especially in Newport.

Another question is whether items were removed from an estate before the appraisers arrived. All across the Atlantic, porcelain dishes had a strong association with women, as discussed in the next chapter, and it is conceivable that small dishes were removed by widows or daughters who had no legal claim to an estate unless a will survived specifically designating them as beneficiaries.[144] Many of the estates represented by the inventories in my collection were intestate, in which case creditors—and almost everyone had debts[145]—would move in claiming stake to personal possessions before anyone, including widows. Women buried porcelain dishes during the revolution to preserve them, and it is quite possible that this practice of secreting away treasured possessions occurred throughout the colonial period whenever women faced a threat to what they perceived as *their* property.[146] Such a practice would skew the amount of inventoried china downward.

A final caveat in using inventories concerns the date. It may be a precisely fixed historical fact that an inventory of possessions was taken on the date recorded—and historians tend to enlarge on any such accurate chronological information—but it must be remembered that this is a death date. It tells us what a person owned at the end of his or her life, not during it or how long the object had been in the home. In most cases each china object listed in the inventory had probably been around the house for some time, but we do not know exactly when it entered the home. We see in figure 1.2, for example, that in 1730 42 percent of probated estates for the Boston area contained porcelain. It is possible, however, that in 1725 or 1720 or even earlier, most of those households contained this very porcelain. We should, therefore, read the inventory data as telling us something about a community during the preceding years, understanding the dates as end points.

Historians have noted, based in large part on estate inventories, a broad increase in imported household items following the 1730s.[147] But if these items appear in 1730s inventories, they were probably in circulation before that date, especially given the way porcelain was "recycled." In 1720 in Boston, only 15 percent of the inventories in figure 1.2 contain porcelain. Looking at these two data sets, 1720 Boston and 1730 Boston, one might infer that china ownership begins to increase *after* 1730. But china ownership may actually have begun to climb after 1720, and maybe earlier. This distinction is important since conventional wisdom about the role of consumer goods in the events preceding the revolution rests on the assumption that "the cultural landscape of colonial America changed perceptibly during the middle decades of the eighteenth century."[148] A more careful reading of the probate data, one that views the dates attached to inventoried objects as end points and one that contextualizes the estate information within colonial commodity circuits, argues for placing the surge in imported objects in the northern plantations somewhat earlier. We have seen that Americans had a voracious appetite for manufactured goods from across the globe, not just across the North Atlantic, from at least the last quarter of the seventeenth century when their shipping infrastructure passed a critical threshold. Their exposure to a *profitable* "world of goods" in the Caribbean Sea, southern Europe, and the Indian Ocean from that time set them invariably on a path of mass consumption, and a rise in the use of imported wares within colonial homes followed.[149]

Table 3.1 compares the percent of inventories containing china to those in the same sample containing silver. "Silver" includes "plate" and coins (bullion) and silver dishes. An inventory would not be counted as containing silver if it only had a few silver spoons or a silver cup (often related to baptism rituals). This comparison achieves two things. First, when silver is viewed as a monetary measure of wealth, this ratio offers a wealth control for china ownership. In other words, we are able to determine the overall wealth of the sample at one point and relate the degree of china ownership to wealth, over time and across regions. In Philadelphia from 1720 through the 1740s, for example, it appears that as wealth (measured by silver) increases or decreases, china ownership follows. But then in the 1750s, wealth based on silver decreases while china ownership shoots up. The data indicate that in Philadelphia a correlation between wealth and china ownership existed until about the decade of the

Table 3.1 China holdings compared to silver holdings in estate inventories of five towns (% with china / % with silver)

Year	Philadelphia	New York	Newport	Boston	Salem
1690		30/55			9/40
1700	0/53	19/48	5/30	0/85	9/33
1710	0/36	20/70	21/68	0/75	0/15
1720	4/35	14/20	32/60	15/70	0/20
1730	20/44	38/50	45/45	42/53	20/20
1740	36/52	25/30	55/45	38/48	0/25
1750	24/36	30/20		64/52	10/30
1760	46/26	65/35		60/35	20/25
1770	68/48	62/35		85/40	35/35

Note: See chap. 3, n. 149, for sampling strategy.

1750s. But silver can also be viewed as a commodity. In this case, we might say that the overall growth in wealth in Philadelphia from the 1710s through the 1730s allowed both china ownership and silver ownership to rise, while in the 1750s, people made a choice to expend more of their wealth on china than silver. (Of course, the increased use of paper currency and bills of credit is also a factor in the falling off of silver plate holdings).

If we turn to nearby New York, the situation is a little different. China ownership existed here from the seventeenth century, with 30 percent of estate inventories containing china in 1690, indicating a strong presence during the 1680s. China ownership in New York remains higher or equivalent to the other towns until the 1720s. I believe this reflects the Dutch predilection for colorful ceramics as well as the more expansive trade connections afforded to those with Dutch and Jewish kin networks around the Atlantic and the world. The dip in ownership recorded for 1700 supports the conclusion that Lord Bellomont led a crackdown on East India imports into New York. The only other towns with as much porcelain this early on are Newport and Marblehead. In Newport the incidence of inventoried porcelain surpasses New York in the 1710s, and this supports the view here that a weaker admiralty apparatus in Rhode Island made it easier to bring imported contraband into circulation. Looking at Table 3.1, we see that the increases in porcelain ownership in Newport are accompanied by increases in silver, which can be interpreted either to mean that Newporters were getting generally richer or, within the empire perhaps more likely, that their maritime presence all over the West Indies had strengthened and more silver and china were entering Newport. Marblehead accounts for all the china ownership from the 1680s to 1710 in the Salem region, and the trend here closely follows New York. Marblehead, as mentioned, was a maritime community with few mercantilist or religious constraints until the 1720s.

In all four of these seaport regions, about a quarter to a half of the inventories consistently hold silver, while porcelain ownership falls or is nonexistent at the beginning of the century and then begins a continual rise shortly after 1710. Boston inventories present a very different picture in that the incidence of silver is initially much higher than in the other towns. Three-quarters of the households in the sample hold silver before 1720 compared to only about a quarter of the sample after 1700 in nearby Salem/Marblehead. Moreover, unlike Newport where china is present from the beginning of the century and a rise in silver ownership is accompanied by a rise in porcelain ownership, no porcelain appears in Boston inventories until 1720, despite very relaxed port oversight during the early decades of the century.[150] But from the decade of the 1720s forward, we see a precipitous rise in china in Boston accompanied by an equally marked decline in silver. This inverse relationship of Chinese ceramics to precious metal points to a cultural shift in Boston examined in chapter 4.

It is important to caution that these inventory data are impressionistic. For the large seaport towns of New York and Boston, samples of twenty to twenty-five inventories per decade represent only a small portion of all inventories available, especially in the latter part of the century.[151] Moreover, as stated above, not everyone had their estates inventoried at death. But the sampled data do allow us to see broad trends within regions and shadows of differences between them. General patterns of china ownership emerge that, when set next to an awareness of the avenues of trade and commerce in East Asian wares in the western Atlantic, open up an entirely new perspective on middle- and upper-class colonial Americans in northern seaports. The inventory data that show porcelain ownership ranging from 5 to 30 percent of New York, Newport, and Marblehead estates at the turn of the century—a relatively high figure for British people outside London at this time[152]—help us understand the concerns of Lord Bellomont and Crown officials at the turn of the century over East India goods entering the colonies.

Some of the patterns emerging from this inventory data raise questions relative to this study. We see that Chinese porcelain was present in northern colonial homes from the beginning of the eighteenth century, falling somewhat in its early years. Was this drop, which is not registered in Newport, related to the explicit Crown crackdown on East India goods in the major seaports? After Bellomont's death, porcelain ownership rose dramatically in all regions throughout the century (Salem was a bit slower), punctuated by a dip in the 1730s (a bit later in Philadelphia). This dip in probated porcelain in the 1730s supports the contention that much of colonial American chinaware entered as privateering booty, since the period 1720–39 was the single extended period of peace in this century between England and the other European states. The resumption of war in the 1740s, especially King George's War (1744–48) in which colonial privateers participated heavily, brought a new influx of valuables, including porcelain. Porcelain ownership rose in the 1760s to between 65 and 70 percent of probated inventories, except in Salem (Essex County) where it only ever reached a level of 35 percent. From the second decade of the century, Boston led the pack in porcelain ownership, so it is interesting that its neighbor Salem—with all the close family ties that existed between Boston and Salem—remained seemingly so much less interested in owning china.

Patterns that are not visibly apparent on the chart but that I observed during data collection include the wealth, professional affiliation, and other co-occurring possessions of probated estates containing china. Many wealthy estates were inventoried in each decade that did *not* contain porcelain. Dow Ditmas, a yeoman outside New York City, died in 1750 with a substantial estate of £1,006 but no china; Thomas Flagg, a tailor in 1740s Boston, died with an enormous estate of £1,729 but no china. Similar examples of porcelain naysayers, including even a number of merchants, occur in each sample. On the flip side we see some middling sorts owning porcelain, such as fisherman Michael Coomes in 1731 Marblehead (£508) or Austin Paris, a founder in 1730s Philadelphia (£136). Daniel Tucker, a tailor in 1740s Boston like Flagg, had an estate that was a tenth of Flagg's (£175), yet Tucker owned china. It is clear that interest in owning china in all the northern seaports was not linked to wealth or to profession. In the early decades of the century, however, one does find china more often in the estates of those directly involved with maritime commerce, such as captains, merchants, and their widows. But the inventory data do not tell us which parties had close connections to maritime trade. Tucker's brother, father, or uncle might have been a sea captain or merchant, while Flagg's relatives might have been farmers. In the end, we need to rightfully assume that everyone in a seaport had connections to maritime trade, and therefore access to the fruits of global commerce was widespread.

A more pronounced correlate of china than wealth or profession emerges in the inventories. There is a strong association between owning china and owning certain other specific items, such as books, maps, pictures, and navigational instruments. Founder Austin Paris in Philadelphia owned "4 Mapps" along with his china, as did the modest merchant John Thomas, who also died in 1730 in Philadelphia with only £65 but two sets of china and a "Mapp." Sometimes the area of the globe depicted on the map is mentioned, such as "Map of ye World" in the 1709 Salem estate of Benjamin Pickman, who also owned "China Ware." Similarly we are sometimes given a global region for the prints, pictures, or "Landskips" hung on the walls. A number of these have Asian subjects, such as "India Pictures" in the 1760 estate of New York gentleman John Pinhome. Pinhome also owned "2 china teapots, 6 china cups & saucers, and 1 china mugg & bason," but he owned no silver and his estate valued at £149 was hardly lavish for this prosperous wartime period.

Pictures and maps of the various regions of the world coinciding with Chinese porcelain is indicative, for certain colonial Americans, of their awareness of and interest in the wider world and their place in it. It also might tell us that those who owned porcelain appreciated, or at least were comfortable with, porcelain's cosmopolitan cachet—even its imagined Eastern cachet. Those who chose to make Chinese ceramics part of their household retinue, like sign painter William Gibbs in Newport who covered his walls with imitation lacquer, were embracing an oriental aesthetic that was at once bold, cosmopolitan, capitalist, and perhaps imperialist.

This examination of Atlantic commerce shows that an increasing number of European as well as American merchants and seamen were benefiting from the most lucrative of all trades, the "East Indies trade," over the course of the eighteenth century. In conjunction with this prosperous traffic, inventory data show an increasing number of colonial Americans of all classes in the northern seaports choosing to display china in their homes. The cultural work of porcelain in colonial homes is the subject of the next two chapters. Here it is important to acknowledge that colonial Americans were deeply involved in buying, selling, and owning Chinese porcelain long before direct, nationalized trade in the East. Globally and locally they sought out entrepreneurial gain in the commerce of tea and porcelain, and they were discriminating consumers of these Chinese commodities at home. It would be a shame to trivialize both the economic significance of this trade and the locally constructed cultural interpretations surrounding its fruits by asserting that Americans were merely imitating British courtiers in their consumption of china.[153]

Americans in the northern seaports found themselves in a dramatically different situation from that of their class-equivalents in Great Britain. The cultural inexperience ascribed to them in Bushman's emulative model was hardly a reality. Indeed, being closer to both the Caribbean and to seafaring in general, Americans held advantages over their chinoiserie-rapt counterparts across the ocean. It is tempting to suggest that the picture of a dependent, simple, marginalized American colonist, out-of-touch with the rapidly globalizing world of the eighteenth century, has been handed down over the ages by two powerful ideological strains, that of the potency of imperial England and that of the purity of reformed Protestants. As we shall see, this very tension between potency and purity intensified over access to Chinese commodities in the decade preceding the revolution.

4

The Oriental Aesthetic in Old Yankee Households

China in Northern Colonial Homes

> When you incline to buy China Ware, Chinces, India Silks, or any other of their flimsy slight Manufacturers . . . all I advise, is, to put it off.
> —Poor Richard, 1756

> One piece of China-ware, before it is fit for the furnace, passes through the Hands of above twenty Persons, and this without Confusion . . . after it is baked, [it] has passed the Hands of seventy Workmen.
> —Père Du Halde, 1736

Beginning in the Ming dynasty in the fifteenth century, Chinese potters would "sign" the bottom of their pieces with a four- to eight-character mark acknowledging the reigning emperor and imperial standards in the production of the pots. By the time porcelain was streaming into the Atlantic on ever-larger vessels of competing European states, the great Manchu emperor Kangxi (1662–1722) had outlawed the use

of his mark on exported wares.[1] Despite the insult to export ceramics, these
bastard offspring of the potteries of Jingdezhen held firm ground in Western commodities markets and homes. The quality, craftsmanship, and allure
of Chinese porcelain remained superior to that of any other commercially
available ceramic product, and superior even in the minds of many Westerners to the family pewter.[2] During the first half of the eighteenth century in
one North American household after another, the pewter that had graced the
seventeenth-century "bofat" or "manteltree" was moved out of view into the
kitchen to be replaced by "Chaney" ware, with or without the Chinese emperor's seal of approval. Porcelain held a position in the front and best rooms
of the home next only to silver dishes. An article in the *Boston Gazette* in 1722
sums up the place of Chinese porcelain within the Western universe of dining.
It reports that the "Ambassador Plenipotentiary of his Britannick Majesty"
celebrated the king's birthday in Cambray with other dignitaries in a dinner
of four courses. The first was served on silver, the second on silver gilt, the
third on gold, and the fourth on "the finest of China." Among court nobles
in Europe, Chinese porcelain ranked in the ultimate position alongside dishes
of traditional precious metals, and as the description of the dinner appeared
in a Boston newspaper, we can safely assume that Americans vicariously participated in aristocratic European dining standards. Since individual historical
circumstances condition responses to foreign objects, however, Americans did
not necessarily adopt this hierarchical ordering of dishes uncritically. People
across the Atlantic took on this perspective in a contextually contingent way.

While some very solid scholarly work has come out in recent years assess-
ing the cultural work of chinoiserie and Chinese objects within eighteenth-
century English or Dutch interiors, we cannot directly apply these insightful
analyses to colonial Americans, complicating our task of understanding the
place of Chinese porcelain in colonial homes.[3] William Hogarth and Joseph
Addison, whose creative responses to Chinese porcelain provide fertile material for scholars of early modern England, were well known and appreciated
in the colonies through publications such as the *Spectator* and *Tatler* as well
as off-print engravings, but their work sprang from a different socioeconomic,
political, and cultural scene in which classes were more rigidly defined and the
maritime economy was balanced or overshadowed by an emerging industrial
sector.[4] To best understand the place of Chinese objects in Anglo-American
homes, we need to first acknowledge that there were plenty of them around.
Second, we need to approach critically assumptions that Chinese commodities were treated the same in colonial homes as in English ones, even though
many cultural prejudices were shared, were transatlantic. The china dish was

a beautiful and useful commodity that, unlike tea and silk, retained a vibrant Chineseness for generations to come. Porcelain was not only produced in China, it inescapably looked Chinese. What this complex global commodity meant to Americans in the eighteenth century was related to their own market-oriented, maritime economic life, to their reformed Protestant culture and social roles, and—in short—to the innumerable distinct experiences of colonial American living.

It is not useful to approach the use of porcelain in America as simply imitation of English high society. One never says that in executing presumed witches, New Englanders were simply imitating Europeans, who in the same period persecuted more women as witches than Americans did. Even though the witchcraft hysteria began in Europe, we view it as a pan-Atlantic cultural phenomenon in which Americans, as situated within a distinct category of European culture, participated in a particular way. They defined and persecuted "witches" in a way that was particular to their cultural place in the world— particular to the beliefs, experiences, and physical constraints accumulated over several generations on the American continent. Likewise, Americans did not merely imitate Europeans or English court society in using Chinese porcelain objects at home. They participated in a pan-Atlantic phenomenon— orientalism, a visual culture that promoted chinoiserie, and a surging demand for East Asian commodities—in a way that was particular to their own societies and cultural context. With so many families on their third, fourth, or fifth generation in America, we must view eighteenth-century colonial consumption of Chinese porcelain as having *American* roots.

Our task of recovering the attitudes toward china actually at play in northern colonial homes in the first half of the eighteenth century is further complicated by the prescribed place given to Chinese porcelain in American colonial history by nineteenth- and twentieth-century collectors and curators. Meanings have been read back into the colonial period that were, in fact, only elaborated later, after the country emerged as a nation-state, victorious against a great sea empire, and had established face-to-face commercial relations with the Celestial Empire.[5] Nineteenth-century wives and daughters of American China traders collected porcelain dishes in order to interpret these spirited events. Such women were highly instrumental in projecting new meanings onto the Chinese pot, thrown away with disdain from the emperor's kilns. Those meanings *domesticated* this little illegitimate and exotic commodity, giving it a place in the pantheon of hardy, blue-blooded, old-monied American seafarers—"Yankees" in fact.[6] An earlier generation of historians have affectionately known these early national northeastern merchants and mariners as a "breed" or a "race," and if one is to be part of a race, a place-based genealogy is required.[7] Colonial American popular history, and especially that of New England, has been deeply impacted by a Yankee mythology, and a number of objects, including Chinese porcelain pots, are implicated in these influential traditions. This is evident in Northeast Auction's popular "Marine and China Trade Auction," hosted every year in Portsmouth, New Hampshire, which ties together Far Eastern trade goods with early New England folk art, locally made furniture, and maritime artifacts, deepening and perpetuating a popular culture of Yankee seafarers, who from the earliest days of their association with American soil are seen as both local folk and masters of the most illustrious and lucrative trade routes of their time. Significantly, Chinese porcelain is included under the heading "Americana" by many American antique dealers and estate auctioneers.

If Benjamin Franklin were to walk the earth today, he would certainly not be surprised to see Chinese porcelain in museum period rooms portraying the colonial northeast for, as we have seen, there was plenty of it around throughout the eighteenth century. As Franklin pointed out in his 1770 *Public Advertiser* article, American mariners were indeed successfully competing for a place in the lucrative East Indies trades. What he might find more surprising, however, is the cultural continuum proposed by the period rooms or the auctioneers' presentation of objects, a presentation that links the folksy, homespun articles near and dear to Franklin's heart with foreign—not yet domesticated—objects, indeed, with commodities that were Asian and "flimsy." In Franklin's time, the place of Chinese porcelain in northeastern American homes was socially and politically contested terrain, cultural currents not conveyed in today's historic period rooms. The Yankee identity had yet to be fully fashioned that would allow Asian imports to easily breathe the same air as the products of American labor. Moreover, since much of the porcelain was recycled or contraband of one form or another, it was much more politicized than it would be after the mid-nineteenth century when, "old" and "graceful," it acquired an American heirloom patina and entered the lifeless halls of colonial period rooms.

Having established that Americans in and around the northern colonial seaports had ready access to Chinese porcelain, we can seek to uncover the social content of this specific commodity in America. Northern Anglo-Americans were not merely imitating European aristocrats in using porcelain, nor were they expressing Yankee pride, which came later. Moreover, ownership of porcelain was not based on wealth or economic status alone. Many wealthy individuals shunned porcelain, which was easily available to middle-class widows in seaports or to German peasants in upstate New York. The goal of this chapter, therefore, is to give a more rigorous reading of the avid consumption of this refined Chinese manufacture by so many—but not all—colonial Americans.

Locating Porcelain in the Colonies

The probate evidence from chapter 3 (see fig. 1.2) comprises hundreds of estate inventories from the principal northern seaports and their environs over the course of the eighteenth century. Taking this vast data set together with collected pieces and archaeological collections, we are able to locate Chinese exported porcelain over the geographical and social landscape of the northern plantations. We can also observe trends in the expansion of china ownership beyond original loci over time. At the opening of the eighteenth century we generally find chinaware in three places: in Dutch New York,[8] on manor estates along the Long Island and Rhode Island Sounds, and in seafaring communities lacking a dominant religious presence. In Dutch New York, "parslin" existed in great quantities everywhere in the city and along the Hudson River to Albany.[9] The manor estates included places such as Colonel William Smith's St. George's Manor on Long Island or the estate of Governor Theophilus Eaton in New Haven.[10] The freewheeling seafaring towns included Marblehead and Pemaquid in Maine. Although rooted in the seventeenth century, these northern colonial cultural loci for chinawares confer imaginative associations on eighteenth-century users and owners of Chinese pots that were as influential to later generations of Americans as meanings elaborated on the other side of the Atlantic. All were marked by private enterprise and operated outside of or beneath the notice of British imperial authority. In one form or another, these places asserted independence from local governing structures. While New Netherland was taken over by the English in 1664, many of the Dutch free-trade practices, local economic and legal structures, and Dutch trading connections continued into the next century. In many respects, New York remained non-English into the eighteenth century.[11] Manor estates, whether in New Netherland or British America, were by some combination of legal and cultural practices relatively independent of local control. Finally, many fishermen and traders in coastal communities spent long periods of time at sea and many answered to no higher religious or state authority than maritime profit; these agnostics, dissenters, and mavericks tended to find each other, locating together along the coves and peninsulas of New England.[12]

While there are exceptions to this admittedly simplified framework, with early instances of porcelain being found in elite Boston or Pennsylvania families, such exceptions make weaker emblematic contributions to china's place later in eighteenth-century homes because they were more isolated, less provincial, and generally later.[13] By the second decade of the century (hence probate data from the 1720s and early 1730s), Chinese porcelain appears to have spread to almost every sector of the colonial landscape, with ownership evidently depending more on individual choice than wealth, profession, or remoteness of location. As the meanings attached to Chinese porcelain in the seventeenth century continued into the eighteenth in America, it is important to look back beyond the year 1700 and examine the place Chinese porcelain traditionally held in America prior to its rapid expansion throughout society. Using the broader perspective afforded by the probate data and the discussion of American trade in the previous chapter, an examination of individual pieces of chinaware and inventories allows to us to link known people with specific china dishes within an established context, enabling a more concrete analysis of the cultural place of this Chinese commodity within the northern colonies.

Dutch Tastes and Manor Estates: The OpDycks of Rhode Island and a Local Cultural Legacy

The impact of Holland's dynamic global trade network, spanning from Nagasaki to Albany, on Anglo-American taste cannot be overstated.[14] Seventeenth-century Americans, culturally nurtured with commodities of the world directly disseminated by irrepressible Dutch businessmen, left a profound legacy for subsequent generations, a cultural patrimony certainly as influential on the material tastes of their eighteenth-century descendants as secondhand descriptions of metropolitan fashion across the ocean. Many, many colonials at the dawn of the eighteenth century were third- or fourth-generation Americans. The *American* parents and grandparents of colonial Americans certainly formed important points of cultural reference rivaling European sources, and in seventeenth-century America, Dutch settlers and traders loomed large.[15]

In the winter of 1652, for example, John Warner, a religious radical transplanted ten years earlier from the Massachusetts Bay Colony to Warwick (present-day Rhode Island), housed a "crew of small Dutch vessels," or traders, in his coastal home for two months, storing their goods for sale. One of the Dutchmen later sued Warner for damages and, regardless of state affiliation, won.[16] Trading with the Dutch, apparently, garnered no sympathy for Warner among town officials. A year later in 1653, after the declaration of war between Holland and England, New Haven magistrates, located just a day's ride from

Rhode Island, turned their attention to more tainted Dutch commerce. Town meeting records read: "Mr. Atwater was complained of for trading with the Duch Jurisdiction. It was said others traded as well as he, as Lieutenant Seely and Sarjent Jeffery . . . Mr. Atwater confest he traded wth one of Hempsted for one hundred pound of sugar, one anker of liquors & 12 l. of candells."[17] War or no war, English settlers were clearly carrying on a brisk and complex trade with New Netherland from the earliest days of settlement, fortified by ties of marriage. The Dutch had a shipping advantage from the beginning, and English colonists were drawn to the opportunity to widen the market for their meager produce by using Dutch bottoms.[18] Over time the English gained a demographic advantage, with increasing numbers of English people settling in southern New England, pushing west to the Hudson, and swarming south onto Long Island. As each new English migrant jockeyed for land to secure his family's place and rise above subsistence, the temptation to trade with these foreign masters of global commerce was irresistible.

Richard Smith was one who did not resist. In fact he, like many early English colonists, maintained close ties with the Dutch, who showed more tolerance for all forms of religion and irreligion than the Puritan oligarchs in Massachusetts. Along with Providence's Roger Williams, Smith built a blockhouse and trading post on a tract of land purchased in 1637 from the Indians on the western shores of Narragansett Bay. In 1641 Smith fled Plymouth Colony for New Amsterdam with an exiled minister and thereafter maintained homes in Manhattan and present-day Queens, giving his Rhode Island trading post clear commercial advantages.[19] Smith carried furs bought from Native Americans to New Netherland in his sloop *Welcome*, which returned to Rhode Island loaded with manufactured trade goods, including ceramics. Like so many others he cemented his business deals with ties of kinship, marrying his daughter Katheryne in 1643 to Gysbert OpDyck, a physician and rising star in the Dutch West India Company. In 1666, just after the English took over New Netherland, OpDyck, Katheryne, and their seven children settled permanently on the Rhode Island property, a place labeled "wilderness" by Cotton Mather as well as by Americanist scholar Perry Miller generations later.[20] Archaeology conducted on the property in the 1990s, however, reveals another story. Archaeologists excavated nearly two hundred shards of colonial-era Chinese porcelain, representing over two dozen dish types, from the grassy waterfront area of the Smith-OpDyck estate, today maintained as a historic site in Wickford, Rhode Island.[21] While centuries of disturbance to the grounds around the circa 1678 house (which replaced Smith's original blockhouse) have made precise archaeological dating of the shards impossible, it is likely that much of this porcelain came to the site in the second half of the seventeenth and early eighteenth centuries, during the family's period of intense interaction with New York.[22]

Some of the earliest and largest quantities of Chinese porcelain in North America are associated with Dutch New Netherland. Porcelain ownership remained widespread there even after the English took over the colony, which they renamed New York. It was only following Lord Bellomont's persecution of those suspected of trading and owning East India goods that we see a drop in porcelains recorded in probate records. With permanent trading posts on the Indian coast, in Indonesia, on Taiwan until 1664, and in Japan during the upheavals of China's "transitional period" (ca. 1620–80), the Dutch had a much stronger presence in Asia in the seventeenth century than the English.[23] Moreover Dutch trade laws were less stringent than English mercantile burdens, allowing Dutch East India traders to import goods directly to the colonies and tolerating independent traders.[24] Given the Dutch preeminence in colonial shipping, Dutch traders are certainly responsible for most early porcelains found throughout the northern and southern colonies, including those found in Native American communities.[25] The Dutch maintained trade relationships up and down the Atlantic coastline, cementing their business relationships with marriage, as we have seen, and thereby spreading to their neighbors not only vendible commodities from all over the world but their personal tastes and family possessions as well. As early as 1595, Elizabethan soldiers arriving in Holland as allies were awestruck by the extent of material prosperity and the luxuriousness of people's possessions, despite two decades of war with Spain.[26] The Dutch carried their love of cupboards filled with colorful ceramics to the New World. Their nearly direct access to the kilns of China and Japan throughout the seventeenth century, and their close ties with neighboring American colonies, was a key factor in the contagious spread of a taste for Chinese porcelain throughout America by the early decades of the eighteenth century.[27]

Although each manorial estate in New England, Long Island, and the Hudson River Valley presents a cultural pastiche peculiar to its owners and their particular experiences—legal, ethnic, religious, political, and socioeconomic—the Smith-OpDyck estate did share a number of important features with other manorial plantations, features that were ultimately implicated in the material culture choices made by their overseers and, hence, important to our understanding of the historical place of porcelain. In early modern Europe landed estates were the backbone of regional or state power. Tracts of land with well-defined juridical boundaries that were built on, lived on, and farmed empowered the English in their New World territorial claims as well. New Netherland responded to deepening encroachments by English (and French) settlements by also fortifying itself with large land patents, either as vast "patroonships" or smaller "manor estates."[28] Wealthy, powerful Europeans from all walks of life desired to set themselves up on enclosed manorial compounds modeled on the estates of European feudal lords, something impossible for younger sons and professional classes in the densely populated, rigidly hierarchical landscape of northern Europe that could become a reality in the New World.

The "wilderness" of North America allowed easy access to land, and lavishly furnished manor houses provided the framework for self-fashioning and power building. Robert St. George's analysis of Samuel Desborough's estate in New Haven colony provides us with masterful insight into the sorts of cultural metaphors guiding the material choices made by proprietors of seventeenth-century manor estates (Guilford compound, ca. 1641; fig. 4.1). St. George describes these compounds as outposts of production, profit, and processing, places in which private interest and commercial activities were protected under "a veneer of ethical aristocracy."[29] "Enclosed domestic compounds like those built for Eaton and Desborough"—and for Philipse and Livingston on the Hudson, Lyon Gardner on his island, Winthrop in Saybrook, OpDyck on the Narragansett, and Philip English in Salem—"allowed for a comfortable embrace of commercial capitalism, but, by suggesting the persistence of

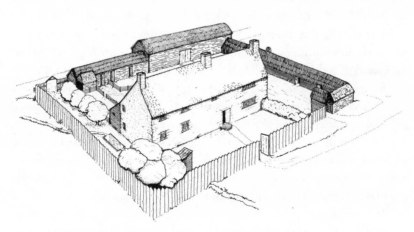

4.1. Drawing of a Guilford, Connecticut, compound, ca. 1641. Illustration by Robert Blair St. George in his *Conversing by Signs: Poetics of Implication in Colonial New England*, University of North Carolina Press, 1998, p. 20.

a quasi-feudal, organic social order, they conveniently legitimized keeping the uninvited from seeing their material possessions too closely."

Here "the uninvited" St. George refers to were the lower classes, whose mere presence might debase elitist pretensions built around worldly possessions. But, one might also add, jealous public officials and governments equally threatened the imaginative styles signified by worldly possessions. From the beginning men of means were enticed to "plant" themselves in the New World, in the name of their sovereign, with the promise that their manor estates would be exclusively theirs to rule over as they pleased. *Private* property ownership was the most fundamental founding principle of the British colonies.[30] As seen in chapter 1, one of the main advantages to be found in the New World was precisely the juridical and physical *distance* from a grasping authority, whether religious or political (which in fact were one and the same in New England at this time). Émigrés to America coveted Chinese commodities and Asian styles with as much zeal as their European counterparts, but in America one did not have to be a lord to elaborate private spaces that allowed the *unharassed* enjoyment of worldly pretensions, including, if one so chose, an imagined East Indian decor.

Colonel William Smith offers an obvious example. As a dutiful civil servant to the king of England, he was appointed in 1674 mayor of the new English "possession" of Tangier, Morocco. By 1683 the project was a bust, and Smith was recalled. But having had a taste of the world, Smith found England oppressive, and so he set sail for New York. Within a few years he had set himself up as a manor lord on Long Island. The patent issued to "Loving Subject, Coll. William Smith" on October 9, 1693, sets forth that "the said lordshipp and manour shall be and forever continue free and exempt from the jurisdiction of any town, township, or manor," and, moreover, these privileges pass unencumbered directly to Smith's chosen heirs.[31] "Loving subject" Smith was free to create his own set of ruling standards, his own microcosm of worldliness, untouched by any meddling local authority.[32] The parallel and interrelated colonization of India and of America engendered in the English subject what Michael Warner calls a "provincial belonging to the world."[33] The full extent of Smith's engagement with Eastern tastes are apparent in his 1705 inventory, which lists spices, chinaware, "Jappan" furniture, Venetian glass, silk cushions, oriental carpets, a Turkish scimitar, and East India sashes.[34]

Unlike William Smith, whose patent was confered directly by the Crown, Richard Smith, his OpDyck descendants, and most presumptive manor lords were never granted such outright privilege. By forming close alliances, however, with power brokers within the colonies, such as officials of the Dutch

West India Company, the Winthrops in Connecticut, and various other colonial governors, Richard Smith and many others were informally granted identical jurisdiction. Where alliances in the colonies were difficult, as in the case of Rhode Island's Roger Williams of Providence or Samuel Gorton of Warwick, one could always sail to London and seek out a friendly backer. However it happened, many independent and elaborate manor estates appeared in the second half of the seventeenth century, and historians have a lot more to learn about exactly what sorts of producing and commercial activities were going on within the protected, often hidden, confines of these estates, to say nothing of the imagined identities generated by such protected wealth and privacy.[35]

A few of the porcelain shards from the OpDyck property are of special interest to our understanding of the culture of independent manors and the domestic impact of global commerce and objects such as Chinese porcelain. Two small broken edges of a pure white *blanc-de-chine* statue complicate conventional narratives about the reformed Protestant household in early New England. Such statues were very popular with the Spanish and Portuguese, and their broken remains are littered across Mexico. Their most typical form was that of the Guanyin, the Chinese goddess of mercy, who Europeans mistook for the Virgin Mary, a misperception encouraged by savvy Chinese potters who soon discovered that placing a babe in the Guanyin's arms dramatically boosted sales to Catholic Europe (figs. 4.2 and 4.3).[36] Buddhas, other divine figures, and little animals were also common figurines (see figs. I.1 and 3.9). These are occasionally found in northern estate inventories of the late seventeenth and early eighteenth centuries listed as "alabaster toys," "India images," or "Indian Babyes" (as in the 1695 will of New Yorker Margrieta van Varick). But, interestingly, none of these little statues have been preserved or collected in the north. This may be because they reeked of idol worship, and devout Protestants ostensibly took very seriously the injunction of the second commandment, which forbade the making or worshipping of images.

Orthodox Puritan Samuel Sewall of Massachusetts, for example, exhorted his countrymen in verse repeatedly in his diary: "So Men shall God in Christ adore, And worship Idols vain, no more."[37] Although today we partition "religion" as a discrete category of analysis, among early Americans religious beliefs thoroughly permeated all aspects of life, impacting even secular, nonworshipping communities. In most people, whether they attended church or not, the core values of reformed Protestantism were simply part of the mental grounding they brought with them to America.[38] One aspect of such a belief structure was a deep-seated suspicion of the seductive power of decorative objects. In dress and household furnishings, a dialectic emerged between necessity and

4.2. Soft-paste porcelain Guanyin (Bodhi-
sattva), standing. Qing dynasty, Dehua,
China. Museo Nazionale d'Arte Orientale,
Rome, Italy. Photo: Scala / Art Resource, NY.

masculine functionality on the one hand and superfluity and feminine frivol-
ity on the other.[39] Intimacy with an ornamental schema associated with a foreign people widely believed to be both idol-worshippers and under the spell
of despots would certainly cause discomfort if it were not first sanitized by an
overriding Western narrative. Proximity to the East aroused fears of going native as expressed repeatedly in American newspaper accounts of the Jesuits in
China, as discussed in chapter 2. Such anxieties remained strong throughout
the colonial period, appearing in the early years of the American China trade
when Americans themselves were actually spending extended periods of time

4.3. Soft-paste porcelain Guanyin (Bo-dhisattva), seated with babe. Kangxi period (1662–1722), late seventeenth century, Dehua, China. Porzellansammlung, Staatliche Kunstsammlungen, Dresden, Germany. Photo: Bildarchiv Preussischer Kulturbesitz / Art Resource, NY.

in China. One late eighteenth-century Providence lady remarked of a beau on a China voyage that she anticipated he would "appear among us a regular Chinaman.... How people will stare! You may expect to see yourself an eighth wonder of the world."[40] Close contact with a seductive, alien people clearly had contagious qualities, capable of transforming one from a vital human being into a freak, "an eighth wonder of the world."

Situated in the Protestant heartland of New England, these traces of Chinese statues made in the image of Buddhist deities were revered not as objects of worship, of course, but as icons of exotic riches, revealing the complexity of reformed Protestant culture. The colonist's propensity for religious freedom, whether as a devout Puritan or a nonbeliever, perhaps signals an even broader sense of freedom, one that included freedom to trade in *any* productive market, to value the fruits of trade with idol worshippers, and even to place their very idols on one's mantel, if, that is, they were valuable. The irresistible allure of global commerce—not just its fruits, but the freedom to voyage, trade, and import in and of itself—outweighed even a sin as great as idol worship. Writing nearly a century later, Mercy Otis Warren, who grew up in the lap of reformed Protestant culture in Plymouth, expressed customary Puritanical apprehension about mixing freedom, commercial wealth, and idolatry. In a passage on Washington's wayward general, Charles Lee, she wrote,

> Without religion or country, principle, or attachment, gold was his diety, and liberty the idol of his fancy; he hoarded the former without taste for its enjoyment, and worshipped the latter as the patroness of licentiousness, rather than the protectress of virtue.[41]

The enduring Puritanical message here is clear: commercial freedom can lead to licentiousness and the worship of idols. It is no wonder that wealthy Protestant merchants and farmers participating in commerce in far-flung markets built high walls around their estates. Historian Robert St. George has asked that we rethink the conventional figuring of these enclosed colonial compounds solely for defense against Indians, who in fact the Puritan colonists fully and comfortably exploited for purposes of enhancing their position in the world's commercial markets.[42] There is no doubt that local Indians posed a threat, both in terms of sheer force and in the potential contagiousness of their idolatry, but there were many other perceived threats as well, from within their own English communities. In owning and displaying Chinese porcelain statues, "India Images," the OpDyck family bravely ventured along the moral precipice of commercial freedom, using the remote and privatized space of their manor as a means to more safely indulge in the enticing, commodified trappings of mercantile independence and success. The Chinese statue or pot was a pawn in this game of capitalist self-aggrandizement, and its artistically Chinese forms were subsumed within the Western mercantile aesthetic. Even when as blatantly idolatrous as an image of Buddha himself, what mattered most was that the image manifested one's mastery of overseas trade.

Another pair of china shards from the Smith-OpDyck estate show traces of a blue underglazed shield and crown, part of a coat of arms (fig. 4.4). Private

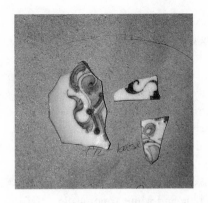

4.4. Shards of blue-and-white armorial porcelain, pre-1730. Friends of Cocumscussoc Association. Author's photo.

orders of blue-and-white armorial-decorated porcelain were popular with the Portuguese from about 1540 to 1630. The Dutch showed little interest in armorials until the end of the seventeenth century. At that time their presence in the South China Sea was strong and the market for Chinese porcelain at home even stronger. The English were only permitted to trade in China, or more precisely, Canton, where special order porcelain was procured, after 1700, and private order china with heraldry quickly became very popular throughout the British Isles. Such orders were facilitated when the English built a permanent factory in Canton in 1715. The French, Danish, and Swedes built factories ten to fifteen years later, but the Dutch did not set up a permanent post in Canton until 1769. This tardiness may account for the small number of Dutch armorial porcelains compared to the other European states. The English ordered thousands of armorial sets compared to only about 250 known for the Dutch. By 1730, almost all armorial designs were executed in overglaze enamels, not in underglaze blue.[43]

What are the chances, then, that this armigerous pot shard can be directly attributed to the OpDycks? As the crest is painted in underglaze blue rather than the colorful enamels, we can assume the shard was part of a dish or set of dishes that predates 1730. Both the Smiths and the OpDycks had family coats of arms in Europe, and while such worldly pretensions may have been left behind by the founding generation in America, subsequent generations may have been more interested in this sort of status symbol. Richard Smith Jr. had been a Cromwellian soldier and aligned himself with the Church of England rather than the Puritan oligarchy in Boston. Lodowick OpDyck (d. 1737), son of Gysbert, inherited the Rhode Island estate in 1692 and also maintained close ties with the Anglo-centered establishment in Connecticut (as opposed to his more radical Antinomian neighbors in Rhode Island). He was a sea captain and grandson of Richard Smith Sr., and he married another Smith grandchild, permanently bringing together the two families under the anglicized name "Updike."[44] If Lodowick had any connections to the Dutch East India Company or to the English East India Company, he may have ordered the blue-and-white armorial service for himself. Given his relative remoteness, however, from European metropolitan centers where such orders were placed and received, it is more likely that this armorial dish was made for someone else and pirated. It may well have been picked up in the Indian Ocean from a Portuguese vessel out of Goa, or any of the other numerous Portuguese settlements around the coast of India, and subsequently carried to New York. Indeed, the bulk of blue-and-white armorials in circulation were Portuguese (see, e.g., fig. 4.5). Alternatively, it may represent prize booty that had been in the OpDyck family for generations. In 1602 and again in 1604 the Dutch attacked and captured Portuguese ships carrying

4.5. Chinese porcelain ewer, with upside-down blue-and-white armorial design, made for the Portuguese market, ca. 1520, h. 7 ⅜ in. Metropolitan Museum of Art, New York, NY. Helena Woolworth McCann Collection, Purchase, Winfield Foundation Gift, 1961 (61.196). Image © Metropolitan Museum of Art / Art Resource, NY.

enormous cargoes of porcelains, which were subsequently auctioned in the Netherlands.[45]

Thinking in terms of a cultural identity that is amplified in the use of Chinese armorial porcelain at home, the metaphorical distance between using dishes with one's *own* coat of arms and those of another from an alien state seems vast. The social, symbolic message is simply not the same, unless one ignores the decorative motif or mentally replaces it with another imagined symbol. In the case of the OpDyck "borrowed" armorial porcelain, it is likely that a family member or a vessel with which the family was associated had proudly pirated them. Therefore, the dishes, with their coat of arms, represented victory and served to reinforce an element of manly conceit related to individual commercial, maritime prowess, as opposed to one's subject status within a kingdom or proximity to state powers as symbolized by one's own family crest. Here the European armorial design inflated the fact that the dishes came from China and thereby reinforced their status as a manly trade good. Since the means and privilege to trade directly in China represented the highest commercial attainment of the seventeenth and eighteenth centuries, these Chinese-manufactured household commodities, placed in the hands of one's wife, marked a feather in the cap of a worldly sea captain such as Lodowick Updike, a trophy on his manteltree. The armorial indicates success in competition with other European states.

Lodowick's son Daniel Updike (1694–1757) sailed across the bay, taking up temporary residence in Newport as a merchant. Judging from the archaeological remains at his Wickford estate of large quantities of *famille rose* and *grisaille* porcelain shards—porcelain types only arriving in America after 1725 and popular from 1730 to 1770—he appears to have been as successful as his father. Many vessel forms are accounted for in these shards, delicately overglazed in pink, yellow, and silver-gray enamels and edged with gold gilt. While the typical ratio of overglazed china to ordinary blue-and-white in colonial archaeological assemblages is about 1:12, or 8 percent of the porcelain being the more expensive enameled wares, the ratio at Updike's manor is 1:5.5, or 18 percent of the porcelain assemblage accounted for by enameled pieces.[46]

The Updikes' large and somewhat costly collection of Chinese dishes would make Daniel and Daniel's son (who lived on the manor until 1804) participants in what some historians today refer to as the "anglicization" of colonial Americans, described as a "English renaissance" occurring in the decades preceding the revolution.[47] But we need to consider that Daniel and his son were fourth- and fifth-generation Americans of both Dutch and English heritage who had grown up surrounded by worldly goods, including chinaware.

4.6. *Taste of High Life*, engraving by William Hogarth, ca. 1743, based on his own
original painting.

Arguably their model for the use and care of china—the source of their attitudes toward this refined Chinese import—was not high society in England
but their own parents and grandparents, for whom china had been an icon of
maritime and territorial liberty and power. It is much more likely, in fact, that
neighborly visitors, local artisans, servants, and the whole host of local folk in
the small, interdependent society of southern New England plantations and
seaports, referred *not* to the English but to the likes of Lodowick Updike for
their social understanding of Chinese porcelain. The "consumer revolution"
did have important roots in seventeenth-century American society, which
from the beginning depended on imports from and exports to all points of
the globe. While the culturally complex Georgian response to Chinese objects
in England was felt in America, that response was filtered through American
experiential circumstances in which the semiotics of Chinese objects, indeed
that of all foreign, exotic imports, remained much closer to the freewheeling days before the East India Company's exclusive grasp on trade. It is noteworthy that one scholar of the early American China trade has observed that
American captains arriving in Canton at the end of the eighteenth century

by and large resembled seventeenth-century adventurers.[48] Chinese porcelain invoked a masculine liberty to make one's own rules and mastery at sea and on land. As Moses Marcy's portrait (fig. 3.5) shows, in the colonies porcelain manifested precisely the opposite of the slavish devotion to feminine fashion suggested in Hogarth's visual commentary on china's place in English high society (fig. 4.6).

Ephemeral and Effeminate: Brittleware and Broken Dishes

By the second decade of the eighteenth century, china ownership had spread beyond mansion and manor walls, beyond Dutch cupboards and fishermen's taverns, to almost all sectors of northern colonial society. At this point it becomes more difficult to generalize about the significance these Chinese objects may have had for Americans. What porcelain meant to middling women shopkeepers, such as Mrs. Pratt of Newport , or to Prussian peasants on Livingston Manor, or to aspiring Massachusetts merchants such as Thomas Amory or Thomas Gerry (see fig. I.4) was certainly different than what it meant to colonial elites such as Daniel Horsemonden in Flatbush, New York, or to colonial officials such as William Penn, or to affluent merchants' wives such as Catherine Livingston. But there were specific repetitive—*dominant*, one might even say— discourses related to china that emerged with increased consumption, discursive evidence that reveals ambivalence across the board toward china's attributes and its place in American homes. Two of these perceived qualities will be discussed here: china's ultimate fragility and china as a feminized foil to masculine strength. In both cases china—and perhaps China—was set up as a chimera or a femme fatale, leading capital-healthy men into a capital-sucking trap.

On March 25, 1742, the *Pennsylvania Gazette* reported on a curious incident that took place in Philadelphia's public market.

> Benjamin Lay, the Pythagorean-cynical-christian Philosopher, bore publick Testimony against the Vanity of Tea drinking, by devoting to Destruction in the Market place, a large Parcel of valuable China, &c. belonging to his deceased Wife. He mounted a Stall on which he placed the Box of Ware; and when the People were gather'd round him, began to break it peacemeal with a Hammer; but was interrupted by the Populace, who overthrew him and his Box, to the Ground, and scrambling for the Sacrifice, carry'd off as much of it whole as they could get. Several would have purchas'd the China of him before he attempted to destroy it, but he refused to take any Price for it.[49]

Dissecting this bizarre account, we see that it involves three parties representing three distinct perspectives on china in colonial Philadelphia. First there is Lay, a zealous Quaker and one of the region's earliest abolitionists and animal rights activists, known for expressing moral disapprobation through public stunts of this sort.[50] Second, we have the china-crazed populace "scrambling for the sacrifice" like starving animals, willing to pay "any price" for the fragile Chinese commodity that will relieve their wants. Third, of course, is the cool-headed reporter whose interest and very description tell us that a cultural tension provoked by china and tea drinking really did exist in 1740s Philadelphia, but that it was possible for some—the reporter, for example—to retain composure when confronted with a valuable Chinese commodity.

Let's examine Lay's response to china first. How are we to interpret this particular outburst against the "vanity of tea drinking" and its principal prop, china? What socially relevant comment is Lay making on the use of china here, especially his unwillingness to exchange it for a price? Lay was a Quaker and china was, as we have seen, often obtained as war booty. Other Quakers avoided porcelain exactly because of its association with acts of war. William Wilson, a Philadelphia merchant and a Quaker, specialized in buying and selling household goods such as earthenwares, pewter, metal pots, and tea, but his accounts do not once list porcelain and, moreover, he gives specific instructions to his captains to avoid ill-gotten gains.[51] England's so-called King George's War (1739–48) began to be felt along the colonial coast in 1740,[52] and it is probable that in the years preceding Lay's public scene, increased quantities of chinaware had flowed into town as war booty. The Society of Friends preached pacifism and resistance to "vain and superfluous things," but many midcentury Quakers comfortably lived otherwise.[53] In any event, the maniacal quality of Lay's bizarre outburst stems from deeper cultural roots than the level-headed enactment of a religious injunction against warlike behavior, such as Wilson's. As Foucault has shown us, the madman can plainly evince the power of real cultural contradictions suppressed in everyday life by the sane.[54] In this case, the sane reporter confronts mad behavior on the part of both Lay and the "populace," the vanity-stricken consumers—not privateering procurers—of china. The fanatical behavior described in the article reveals a society struggling to remain detached from narcissistic desire provoked by a Chinese commodity that is here cast by Lay as a brittle chimera.

Lay's display purposely focuses attention on the fragility of china, and not any other sort of war booty. The breakable quality of china, in fact, comes up repeatedly in eighteenth-century American discourse. This fragility seems to irk provincial probate appraisers, who never miss recording chips and cracks as they lump china dishes under the heading "brittlewares."[55] In the regularly occurring newspaper reports of seismic tremors, the force of any earthquake is invariably measured by how much china falls from the mantel and breaks.[56] Even ordinary thunderstorms break china, as seen in the 1739 *Boston News-Letter* report about a "very severe Clap of Thunder, which struck the House of Andrew Hamilton, Esq.; but did no Damage only broke some China."[57] Like severe weather, overenergetic male behavior posed a risk to china. A *Boston Evening Post* article of Christmas Day, 1738, told of a group of gentlemen seated around a tea table, who, jumping up to look out the window at a passing group of "jovial Blades," "overset the table, by which all the China Ware was unhappily broke." What is perhaps more telling than all these broken dishes is the fact that broken china was considered so newsworthy that such seemingly trivial tales claimed valuable newspaper space. The cultural contradiction contained in the example clearly had implications for American consumers. Chinese porcelain was simultaneously the esteemed icon of masculine commercial fortitude and yet so delicate that any rough disturbance to the domestic fireside or tea table could shatter it.

Over the course of his long life, Benjamin Franklin also frequently invoked the breakability of china. Under the precocious spell of Joseph Addison, picked up in the piles of *Spectators* brought home from London by his brother James, Franklin, as "Silence Dogood," wrote a clever piece in the *New England Courant* in 1722 in praise of the fair sex. In his example of how refined women maintain composure and eloquence in the face of adversity—as opposed to men who overturn china tables—he tells us that a lady is able to "chide her Servant for breaking a China Cup, in all the figures of Rhetorick."[58] In other words, if ever an accident would try the patience of woman, it would certainly be the mishandling of the fragile family china by a servant. But perhaps Franklin's most famous reference to broken china is found in a letter to Lord Howe at the outbreak of the revolution. "Long did I endeavor with unfeigned and unwearied Zeal, to preserve from breaking, that fine & noble China Vase the British Empire," he claimed with feigned remorse.[59] In comparing the empire to a china vase, Franklin wishes to underscore not only its fragility but, just as Lay did, its chimerical qualities. The china—and the China trade within the china—deceived men, leading them into far-reaching, capital-consuming exploits, only to break apart. Franklin had indeed witnessed such a deception in the financially devastating collapse of the South Sea Company in 1720, in which an elusive opportunity to break into Spain's Pacific trade with China led London investors to fall off a speculative mantel and break apart.[60]

For Franklin, the china vase was indeed a "flimsy manufacture." But the derisive force of the metaphor owes as much to the crazed longing American consumers felt for porcelain as to china's inherent fragility. Given the apparent ease with which a china owner could cross the fine line between enjoying a whole vessel and sweeping up broken pieces, why did the "Populace" watching Lay want the porcelain so badly they would pay any price for it? Why, more to the point, would they waste their money? Social pundits of all stripes consistently posed this question, invariably arriving at the same answer: china purchases amounted to a useless drain of scarce colonial capital. Note the didactic commentary in the *New York Weekly Journal* in 1742:

> I am credibly informed, that Tea and China Ware cost the Province yearly near the sum of Ten Thousand Pounds; and People that are the least able to go to the expence, must have their Tea tho' their Families go hungry.

Yet even Franklin, who had long preached the virtues of frugality in *Poor Richard's Almanack*, could not control his urge for this Chinese commodity. He relates in a well-known passage in his *Autobiography* how suddenly one morning he innocently found that his wife had replaced his two-penny earthen porringer with an expensive china bowl, giving as an excuse the remark that her husband deserved the same as his neighbors.[61] As Franklin tells the story, he chose to indulge his wife's vanity—not his own, of course—and ate from china happily ever after. This we know with some certainty because archaeologists have recovered a large quantity of ceramic shards from the Franklins' home, 12 percent of which were Chinese and Japanese porcelain. Given the greater care usually given to china—and the keen popular attention paid to its breakability—I would suggest that more than 12 percent of Franklin's household dishes were porcelain.[62]

The real economic vulnerability hidden in the eye-stopping, vanity-stroking *whole* china vase was suddenly and shockingly revealed when it broke and all its presumed integrity was lost. The true worthlessness of china was contained especially in the fact that Americans did not produce it and Americans did not control its trade. A love for "homespun" was not something that sprang up only in revolutionary America. Northern colonists carefully cultivated a love of home manufactures and locally generated commerce over the course of the whole colonial period. We see this sentiment nurtured in a 1728 poem entitled "A Description of Pennsylvania," penned by Thomas Makin, an early settler and local Latin tutor. While acknowledging that Philadelphia was a world-class seaport, the author reserves heartfelt appreciation for Pennsylvania farmers and their home manufactures.

To this long known & well frequented port
From sundry places many shipps resort.
In merchandizing most men are here imploy'd:
All usefull artists too are occupy'd.
The frugal farmer, like yᵉ carefull Ant,
In Sumer 'gainst cold Winter provident,
His barn, well cover'd to keep out yᵉ rain
Fills wᵗʰ good hay & diverse sorts of grain.
Neglecting costly cloathes & dainty food,
His own unbought provisions sweet & good.
Weary wᵗʰ labour takes his ease & rest:
His homespun cloathing pleasing him yᵉ best.[63]

For Makin, all was virtuous in the province of Pennsylvania, even the merchant in his cosmopolitan, "long known" port of Philadelphia. But the "frugal farmer" was the truly estimable American, living on "His own unbought provisions."

Enterprising Philadelphians, Quaker and non-Quaker, may have been perturbed by porcelain's lack of local genesis. In response Philadelphia can boast a number of firsts in the American china market. The first American porcelain manufactory was the Bonin & Morris enterprise founded in Philadelphia in 1770, and although it lasted only two years, it showed a solid output of soft-paste porcelain during that time, with a few pieces even surviving today.[64] It exemplifies better than any rhetorical gesture can the great need these people felt not only to make their own china, but to make china their own. More famous than the porcelain manufactory is the first United States vessel to sail to China, the *Empress of China* (not, interestingly, the *First Lady of America*), financed by Philadelphia merchants before the peace treaty with Britain was even signed; the ship was launched within days of the end of the revolution. Americans wasted no time in making the China trade their own as well. The trade would prove as fragile to manage as the object and, while it made many great fortunes, many traders were broken to pieces by its charms. It was a chimera, as the skeptics had warned all along.

Strong Metal Men and Beguiled Porcelain Women

Another central aspect of Chinese porcelain becomes apparent in each of the above examples in addition to, or in conjunction with, its veiled lack of substance. There was in colonial America an alleged affinity between conniving

women and this materially and morally weak commodity of the Orient. A
discourse linking women to porcelain playthings within a conspiratorial or
hedonistic domestic setting developed in the West over the course of the eighteenth century, and in America it existed alongside the opposing discourse
from earlier times that linked brave, virile, mercantile men to china trophies.
In England the burgeoning consumption of Asian commodities, and tea in
particular, was accompanied by a vigorous debate on tea and china's presumed
power to sap masculine vitality.[65] Dr. Samuel Johnson perceived vitiating effects on masculine strength: "Tea is one of the stated amusements of the idle
and luxurious. The whole mode of life is changed, every kind of voluntary labor, every exercise that strengthened the nerves and muscle, is fallen into dis-
use."[66] Gradually the masculine aura once granted china in England gave way
as porcelain vases and tea sets, stacked in ladies' parlors like those observed
by Oliver Goldsmith's Mandarin, became the defining trope of a languid, ir-
responsible femininity. Collecting porcelain and sipping tea afforded women
too much leisure and an aversion to maternity. In 1740 an English visitor to
Boston observed, "the ladies here visit, drink tea and . . . neglect the affairs of
their families with as good grace as the finest ladies in London." By midcentury in England, gender-based arguments against tea and china had become
more tightly synthesized into a class-based discourse. Tea-induced familial neglect was less seemly when the abusers were washerwomen or, for that matter,
colonial women. Simon Mason was one of the first to distinguish between an
upper-class and lower-class use of tea in his 1745 book, *The Good and Bad Effects of Tea Considered.*[67] In brief, Mason allowed the medicinal benefits of tea
to those who consume large meals and strong drink as well as to those who can
benefit from the inducement it provides for intelligent conversation. For the
lower classes it was merely a waste of precious time and labor that promoted
gossip and malicious behavior.

Americans, especially urbane Americans, participated in this chauvinist
mind-set emanating from the metropolis. In 1759 John Adams wrote to Josiah Quincy while traveling in the countryside about embarrassing "Indiscre-
tions" on the part of country revelers at a local tavern, "shoe string fellows that
never use Tea and would use it [as awkwardly] as the Landlady did."[68] Her
"unguarded" behavior in mishandling the tea service inappropriately spread
to the men about her. In general, however, elitist pretensions in America—
those called forth by the emulation thesis in interpreting the tea ritual—were
secondary to anxieties about the loss of fiscal self-determination brought on
by tea-drinking women. Whereas the English were most anxious about the
mockery female consumers could make of deeply rooted, class-based preten-

sions and a hierarchal world defined by an exclusive male, landed aristocracy,[69] Americans were much more pointedly concerned with the draining of scarce colonial capital and a resulting state of dependency. The early Massachusetts Bay government, aware that overseas commerce was indispensable to the survival of their colonial experiment, had flirted with sumptuary laws explicitly to control depletion of local resources caused by too many community members consuming unneeded imports.[70] Legislating social control may have failed in New England, but this anxiety about excessive consumption of imports endured despite robust colonial economies and rising wealth. In the eighteenth century anti-British whiggery and evangelical Protestantism became discursively linked through attacks on excess consumption of imported fineries.[71] Tea and china were singled out for special vilification. One New York gentleman wrote in 1762, "Our People, both in Towne and Country, are shamefully gone into the habit of Tea-drinking."[72] Indeed, men as well as women were drinking tea from china cups (fig. 4.7).

In 1732 Franklin borrowed from Addison once again to satirize those anxieties before an American audience. He created a decent working fellow named Anthony Afterwit, who, deceived by his paramour's father, found himself with an import-crazed wife and a financially precarious marital situation. Being dissatisfied with his "tolerably furnished" house, his wife first bought a "large looking glass," to which Afterwit comments, "Had we stopp'd there, we might have done well enough." But his wife proceeded next to a "Tea-Table with all its Appurtenances of China and Silver," followed by a clock and £20 riding horse. At this point she had drained the victimized husband of not only his earnings but his very masculinity, evident in his confession, "I . . . had not Resolution enough to help it." It took a two-week absence by his wife for him to regain a healthy manly resolve, at which time he replaced each luxurious import with an article related to domestic industry, objects used for production as opposed to idle enjoyment: a spinning wheel for the tea table, flax for tea, and a cow for the horse. Here china and tea drinking figure foremost among the villainous, emasculating imports, and it is only through reselling them that this otherwise modest man is able to pay his debts and return his house to order. It was idle women and their intemperate desires who led men into a servile state. Mr. Afterwit is indeed fortunate that his china did not break, or it would have been more difficult to reestablish his patriarchal authority.

Contrary to this pan-Atlantic stereotype so readily indulged by Franklin, however, American women were certainly also worried about servility. A woman desired porcelain not so much to relish the pleasures of upper-class living, which were often repugnant to lingering Protestant mores, but rather to

4.7. John Potter and Family, anonymous overmantel painting, ca. 1742, Newport. Collections of the Newport Historical Society.

demonstrate, to herself as much as others, that she had secured "a sufficiency"—that she had, in other words, sufficient family wealth and was free of servility.[73] The second half of Puritan minister Samuel Sewall's diary (ca.1700–1729) consists in a continual round of social drinking, tea in the afternoons and Madeira or punch in the evenings. Daily offhand references to tea parties and soirees around the punch bowl denote his self-satisfied, "elect" state of life.[74] It is certainly not lavish, high-style living that interested Sewall and his hostesses but rather signs of salvation. In examining midcentury, middle-class Newport women, archaeologist Christina Hodge discovered that both feminine sociability—marked by the use of porcelain tewares—and deep anxieties about debt and servility emerge prominently from the documentary and material evidence of their lives. The poor and the enslaved—and the widowed if a woman were not careful—were socially and legally defined by their lack of property. In a society that incarcerated the poor and viewed poverty as a socially deviant state, it is not surprising that women, whose husbands were at sea and whose property had scant legal protection without them, would find themselves obsessed with signs of material security.

Being in a position to buy and display Chinese goods made the best statement possible of personal financial freedom. This John Francis well knew when he responded in 1787 to his father-in-law's request that he sail the first Rhode Island vessel to China. Francis was very ill at the time, but the request from his wife's father was difficult to disregard. "When you come up I shall determine whether to go or not in the Indiaman," he wrote to John Brown.

"The idea of obtaining a sufficiency to support my dear A[bigail] and myself in a decent manner would induce me to encounter any Danger."[75] Here we see that Francis's wife, Abigail, through her father, was implicated in leading her husband into a reckless attempt at china, and China. Benjamin Franklin's wife, in her quiet conniving way, as he described the situation, manipulated him into the use of a china bowl in order that the neighbors not think they were struggling. But Franklin feared the china bowl was but a camel's dainty nose under the domestic tent. Its promise of material comfort was a deception, the first step to financial and moral ruin. The china pot was, after all, an imported commodity, not a thing of substance. Benjamin Lay, the Quaker ascetic who carried to the public square "a large Parcel of valuable China, &c. belonging to his deceased Wife," was sure of this, and he also had his wife to blame for the threat of a dissolute lifestyle.

In the print culture of the eighteenth century, American men entered a semantic rivalry with women over the figurative role of Chinese porcelain in colonial communities. In this contest, men were the producers of wealth and women the consumers. It was women, in fact, who could lead men and society into a barren state of fruitless labor and dependency, as the biblical Eve had done, and the only way women could compensate, of course, was by producing offspring. Indeed frugality and fertility were closely linked in Enlightenment discourse. Franklin believed, for example, that population increases in the highly revered "ancient states" of classical times were attributed to "Simplicity of taste, frugality, patience of labour, and contentment with a little."[76] Maxim number sixteen of his *Observations concerning the Increase of Mankind* (1755) states that foreign luxuries "increase the People of the Nation that furnishes them, and diminish the People of the Nation that uses them," and in the very next maxim Franklin singles out Asian imports. "Some European Nations prudently refuse to consume the Manufactures of East-India. They should likewise forbid them to their Colonies; for the Gain to the Merchant, is not to be compar'd with the Loss by this Means of People to the Nation."[77] In other words, women preoccupied with Asian luxuries, and men preoccupied with providing them, will somehow lose their sex drive; they will become depleted and their society depopulated.

Imports, as opposed to home manufactures, were associated with dependency in yet another way related to one's ability to command power during an exchange. In her examination of early Newport furniture makers, art historian Margaretta Lovell observes two types of producer-consumer relationships. The first involved artisanal or manufactured objects in which the producer's identity had been obliterated. In the case of porcelain, the producer was the distant, unknown Chinese potter. In this faceless relationship not only was the potter's work exploited, but his very self was viewed as exploitable. Both the nameless Chinese potter and his output were subservient to Western capital.[78] The purchaser, a Western captain, emerged as master of both the potter and his work. The porcelain was, in this relationship, a trophy signifying the servility of Asians (and/or Catholics from whom it may have been pirated) and the dominance of Protestant mercantile men. The object became ever after identified with the Western procurer rather than the Asian producer.

The second type of producer-consumer relationship identified by Lovell involved a craftsman who, unlike the former example, personally forced himself into the transaction, asserting his pride of place vis-à-vis the object he produced. The producer commanded the price and signed his work. American artisans, such as furniture makers, clockmakers, and silversmiths, fell in this second category. Noticeably absent from this list are women, who did not sign the clothing they made or their other household productions such as candles, soaps, and cheeses. A woman's products, like those of American slaves, were already owned. In this race-based, patriarchal society, women and slaves could not produce their own commodities, and Asian producers could not be recognized. Only white, masculine merchants and craftsmen were acknowledged on objects and identified with them.[79] The male producer made sure he was not alienated from the fruits of his labor the way his wife, his slave, or the Chinese potter were. He demonstrated his mastery over the exchange and his personal association with his products for eternity in various ways, but most notably by signing the object. Such master-artisans as John Goddard or Joseph Richardson—or even japanner Robert Davis—have claimed a sanctified place in the pantheon of colonial American artisan heroes, evident still today in the extremely high prices their works command in auction markets.[80] Their worthy products certainly form the canon of colonial American material culture.

The operative duality of masculine, masterful, durable home manufacture versus effeminate, exploited, "flimsy" Asian import is glimpsed in two portraits by John Singleton Copley (figs. 4.8 and 4.9). First we consider *Mrs. George Watson*, painted in 1765. On the right, the delicate blue-and-white porcelain vase, carefully elevated in the feminine grasp of the idle merchant's wife, amid yards and yards of Asian silk and imported Dutch tulips, mimics her female shape, becoming a logical extension of the woman's body. Her eye contact with the viewer is made ambiguous by the playful coquetry of her cocked arm and half-smile, reflecting the hollowness of the vase. Compare now *Paul Revere*, painted in 1768. Revere's gaze, in contrast, is direct, unambiguous, and challenging. The tools on the table tell us the stout silver teapot cradled in his

4.8. Mrs. George Watson, by John Singleton Copley, 1765, oil on canvas, 49 ⅞ × 40 in. Smithsonian American Art Museum, Washington DC. Photo: Smithsonian American Art Museum, Washington DC / Art Resource, NY.

4.9. Paul Revere, by John Singleton Copley, 1768, oil on canvas, 89.22 × 72.39 cm. Gift of Joseph W. Revere, William B. Revere, and Edward H. R. Revere. Museum of Fine Arts, Boston. Photo © 2011 Museum of Fine Arts, Boston.

strong hand is his own work. He is wigless and clothed in homespun, lacking imported pretension. The only possible artifice in this straightforward portrait of a native man and his work is his reflection seen in the mahogany table, and this serves to deepen the impact of his persona, giving it a natural refinement. Men were very rarely depicted with porcelain, and then only with women in taking tea or, if alone, with large punch bowls of rum punch (see figs. 3.4, 3.5, and 4.7). American men, as we see, were more appropriately associated with American silver than Chinese porcelain.[81] Like men, silver was strong, durable, and figuratively and actually linked to *real* wealth.

Throughout the first two centuries of Euro-American history, women could claim a right only to movable or personal property while men inherited land and homes, *real* property. Like the ethereal security of women in a patriarchal society, porcelain was alluring but might shatter and break at any time. People of English descent never passed on porcelain in their wills, unlike Dutch Americans such as Margrieta van Varick, who explicitly willed chinawares and "East India Cabinets" to her daughters. English Americans typically name only real property and objects made of precious metals in their wills. Of interest, then, is the dramatic inverse relationship observed in Boston in the ownership of silver and Chinese porcelain, seen in table 3.1. In 1700, 85 percent of the Boston inventories sampled contained a substantial quantity of silver but no china. By 1760, however, silver ownership had dropped to 35 percent while china appears in 60 percent of the inventories. Given the striking metaphorical association of silver to secure patriarchal dominance and of Chinese teawares to effeminate servility, we as historians might be correct to assume that an air of uncertainty hung over midcentury Boston, with many men feeling less secure than before.

Chinese porcelain objects in colonial homes, despite their perception as ephemera, were always entangled with the disposition of American maritime capital and the men who controlled it. American colonists were not simple, self-sufficient people living outside empire, even though they circumvented its decrees. As the screws tightened on mercantile regulation from the metropolis, the material well-being of everyone in the hinterlands was impacted, especially that of American merchants and consumers who had benefited from a degree of commercial autonomy in the first half of the eighteenth century. As imperial ministers once again targeted East India goods, as they had seventy years earlier, the most patently obvious Asian commodity in circulation, chinaware, emerged as a heightened symbol of the power struggles within the British imperial political economy. This is exemplified in Franklin's china vase allegory.

Consumer demand should never be understood merely as growing out of primitive individual human desires and needs; it is always a function of complex sociocultural practices, and, as Marx alerted us, in a capitalist society consumption is shot through with the exigencies of political economy.[82] In colonial America, local consumption practices developed in relation to larger regimes of value related to imperial practices. Consumption was unavoidably political. One other point of interest in the Copley portraits is that Revere was a staunch Patriot and Mrs. Watson a Loyalist. We will see in the next chapter how the political dimensions of this Chinese import, based on its status as an icon of contested but potentially ephemeral mercantile capital, eclipsed all its other features. Out of the trash heap of imperial profit mongering, Chinese porcelain lost its dignity in America, and in the hands of self-assured Yankees, it took on powerful auras of commercial and gender conquest.

5

Manly Tea Parties

The Idea of China in Boston's Rebellion

Squash into the deep descended
Cursed weed of *China*'s coast—
Thus at once our fears were ended:
British rights shall ne'er be lost.
—*Boston Evening Post*, January 24, 1774

About an hour after dusk on December 16, 1773, Captain James Hall paced beneath a dangling red-and-white striped flag along the quarterdeck of his large, creaking ship.[1] His uniform was crisp and starched, his piece polished and shiny under the moonlight. The calm, frigid sea lapped quietly against the hull. He peered over the water, beyond bobbing sloops and sturdy Griffin's Wharf toward a row of buildings along the shore and, behind them, to more structures, all unusually illuminated with candlelight flickering in every window. Across the eerie calm he made out a low rumbling din. He knew what was coming. He had been anticipating this for two weeks now. At sea he would simply unfurl his sails and outrun the outlaws, as he had done many times. But here his vessel was a sitting duck, forced to remain at anchor on pain of the governor's cannon at the mouth of the harbor. Distinct sounds grew louder above the dull roar, all at once turning into "hideous yelling" and "war-whoops." A mass of dark forms appeared on the waterfront.

The captain braced himself as men with blackened faces clambered over the boards, carrying clubs and hatchets. "Savage moors!" they were later called in the press, and indeed that was exactly how he himself imagined them in this instant. More than once dreadful Barbary pirates had chased his vessel in the eastern Atlantic. More than once, over exquisite china bowls filled with comforting rum punch, he had listened to horrifying tales from brave compeers whose vessels had been boarded by "Indians come from distant shores." Now their untailored, ragged clothing and the darkened color of their skin marked these freebooters as alien, non-European, "heathen."[2] But once on board, the frightful savages wanted only one thing: the "PLAGUE," the "accurs'd tea." Nothing else was destroyed or stolen, not the ship or its valuable rigging, not any of the many valuable English objects found in the captain's quarters or in the ship's cargo hold, not the customs house or warehouses on shore associated with taxed English imports, not even the mighty English ensign, emblematic of the "tyrants" then bent on "enslaving" them. Only the cargo of Chinese tea was of interest.

The "Indians" were surprisingly "brave and bold"—"Like Men you acted / not like savage Moors"—unlike the effeminate sippers of tea in the governor's company then walled up across the harbor on Castle Island, unlike the oppressed Chinese cultivators of tea, and certainly unlike the "heathen" Moors who threatened "valiant" English ships. One by one in orderly fashion these Patriot-pirates carried more than a hundred 340-pound tea chests up on deck and cracked them open. Resisting the temptation thrown in their "copper" faces by the pungent odor of the costly "weed," they dumped the tea overboard.

This account, taken from eyewitness reports and broadsides released days later, recalls a dramatic scene familiar to every American.[3] In both popular culture and academic scholarship, it has legendary status in US history as one of the initial acts of a "free-born" people resisting tyrannical rulers and oppression. It is widely considered the "spark of the Revolution."[4] But why did the importation of tea, at this moment, provoke such a radical response—political, martial, and rhetorical—when colonists had tolerated and excused over a century of antagonistic mercantilist legislation? Was not a standing army in their midst a greater menace to the natural liberties of Americans than merchantmen carrying a Chinese beverage that had been taxed from its first appearance on English soil? The English government had restricted the American colonists' navigation and manufacturing from the mid-seventeenth century (Navigation Acts, 1651 forward, and Iron Act, 1750), and foreign imports had always been taxed (Molasses Act, 1733). Recent restrictions by the English government had blocked colonial expansion, requiring colonists on the western frontier to abandon their settlements and return east (Royal Proclamation of 1763); prohibited colonists from issuing paper money (Currency Act, 1764); and levied taxes on a large assortment of basic commodities such as sugar, paper, and glass (Sugar Act of 1764, Stamp Act in 1765, and Townshend Acts in 1767). The Quartering Act, promulgated by Parliament in 1765, had required colonists to house British troops and supply them with food and every necessity at the colonists' own expense—including the payment of their tavern bills![5]

The earlier laws had not conjured up images of despotism and slavery; they had not provoked meetings of thousands of people as did the Tea Act. The Sugar Act and the Stamp Act did indeed set off louder, more belligerent protests on the part of Anglo-Americans than ever seen before against the British government. Something had clearly changed since the times of the Navigation Acts or the Molasses Act, which actually taxed Caribbean sugar at a higher rate than its later counterpart, the Sugar Act. By 1764 Britain had, in fact, become a major ruling power in Asia as well as America, and the colonists were daily reminded of this by condescending British soldiers in their midst.[6] When the Stamp Act was repealed in 1766, the colonists celebrated. Very little attention was paid, however, to the simultaneous passing of the Declaratory Act giving Parliament sweeping legislative powers within the colonies. The earlier protests lost their focus and energy, despite the implications of the new legislative powers granted Parliament and the continued lack of American representation.

The Tea Act of 1773 allowed the East India Company to import tea directly to the colonies. If we are to accept that the rebellious energy provoked across all Anglo-America by the Tea Act was related to Parliament's unjust power to legislate American colonists, to "tax without representation," as it is still taught today, and that the onslaught on the imported commodity tea, with its association to despotism (Asian and English), was purely coincidental, then we must reckon with two events that contradict this thesis. In 1767, the year following the repeal of the Stamp Act, Parliament passed the Townshend Revenue Act. Various laws relating to the colonies were included in this legislation, including provisions to stringently enforce regulation of the colonists, but the measure that received the most vocal attention from colonists was a new set of duties on paper, paint, lead, glass, and tea. John Dickenson wrote his well-known "Letters from a Farmer" debating Parliament's right to tax colonists, laying out a rhetorical structure that would be used for grassroots organizing by the Patriot elite later on. Boycotts against the taxed items were initiated in several colonies, but by all accounts they were not very effective. By 1770 when the duties were repealed, the nonimportation movement had fallen apart altogether.[7] The most curious point is that the repeal of the Townshend Act was only partial, and the duty on tea was maintained. Yet, between 1770 and the Tea Act of 1773, barely an angry word was raised against the tea tax or English imported tea. Practically no one seemed to care that tea, and only tea, was still taxed.

In 1770, the same year Parliament preserved the tea tax, Patriot John Adams actually *defended*, in a court of law, British soldiers who had gunned down five young American men in the streets of Boston ("Boston Massacre").[8] His defense of the soldiers was so eloquent and persuasive that the American jury sided with him, and the soldiers were spared a murder sentence. Adams was a member of an elite class of educated, cultured American men in Boston. In his youth he had complained about "Shoe string fellows that never use Tea" and would use it awkwardly if they did.[9] Here we see that he clearly aligned himself with the principles, and perhaps identity, of London's ruling class, viewing himself alongside Parliamentary ministers who made their fortunes in East India commodities. Meanwhile, the anger aroused in the streets of Boston dissolved, and people returned to happily drinking tea until 1773.

The Tea Act, which imposed no new taxes, aroused the slumbering masses and elites alike. Popular protest and raucous town meetings had been part of colonial American public life from the beginning, with mobs sometimes reaching two to three hundred people of diverse socioeconomic backgrounds.[10] But the scale and diversity of participants in the meetings over the tea ships sent under the Tea Act, in several towns of several colonies, were unprecedented. Three meetings were held in Boston in late 1773, each over a thousand people (November 29, November 30, and December 14). Five thousand people attended the fateful fourth meeting at the Old South Meeting House in Boston on December 16, nearly one-third of the town's population. Many meetings in smaller towns that fall exceeded five hundred participants, often comprising most town inhabitants. In Philadelphia eight thousand people assembled when the tea ships sailed into the harbor on Christmas Day, 1773, the largest single meeting in colonial American history. Among the many villains occupying the colonial imagination just preceding the revolution, Chinese tea holds the distinction of having been the only *commodity* to be attacked, the only commodity suspected of subversion. We need to ask why *tea*.

Over generations in the telling and retelling of these events, some details have been ignored while others are repeatedly singled out. Based on the traditional archival sources created and deposited by a ruling elite, historians have carefully reconstructed the tax structure and government policy of the tea trade vis-à-vis the American colonies, as well as the economics of tea consumption on the eve of the revolution.[11] But these analyses have overlooked the *culture* of tea in America as a distinct type of commodity, imported from outside the Atlantic and charged with social tension and symbolic content. Tea was Chinese and carried to the Atlantic in one of the most highly contested trades of its time. Moreover, it was associated with an elaborate—also contested—social ritual that depended on imported Chinese dishes.[12] Tea was Asian, cultivated in a region steeped in oriental despotism and, of recent, East India Company oppression. Tea played a role in the opening acts of rebellion in the northern colonies, and in order to understand why the colonists reacted so strongly to the Tea Act, we need to look beyond British prices and taxes to salvage the emotional response to drinking a Chinese beverage in prerevolutionary Anglo-America. I intend in this chapter to associate the empirical outlines of tea consumption with written and visual metaphors, allusions, and symbols about tea, to recover its role in creating or threatening an American identity above and beyond superficially labeling tea and china as status symbols. By peeling away tea's direct references and seeing its indirect references—what Robert St. George calls its "metaphoric compression, symbolic condensation, and symbolic diffusion"—we will gain a better understanding of why Anglo-Americans, as "free-born Englishmen," responded to the tea ships the way they did.[13]

Few historians today would have the hubris to claim that the events leading up to the American Revolution have been properly understood and explained. Was the rebellion about principles or profits, ideas or capital? Was it a teleological social victory of modern democracy over traditional monarchy? Was it an affair of an elite few leading the masses or rather an oppressed underclass pushing colonial society over the brink? In recent times the sweeping explanatory theses of the Whig, Imperialist, Progressive, and neo-Whig schools have given way to more focused and penetrating treatments of prerevolutionary events. These include T. H. Breen's work on commercial life and consumption in the decades preceding the war, Benjamin Carp's examination of urban tavern-goers and congregants, John W. Tyler's examination of smuggling, and St. George's analysis of the metaphorical content of the Stamp Act riots.[14] The opening acts of the revolution, including the Boston Tea Party, were hardly monocausal, and all these studies contribute to our understanding of the event.[15] A generation ago Joyce Appleby urged historians, whether we are focused on commercial imperatives or philosophical ones, to pay closer attention to social details. Her advice then is still valid today: "Examining the content of the revolutionary mind does not relieve the historian of the responsibility for explaining what compelled belief, what triggered reactions, what stirred passions, and what persuaded colonists of the truth of their interpretation of events."[16] We need, in other words, to look behind events and rhetoric to identify the broader emotional basis for this act of rebellion.

In this chapter I would like to peer inside the "Destruction of the Tea," to examine closely its role in prerevolutionary events as more than merely the "the most spectacular in a series of incidents" that preceded the military confrontation with England.[17] That it certainly was, standing toward the end of an incredible string of dramatic scenes of resistance to British authority. A few months following the Tea Party, Britain closed the Port of Boston, setting in motion the colonial unification that made a revolution seem possible. But prior to this political unification, thousands of ordinary men and women across colonial North America had already come together, in spirit and in print, to agree on a few things, foremost of which was that Chinese tea was dangerous to one's autonomy *and* hard to resist. And they forswore drinking tea altogether, even though by all accounts the English were not the importers of most tea consumed in the colonies.

Each and every outburst leading up to the war with England contained specific emotional content that deserves to be analyzed on its own terms.[18] A close reading of the attack on tea as not one in a series of generic mob events but as a specific, meaningful act formed of knowable beliefs, fears, and motivations will yield a better understanding of why so many colonists agreed to rebel and why they did it when they did. The direct importation into America of Chinese tea by the East India Company, prima facie, had such potent symbolic and ideological weight that it touched more Americans than any other prerevolutionary incident and unleashed the collective energy necessary for all classes of colonists to work together over vast distances, pool disparate resources, and overcome prejudices in soliciting help from long-standing enemies. Americans' response to the Tea Act was not merely the last straw or the final moment of maturation in an ongoing resistance movement. Rather, it was a trigger with specific cultural content. It represented a shared fear of having the colonial body force-fed an intoxicating Eastern potion by a mother-turned-Leviathan, of succumbing to a primitive and gendered form of bodily colonization rather than rising to manly mastery in the communion of costly and potentially treacherous Chinese commodities. All of this is the overlooked but singularly identifiable part of the imagined British ministerial oppression that fueled the revolt.[19] Not only merchants but northern Americans of all sorts, including shopkeepers, housewives, wealthy and poor artisans, and farmers situated miles outside seaports, were fearful of Parliament's proposal to open a direct pipeline of Chinese goods into America, a pipeline over which Americans would have little control, much less *self-control*.[20] (Patriot John Hancock certainly had difficulty controlling himself. Until he was snubbed in the summer of 1773 by the East India Company as a carrier for tea into America, he had repeatedly defied colonial nonimportation agreements by shipping tea into Boston.[21])

Apprehension about consumption of specifically Asian commodities and related concerns about Asian colonization and Asian slavery permeate revolutionary rhetoric. Americans were well aware of what had transpired in the East Indies in the recent war: England, and more specifically England's East India Company, had emerged master of all Asian seaborne commerce, its officers becoming rulers themselves in a land deeply marked in the Western imagination by despotism and tyranny.[22] In this chapter we will locate the epistemological basis for the rebellious "destruction of the tea" in two deep-seated, collective convictions current in prerevolutionary America. The first was the individual righteousness and potency ascribed to British peoples at the close of the Seven Years' War, especially when counterpoised to non-European, subjugated peoples, which Americans feared becoming; the second, the potentially unhealthy, contaminating aspects of Chinese tea. Britain emerged from the war as the world's leading colonizer and slave-trading nation, and American life during the prerevolutionary period was marked by an increase in slavery. Yet we will see that both areas of belief—the innate superiority of Englishness and the bodily contamination carried in Asian consumables—were colored by images of *Eastern*, not American or English, slavery.

In addressing the emphatic and radical nature of the collective rant for "liberty" in the 1760s and 1770s, Appleby states, "Our understanding of the Revolution in part hinges upon our capacity to discover what experiences would have prompted this apocalyptic attitude about freedom."[23] This historical question remains open. By looking at these pertinent but historiographically unconventional fields of American experience and knowledge as precursors to the rebellion, we might reach an interpretation that avoids the explanatory traps set by the profound ideological legacy of the revolution. We may, in other words, see something new in this intimately familiar historical moment. We also remark, as in each preceding chapter, the degree to which colonial Americans were entangled in the East Indies trades. Their responses to the "imperial crisis" were conditioned by an understanding that they lived *in*— not outside—a world in which East Asia and its exports figured prominently.

The Valiant English and Subject Peoples

With the development of imperial tensions and revolution so soon after the close of the Seven Years' War in 1763, we have nearly forgotten the moment at the end of the war when many Americans actually celebrated the empire. Then they stood together with the English, writ large as "Britons," within a virtuous circle of national glory. Benjamin Franklin, who had urged colonists to unite with Britain at the outset of the war in his famous "Join, or Die" cartoon (fig. 5.1), was even able at war's end to mount a popular movement in Pennsylvania for changing the colony's independent proprietary status to that of a

5.1. "Join or Die," cartoon by Benjamin Franklin. *Pennsylvania Gazette*, May 9, 1754.

royal colony.[24] The Reverend Jeremy Belknap, writing just after the revolution, remembered this shared sense of imperial pride. England's accomplishments in the Seven Years' War, in his words, "had attached us more firmly than ever to the kingdom of Britain. We were proud of our connection with a nation whose flag was triumphant in every quarter of the globe."[25] Together Britons and Anglo-Americans were vanquishers of corrupt and depraved peoples worldwide. Catholics, Native Americans, and East Indians would henceforth serve them. The many military victories attributed to England by 1763 proved not only that Britons were more valiant fighters but also that they were morally the rightful rulers of subject peoples worldwide, from Manila to the Ohio Valley.[26] Even Boston's smugglers were proud to be British, especially since the capture of French West Indian islands suddenly made the importation of French molasses legal.[27]

Consistent with Calvinist teachings, there was no better demonstration of the elect status of Britons vis-à-vis the subject peoples they now ruled than the worldly treasures that would subsequently accrue to them. The *Pennsylvania Gazette* proudly reported, for example, that defeated but grateful French tradesmen in Martinique presented the victorious British naval commander with an "elegant service of Plate" as he was leaving their island.[28] Likewise, the *Boston Post-Boy* reported that a defeated Nawab in Calcutta, who no doubt controlled a prodigious textile production, was "full of gratitude to [the English] to whom he owed his dignity." While Britons at home construed precious trade goods as a feather in Britain's cap, a manifestation of their moral, spiritual, and military superiority, the fact of the matter was more mundane: the success of the global imperial endeavor depended on subject populations being willing to trade, as demonstrated by England's ultimate failure in the Philippines where local merchants remained aloof despite the Union Jack flying over Spanish forts.[29] Nevertheless, in 1764 American newspapers gloated over the naval prowess and resulting prosperity of the East India Company, reporting figures for company soldiers, ships, and imports across the Indian Ocean with exactitude.[30]

American newspapers carried regular reports of British engagements and victories overseas, and at the close of the war, several papers serialized the "History of the Late WAR."[31] In this account British battles in Asia against both other European colonizers such as the French and Dutch as well as against East Indians are described in rich detail. Terms repeatedly applied to the British include "gallant," "noble," "valiant," and "brave," while those applied to their enemies include "cruel," "treacherous," "deceptive," "cowardly," and "unwholesome." This second set of terms was reserved with ruthless regularity for Asians and Native Americans. At the beginning of the war in India, for example, Britain struggled, and a certain Hollowell was imprisoned in Bengal. In the words of a British chronicler, Hollowell "came out alive to paint a scene of the most cruel distress which perhaps human nature ever suffered." But despite such "inhuman" conditions in India, a few years later the tide had turned, and the ruling Nawab "saw that the torrent of English valour could not be resisted." Although the English were fewer in number, "they had so much advantage in the field, that the Nabob was in short time glad to conclude a treaty of peace, by which the English East India company was re-established in all its ancient privileges." The article continued to report that when the conquered prince saw "himself ruined by the treachery of his officers and the cowardice of his troops," he was grateful to the English.[32]

So as we see—and as people in the American colonies read—"dignity" and "ancient privileges" came with English military "valor." English "joy" at the events in India, however, was "damped by the death of Admiral [Charles] Watson, who lost his life by the unwholesomeness of the country." But not all British peoples succumbed to India's allegedly cruel, diseased, and contagious environment. Colonel Robert Clive lived on "to enjoy the fortune and honour he has acquired by his gallant actions." Clive's notoriously unscrupulous tactics, treacherous even, were completely neglected in these celebratory accounts.[33] Military accomplishments in India, Britain's most significant victory in this global war, were construed as flowing directly from the innate masculine potency and virtue of Britons, which would therefore logically yield the tangible fruits of entitlement *and* fortune, and nowhere was the case more clearly justifiable than in the subjugation of "heathen" peoples in a wealthy land located so near China. The underlying pull of the Celestial Empire is apparent in the shift of British commercial and military resources from the west coast to the east coast of India and the adoption of Calcutta as the East India Company's new center of operations.[34]

Immediately following the war, the godly radiance conferred on triumphant and prospering Englishmen encompassed Anglo-Americans. But a self-righteous imperial identity could have its ugly side. In the summer of 1763, bands of Yankee settlers flush with a sense of entitlement moved into Indian territories along the Pennsylvania frontier, ignoring the legal technicalities of former boundary treaties. Their utter lack of respect for Native American claims and complete disregard for their warnings resulted in some of the bloodiest conflicts of the war in continental North America. The colonials torched Indian villages; the native people retaliated with brutal aggression against the emboldened settlers, who with British soldiers had soon provoked the worst Indian uprising on record.[35] Unfortunately, imperial politics did not confer the same glorified discourse on *American* colonizers. The terms of the Royal Proclamation, recently signed by King George thousands of miles away, had neatly and politely drawn a line between the British and Native American lands in these peripheral territories, restricting Anglo-American expansion. Now brutish American woodsmen, swelled with *misplaced* imperial pride, had soiled the king's imperial map and made an embarrassing mess.[36]

Throughout the 150-odd years of Anglo-American colonization, the American colonists had been portrayed as vulnerable, dependent Britons, chronically in need of sustenance from a "mother country" and protection against the popish French or savage Native Americans. The English had referred to Americans using familial language, typically representing them as children.[37] The very term "mother country," however, has two significantly different meanings in the *Oxford English Dictionary*.[38] The first, which was current throughout the colonial period in North America, defined an ethnic affinity between people in a place of origin and an outlying splinter group. This idea of an ethnic or familial relation between the English and those in North America prevailed until the revolution. A second usage for the term "mother country" began to appear about the time of the Seven Years' War, when Britain made extensive claims to colonies and territories inhabited by non-European peoples. It defined a country in relation to its colonies void of any ancestral or ethnic connection. The relation that now existed between the English and East Indians, of course, offered the most obvious case in point. With their full-blown conquest of India, England explicitly brought a new sort of Briton into the empire, one who would be represented certainly as a child, but less in terms of a natural-born family member and more in terms of a subjugated family member. For Anglo-Americans, a subjugated family member was a slave. If Anglo-Americans were not allowed to represent the vanguard of empire in their own provinces, to participate in imperial glory, then what sort of *colonials* were they to this powerful supreme "mother"?

Fearing Eastern, not Western, Slavery

The preceding chapters have argued that American colonists were not merely imitating the English in using Chinese porcelain, that they were themselves centrally positioned in international commerce and able to fully participate in, rather than just imitate, trans-European aesthetic tastes and consumer preferences. Yet, a host of early Americanists working in the diverse fields of archaeology, literature, and history have all remarked on a heightened con-

vergence in the prerevolutionary decade of colonial and English lifestyles and
consumption.[39] While Americans had diverse models to choose from in using
Asian commodities to self-identify themselves, and their deployment of Asian
commodities sprang from a locally based imaginary and imperatives, they
did indeed have every reason in 1764 to want to appear English. If not English, then what? With a standing army in their midst, with world-renowned,
vainglorious British soldiers—"triumphant in every quarter of the globe"—in
their very homes and taverns, it was certainly preferable for English colonists
born and bred on foreign soil to be family. The alternative looked like debasing
subjugation, even slavery.

Historically English oversight of the North American colonies had wavered
in intensity due to the paucity of worldly goods produced there. The colonies,
according to historian Elizabeth Mancke, remained in "a conceptual march-
land between foreign and domestic affairs."[40] The colonists' subject status as
independent, yet still domestic, would become especially tenuous at this time.
In 1768 a London pamphlet entitled "The Englishman Deceived" was picked
up in newspapers throughout the colonies. Key passages asserted that Englishmen abroad were indeed still Englishmen.

> Englishmen, and their descendants, wherever they go, and wherever they plant
> themselves, are Englishmen, with all their rights, privileges, and freedom. Nor is
> he less an Englishman who lives in India, Africa, or America, than he who daily
> basks in the sunshine of the royal presence. . . . Shall the Englishman, in India,
> or America, for they are still Englishmen, be denied the use and enjoyment of
> their little pocket expenses, while their wealth must center here in England?
> Shall their fidelity be called into question, if, after a trial of 150 years, they never
> did submit to the laws of their country, while they breathed an English spirit?[41]

Here we see America repeatedly paired with India, and the redundant plea
that the English in those places are not "less an Englishman" belies the ambiguity. Clearly by 1768, following the many acts of Parliament aimed at raising
direct revenues in the American colonies, Americans began to worry that they
might become the target of an avaricious military power, themselves the colo-
nized, rather than the virtuous, manly, free-born colonizers. English historian
Stephen Conway maintains that over the course of the 1760s the English began to associate Anglo-Americans more with "lesser" subjects—French Cana-
dians, Native Americans, and Bengalis—than with themselves.[42]

There were even those in the colonies who agreed that Anglo-Americans were an inferior group in need of regulation by a higher authority. In 1773 immediately following the "destruction of the tea," Boston governor Thomas Hutchinson was provoked into revealing his true thoughts on the matter. "Sieur Montesque is right," he wrote, "in supposing Men good or bad according to the Climate where they live. In less than two centuries Englishmen by change of country are become more barbarous and fierce than the Savages who inhabited the country before they extirpated them, the Indians themselves."[43] Once English, Anglo-Americans had over time actually morphed into a lesser form of humanity, "more barbarous and fierce than the Savages." Average Americans, at least vis-à-vis Englishmen, were equivalent to heathen non-Europeans. A few years after Hutchinson's remark, Thomas Jefferson revealed the profound hold such beliefs had on Anglo-Americans by devoting an entire volume of essays to refuting Montesquieu's theory that the American climate produced inferior physical and civic life.[44]

Meanwhile, in 1765 Martin Howard, an American-born English civil servant in Newport, publicly expressed sentiments similar to Hutchinson's, revealing the widespread extent of such pseudo-scientific chauvinism. "Depend upon it, my Friend, a people like the English, arrived to the highest pitch of glory and power, the envy and admiration of surrounding slaves . . . this people will not patiently be dictated to by those whom they have ever considered as dependent upon them."[45] At this time, evidently, there were two sorts in the world, "the English" and "surrounding slaves." Was it only a matter of time before dependent American children living in their unhealthy climate would join the hoards of slavish peoples clawing at the feet of eminent Britons, desperate for dignity? What would it take, finally, to reduce them to this state?

These fears, contained in the breasts of many American Patriots, reached a fever pitch in print literature during the month the East India Company tea ships were en route to colonial seaports. The Seven Years' War had left Britain the largest slave-holding nation in the world. Americans addicted to tea might end up like the growing cohort of enslaved Africans in their midst, or, in an imaginary twist that left American slaveholders unimplicated, like East Indians depicted in chinoiserie, who were emasculated and stifled by an overly luxuriant milieu, ruled over by opulent tyrants. Tyrants were associated with despotism, and despotism was the prototypical political form thought to characterize East Asia, the very same political form responsible for biblical slavery. To understand why English ministers and the king became "tyrants" in trying to tax American consumers, we need to look at the models available to the colonialists. A "Mechanic" writing in the December 8, 1773, *Pennsylvania Gazette* evokes the scepter of slavery perpetrated in "Whole Provinces" of India:

> The East India Company, if once they get Footing in this (once) happy country, will leave no Stone unturned to become your Masters. They are an opulent Body, and Money or Credit is not wanting amongst them. They have a designing, depraved, and despotic Ministry to assist and support them. They themselves are well versed in Tyranny, Plunder, Oppression and Bloodshed. Whole Provinces labouring under the Distresses of Oppression, Slavery, Famine, and the Sword, are familiar to them. Thus they have enriched themselves, thus they are become the most powerful Trading Company in the Universe.

A New York newspaper carried this warning: "A SHIP loaded with TEA is now on her Way to this Port, being sent out by the Ministry for the Purpose of *enslaving* and *poisoning* ALL the AMERICANS."[46] Americans would be reduced to dependent consumers, and, what was worse in the case at hand, they would be consuming Chinese tea, a soporific substance produced by a despotized people. One preacher pleaded with his congregation in western Connecticut, "We have not as yet experienced the galling chains of slavery; tho' they have been shook over our heads. For this reason few perhaps among us, realize the horrors of that slavery, which arbitrary and despotic government lays men under."[47] The whole tea affair was tainted with elements of Eastern despotism and slavery, as Americans recalled repeatedly in an ardent conversation in the press following the passage of the Tea Act. "A Mechanic" and then "A Countryman" in Philadelphia protested, "They [the East India Company] will . . . Ship US all other East India Goods. . . . Thus our merchants are ruined . . . and every Tradesman will groan under dire Oppression."[48] "Hampden" in a New York paper warned, "and the trade of all the commodities of that country [China] will be lost to our merchants and carried on by the company."[49] "If so," a Pennsylvanian added, "have we a single chance of being any Thing but Hewers of Wood and Drawers of Waters to them. The East Indians are proof of this."[50]

This last remark was a biblical reference to enslavement. The full passage from the book of Joshua was certainly familiar to most Christian Americans: "Now therefore, you are cursed, and you shall never cease being slaves, both hewers of wood and drawers of water for the house of my God."[51] The Pennsylvania author imagined precisely this sort of divinely sanctioned slavery perpetrated by Britons in East India and, in this reference, demonstrated the degree to which deep-rooted notions derived from Christian theology saturated the

American consciousness. Even though blatant institutionalized slavery existed in their very midst, colonial pamphleteers habitually called forth some version of imagined Eastern slavery, explicitly Egyptian, Moorish, Ottoman, or Indian. John Adams wrote in his diary the December morning after the tea was destroyed in Boston that landing the tea would have been equivalent to "subjecting ourselves and our Posterity forever to Egyptian Taskmasters," not, interestingly, to Virginia slave owners or Rhode Island slave drivers.[52] This overlooked discourse founded on embedded prejudices and anxieties about the relationship between Anglo ("Western") and Asian ("Eastern") peoples, fueled by commercial prerogatives to Chinese wealth, needs to be interrogated as part of the cultural climate of the Tea Party, and ultimately the identity of American Patriots.

Chinese Tea as Poison

Americans, living so close to slavery in the late 1760s, were made more uneasy by phobias about the perceived enfeebling and feminizing nature of the tea they were consuming than by generalized Calvinist discomfort with costly British goods, as T. H. Breen has proposed.[53] Beguiling Chinese tea, in their view, served as an agent for tyrants, but it also became a metaphor linking the impending oppression of American colonists with Eastern enslavement. It is useful to our understanding of these cultural connotations to first consider the economic context of American tea consumption. In the summer of 1767 Parliament passed the Townshend Revenue Act, imposing taxes on a series of basic imports including tea. By most estimates, Americans were consuming somewhere between one and two million pounds of tea in the late 1760s, with some estimates as high as six million pounds. But only a small portion of that tea came from the English East India Company vendors in London. Both contemporary Company officials and latter-day historians agree that somewhere between two-thirds to nine-tenths of the tea consumed in the North American colonies entered illicitly.[54] But the English East India Company had, nevertheless, become dependant on the American consumer as an outlet for its tea.[55] Over the course of the next two years (1768–70) colonists unsuccessfully attempted boycotts on English imports. In 1770, Parliament repealed the Townshend duties on all imports except one valuable commodity, Chinese tea. Keeping the trade in this Chinese consumable out of the hands of American merchants clearly remained an imperative to jealous imperial ministers. Only with the Tea Act in 1773, allowing the East India Company direct access to colonial markets, did tea come under fire from all quarters in America and, interestingly, not just East India Company tea but all Chinese tea, as if the Chinese rather than the English were threatening American bodies. The *Boston Gazette* reported on December 20, four days after the Tea Party:

> We are positively informed that the patriotic inhabitants of Lexington, at a late meeting, unanimously resolved against the use of Bohea Tea of all sorts, Dutch or English importation; and to manifest the sincerity of their resolution, they bro't together every ounce contained in the town, and committed it to one common bonfire.

The writer added that Charlestown was in the process of following this "illustrious example," but as is made clear in contemporary newspaper accounts, many towns, clubs, and individuals made public shows of destroying tea, *all* tea, both before and after Boston's bold act.

Well before these intense years preceding the revolution—before this *second* confrontation with the East India Company—Anglo-Americans had participated in a transatlantic discourse debating the unhealthy qualities of taking tea. They had, in fact, long been suspicious of the contaminating aspects of tea, years before ever suspecting English ministers of targeting them for bodily enslavement. Yes, tea and china were expensive, frivolous, and feminine habits that unnecessarily drained colonial capital and masculinity. But they were worse, potentially infecting both body *and* soul. As early as 1731, one doomsayer in New York wrote:

> A real Concern for my Fellow Creatures makes me give you this Trouble. I should think myself happy if I could persuade them from a custom of a fatal Consequence (I mean habitual *Tea-Drinking*) which so universally prevails among us. Were it only the Consideration of so much expended on what is absolutely unnecessary, it would not give me much Concern . . . But when not only their Fortunes, but their Health and Happiness are in Danger, I think it my Duty openly to forewarn them, and endeavour as much as in me lies, to prevent their Ruins. . . . The continual pouring into the Body such quantities of what (if not much worse) is no better than Warm Water. . . . Nor does the Body suffer alone, the Soul also is *hindered in the free Performance of its Functions.*[56]

The author concludes that taking tea has "fatal Effects," and, even worse for Protestant America, it constrains the soul! A half-century before the Boston Tea Party, Americans already feared that they could be duped into a corporeal and spiritual enslavement—death without salvation—in the commerce of this

Chinese beverage if they were not careful. Tea, which had become the single most precious Chinese commodity in the West, became the forbidden apple so beloved by Eve but so destructive to Adam and a serene patriarchal society.

The English and Americans were fascinated by tea from its first appearance in London coffeehouses in the mid-seventeenth century, and books published in London on tea were found throughout colonial libraries and bookshops. Americans were heartily engaged in social tea-table rounds by the first quarter of the eighteenth century. While many a verse appearing in *Spectator* and *Tatler* praised the civilizing qualities of tea, especially its taming effect on the brutish side of men, its gendered qualities were more often presented in a negative light.[57] One 1746 text, allegedly translated from an earlier German text and found in Abraham Redwood's original library in Newport, compared tea drinking to the "bleeding" away of masculine vigor. The author strongly advised against exchanging "our salutary Regimen for that of the Asiatics and Chinese by following their custom of drinking tea."[58] Another edition critical of the practice was *An Essay on Tea*, written by Jonas Hanway in 1756.[59] Published in England but popular in the colonies as well, this work was ostensibly directed to two ladies; but the author's intended audience was clearly his masculine cohort:

> Sipping tea . . . has prevailed over a great part of the world; but the most effeminate people on the face of the whole Earth, whose example we, as a WISE, ACTIVE, and WARLIKE nation, would least desire to imitate, are the greatest sippers; I mean the CHINESE . . . that it is below their dignity to perform any MANLY Labour, or indeed any Labour at all: and yet, with regard to the custom of sipping tea, we seem to act more wantonly and absurd than the CHINESE themselves.[60]

Hanway further claimed that the Chinese "adulterated" tea, mixing *used* tea leaves with all sorts of refuse and selling it to unsuspecting Europeans.[61] Tea created weak nerves, trembling, bad teeth and bad digestion, he asserted. Hanway further noted, in a telling comparison, "Habit reconciles us to the use of TEA, as it does the TURKS to OPIUM."[62]

Indeed, the engraved frontispiece to *An Essay on Tea* graphically illustrated Hanway's points (fig. 5.2). Here we see what at first appears to be a bucolic English seaside scene. On closer examination, however, we notice the ordinary sailors are obviously smugglers, carrying ashore large chests embossed with Chinese script. A "tea party" is underway on shore, engaging a man whose house or inn in the background lies in complete shambles; he has evidently

5.2. Frontispiece to *An Essay on Tea*, Jonas Hanway, London, 1756.

lost the strength to "labour" while sipping. The women, so mesmerized by their warm china cups, ignore the child who is about to go up in flames. Their clothes are ragged, as evidence of their inability to perform the tasks assigned to their sex and station in life. To tea, all has been lost, including precious English specie, which is about to be delivered over to the smugglers by the men in the foreground to the left.

By sipping tea, English and American people as well could actually become Chinese and prone to indolent Chinese habits, which would ultimately promote the need for a despotic system of government, just as it had everywhere in Asia. Valiant and masculine officers would of necessity be sent to America to subjugate and enchain an enthralled, feminized people under the spell of a tainted Eastern potion. This image, and the anxieties that inspired it, were at the forefront of the Patriot mind in 1773. The last speech given to the crowd of thousands at the Old South Meeting House in Boston on the evening of December 16 was by Dr. Thomas Young, a physician. Its exact content is unfortunately lost to us, but a report from an observer stated that Young spoke for about fifteen to twenty minutes on "the ill Effects of Tea on the Constitution," interrupted by "the People often shouting and clapping him." According to the observer, Dr. Young stated he had confidence "in the Virtue of his Countrymen in refraining from the Use of it." Chinese tea, not Parliamentary legislation, threatened the patriotic Anglo-American "Body," and short of having total control of its commerce, Americans must abstain from consuming this alluring Chinese "apple" for the sake of manly virtue and autonomy.[63] Samuel Adams, however, was more pessimistic than Dr. Young about the ability of Americans to resist Chinese enthrallment. The anonymous observer noted in his account that Adams had previously said he "could not trust the private Virtue of his Countrymen in refraining from the Use of it." So the tea, and *only* the tea, was destroyed the evening of December 16, a symbolic statement about bodily liberty that was so powerful it could unleash the widespread armed clashes and rhetorical masterpieces that followed.

Endangered Bodies and Germ Warfare

Americans, by so openly demonstrating their desire for contested Asian status objects such as Chinese tea and porcelain, had put themselves at *personal* risk. It was not only "vulgarity" that worried them but, as the discourse above makes plain, the enfeebling nature of consuming a contaminated Chinese brew offered them by a rapacious, despotic parent state. A few days before the tea was destroyed in Boston Harbor, a writer with the Greek pseudonym "ΠΟΝΟΝΧΡΟΤΟΝΘΟΛΟΓΟΣ" reported in the *Boston Gazette* that Captain Coffin's vessel had just arrived, "not only with the Plague (TEA) on board, but also with the Small-Pox." What the author then noted reveals yet an additional Patriot anxiety and may explain their repeated use of the term "plague" for tea. He says, "As Tea is of a Drawing Quality, 'tis suspected it has sucked the Distemper."[64] American consumers were to be sold tea that carried smallpox germs! American shippers had dealt in all nature of commodities and were well aware that tea absorbed the scent of spices or other strong-smelling cargoes. Delicate tea had to be carefully packed away from richly scented Asian commodities. Did Americans thus suspect the calculated use of germ-infused tea to subdue resistant subjects?

Chinese tea sold by the East India Company had quite literally, not just metaphorically, become a lure and vehicle for the bodily destruction of American consumers. A writer in the November 29, 1773, issue of the *Boston Evening Post* pleaded with tea consignees to return the tea as soon as it arrived, for "the good and safety of the People." "Shall this paltry Tea be brought into competition with the Lives and Limbs, Liberties and Properties of multitudes of . . . most loyal Subjects?" The author points out to Governor Hutchinson that "if after these public and private Entreaties and Expostulations, any bad Consequences should follow . . . you and a very few more are answerable." The writer does not specify exactly what "bad consequences" he or she envisioned, but whatever they were, they threatened "lives and limbs." Given the nature of the imagined peril attributed to imported tea, it is no wonder that the core organizers of the Patriot movement from the North End of Boston called themselves "The Body," a term that stuck and was used by everyone. American Patriots were fighting for more than fair taxation and representation within the empire, they were fighting for their personal, corporeal safety *against* the empire. Such language allows us to see more clearly the specific content in the "minds and hearts" of John Adams's fearful compatriots in the years preceding the actual war.[65]

Another writer in the *Boston Gazette* also addressed Hutchinson, comparing him to Balaam, the treacherous biblical prophet associated with a non-specified region *east* of the Jordan River.[66] This author accused Hutchinson, "But pray what business have you with the *Tea affair*, as Gov_r of this province. . . . You have been years used to deal in *Tea*!—Pray what *Tea*—! DUTCH *Tea*—! But those are not DUTCH *Teas*!" Surprisingly, this is one of only a few instances in which a writer distinguished English-imported tea from Dutch. The allusion to Hutchinson's smuggling activities served to demonstrate how irresistible tea had become, and how everyone, even the Loyalist governor, had lost their self-control in the face of this Chinese beverage. Generally *all* tea was considered poisonous to the patriotic American body within the pre-revolutionary anti-tea discourse. As the poem cited at the beginning of this chapter indicates, once the "cursed weed from China's coast" was sunk, "at once our fears were ended." It was a Chinese beverage that threatened the Patriot "Body," turning imbibing governors into perfidious oriental tyrants and besotted American consumers into enfeebled "hewers of wood and drawers of water." Let's look more closely at the imagined role of contaminated tea in subduing Americans.

Throughout the detailed reporting on the battles of the British world war, English and American authors drew out an association between morality and armed engagements. Actual outcomes, whether the conquest of a fort or capture of a prince and all his precious booty, were attributed to some form of ethical goodness on the part of the English. Accolades were usually heaped on a particular named commander, further personalizing the glory for readers across the globe. Such a discourse must be properly situated in the philosophical context of the evolving, and then closely intertwined, fields of natural and international law. The most influential texts guiding political as well as popular rhetoric at this time, such as Emerich de Vattel's *Law of Nations* (1758), personalize the "nation" and confer it with moral rights and actions. Nations were represented in the same light as individuals in a "state of nature," where "natural" principles of morality should prevail.[67] Actual acts of national sovereignty rationalized within this important body of Enlightenment literature, however, often deviated from principle. Heads of state from opposite ends of the globe could wage war across the ever-widening bureaucratic apparatus of empire, allowing them, comfortably located in opulent palaces far from the battlefield, to condone heinous acts that they never had to see, that were in fact abstract acts easily justified by theoretical principles.

In book 3, chapter 8 of *Law of Nations*, entitled "Of the Rights of Nations in War," Vattel argued that a nation has the right to kill enemies "in a just war." "Since the object of war," he states, "is to repress injustice and violence . . . we have the right to put into practice, against the enemy, every measure that is necessary in order to weaken him, and disable him from resisting us and supporting his injustice." For Vattel a "just war" should be one that upholds self-evident laws of nature, defined *outside* of religion and place of origin.[68] He does state, however, that certain acts such as "poisoning" and "assassination" are contrary to both the laws of war and nature, and any perpetrator of these methods should be considered an "enemy of the human race." Nevertheless, throughout his text, he cites historic instances in which such treachery had been defensible. In every case, notably, the victim was Asian, including Egyptians (Farrudge), Persians (several references, especially Darius), Turks (Ottomans generally), and Mongols (Timur). We see here the seeds of a profound change in defining "just" acts of war, in which the law of nations applied explicitly and exclusively to *Western* nations. By 1836 this conceptual shift was complete. In that year an American diplomat, Henry Wheaton, published a treatise on international law in which he states: "The law of nations or international law, as understood among civilized, Christian nations, may be defined of consisting of those rules of conduct which reason deduces, as consonant to justice."[69] A "just war" was no longer one that conformed to universal laws of nature, above and beyond religion. It had become an affair of Christian nations, also known as "the West," and non-Western states would hereafter need to apply for entrance to the civilized world in order to be protected by just rules in international relations.

During the Seven Years' War, British colonizers came into state-level conflicts with non-Christian peoples, and subsequently some of the old rules of war were redrafted.[70] Meanwhile, acts committed on the ground in faraway places were discursively sanitized to fit an emerging *virtuous* national identity situated in eminent philosophical theories. Desperate acts of corruption and treachery were much more widely known than the contemporary popular press or official documentary record reveal. Knowledge of, or indeed firsthand experience with, unscrupulous acts of war perhaps formed the basis of the analogy so many drew at the time between the British Empire and the decadent Augustan state of ancient Rome. Many pundits on both sides of the Atlantic argued that, yes, England had reached its cultural peak, and like Rome, was now poised to decline.[71] Americans were well aware that, no matter how "just" the war or how noble the British people, agents of the imperial government were capable of outrageous deeds.

One very specific type of treachery may have fed the outpouring of fear curiously aroused by the shipments of East India Company tea. We are aware today that disease, and in particular smallpox, inadvertently aided the cause of European colonization in the New World from its earliest days. What we are less aware of is the degree to which Europeans may have fantasized about harnessing smallpox as an extremely effective weapon of war and conquest, and in at least two known cases following the Seven Years' War, the British deliberately attempted to do so. The first of these instances occurred on the frontier during the Indian uprising in 1763, and, despite the existence of firm documentary evidence, its veracity has been debated for over two hundred years, with some historians still calling it a legend. When soldiers in Fort Pitt in western Pennsylvania came down with smallpox, several British officers concocted a plan to send rebellious Indians infected textiles. A journal entry by William Trent, a Pennsylvania militia captain (and son of a member of Pennsylvania's provincial council and namesake of Trenton, New Jersey), reads: "The Turtles Heart a principal Warrior of the Delawares and Malmatee a Chief came within a small distance of the Fort.... Out of our regard to them we gave them two Blankets and an Handkerchief out of the Small Pox Hospital. I hope it will have the desired effect."[72] The act is further substantiated by Fort Pitt account books, which list two blankets, a silk, and a linen handkerchief under the heading: "Sundries got to Replace in kind those which were taken from people in the Hospital to Convey the Smallpox to the Indians."[73] That the idea of such an act was not the least inconsistent with British military procedures is corroborated by an exchange of letters a few weeks later between two presiding officers, Jeffrey Amherst and Henry Bouquet, who apparently did not realize this instrument of war had already been implemented. Amherst wrote to Bouquet, "Could it not be contrived to Send the *Small Pox* among those Disaffected Tribes of Indians," and Bouquet responded, "I will try to inoculate the Indians by means of Blankets that may fall in their hands." Amherst reassured Bouquet that it was necessary to use "Every Stratagem" to "Extirpate this Execreble Race."[74] Most important here is that Americans— the militia captain, the bookkeeper, hospital orderlies, their wives and close friends—would have been fully aware of the stratagem to poison a people deemed ethnically distinct from the British.

The second documented case of a deliberate attempt at smallpox infection occurred at the end of the revolution and was a desperate attempt by Cornwallis's army to infect Americans at Yorktown in 1781. Amid mounting suspicions from American soldiers in Virginia that the redcoats were pursuing such a plan, a British general wrote to Cornwallis, "Above 700 Negroes are come down the River in the Small Pox. I shall distribute them about the Rebell Plantations." Reports of encounters with sick African Americans, turned away from the British forces and directed toward Americans, continued throughout the summer until the end of the war. Indicative of widespread American awareness of the British use of infection in war, Benjamin Franklin recounted the facts after the war in *Retort Courteous*:

> Having the small-pox in their army while in that country, they inoculated some of the negroes they took as prisoners ... and then let them escape, or sent them, covered with the pock, to mix with and spread the distemper among the others of their colour, as well as among the white country people.[75]

Here, as in the previous example, it is hard to ignore the racial underpinnings of acceptable uses of germ warfare. People of non-European origins were vulnerable to unethical attacks—assaults to their very bodies through exposure to toxins—by agents of the British imperial government.

In a similar vein, at least in the eyes of contemporary observers such as Hanway cited above, the British, following the victories of the Seven Years' War, took control of Indian poppy production and the opium trade in the Indian Ocean. Henceforth they began in earnest the conquest of Chinese bodies through a form of commercial chemical warfare, which would end in the destruction of the "Old China Trade" *and* old China by the 1840s.[76] The instrument of British oppression and toxic warfare would be the East India Company. It is in this context that Americans feared the English were beginning to see them also as non-European bodies, and they too were up against the ministers of that very same insturment of oppression, the East India Company.

Rebellion on the part of a prosperous people does not happen without first some hard reflection about *who* they are exactly in relation to their ruling government. In the years leading up to the opening acts of the revolution, Anglo-Americans probed their relationship to British and other identities then emerging in the imperial system. What was an Anglo-American, bred on foreign soil, nurtured in an unhealthy American climate amid savage Indians? In trying to explain why, after their glorious partnership with England—together as Britons, fighting off the Catholic and barbarian threat to Britain's empire—they would then be targeted for exploitative legislation, some colonists pointed to America's wealth, and in particular to what they described as a provocative display of worldly goods. This discourse has been insightfully recovered by T. H. Breen, who places it within what he calls a "Narrative of Commercial Life" that coalesced in the 1760s. The chart of Chinese porcelain ownership in five northern seaports (fig. 1.2) clearly indicates a precipitous rise in the consumption of Asian commodities at this time, especially in Boston. Many, many Americans, as Breen points out, were uncomfortable with this level of "luxury" consumption, but we see that their anxieties went far beyond a concern with moral impropriety and debt. In 1774 Congregationalist minister Samuel Sherwood took it upon himself to inform remote residents of western New England about recent events in Boston and New York. He explained the conflicts with Britain thus: "The common people here make a show, much above what they do in England. The luxury and superfluities in which even the lower ranks of people here indulge themselves, being reported in England by the officers and soldiers upon their return [in 1763], excited in the people there a very exalted idea of the riches of this country, and the abilities of the inhabitants to bear taxes." Sherwood worried Americans had become a target. He cautioned that an engorged, grasping British Empire would seize this wealth for its own disposal, leaving the American people depleted and enslaved—certainly a prescient vision of the subsequent progress of European colonialism elsewhere in the world. The British empowered themselves "to search any body," Sherwood warned, "they may search a man's most private apartments, not even his desk or drawers, or any thing would be secure."[77] In a sermon a

year later, Sherwood described the British state as "Satan," who "unleashed the
Whore of Babylon to ride her dragon on the American continent."[78] Cloaked
in such sexualized and orientalist allegorical terms, Americans fantasized that
they too, like the Indians—of both the East and West—would be physically
violated by the British state, all for the beauty of their wealth (see fig. 5.3).
Sherwood readily intertwined biblical imagery, nurtured on embedded scriptural phobias about Asian decadence and enslavement, with imperial politics
and commerce in sermons defending Americans' right to free trade. He and
many others ultimately related commercial independence to individual bodily
independence. In the 1760s, the nonconsumption discourse reached a fever
pitch that went well beyond devout anxieties about the immorality or impropriety of lavish living, even though such vivid Puritanical rhetoric embellished
their fears. Americans were long aware of the jealousy and competitiveness of
their parent state in the arena of international trade. The colonists had suffered more than a century of restrictive mercantilist legislation and the wrath
of Crown officials such as Lord Bellomont when foreign goods had trickled
directly into their communities.[79] Trade outside the empire was rampant by

5.3. "The Able Doctor; or, America Swallowing the Bitter Draught," *London Magazine*, v. 43
(May 1774); also copied by Paul Revere for *The Royal American Magazine*, Boston, vol. 1,
no. 10 (June 1774). Courtesy of the John Carter Brown Library.

the 1760s and so was consumption of "India tea" and china. Independent American traders were directly undercutting England's importers and merchants, especially the East India Company, at a greater rate than ever before.[80] At the same time American consumers had grown fatter and wealthier than ever before. And they were, many feared, becoming intoxicated. Just as Native Americans put themselves at bodily risk in longing for alluring trade goods such as alcohol or colorful silk textiles bartered by two-faced British officers, and just as the Chinese risked bodily dependence in purchasing opium from the East India Company, so now American appetites for an enticing Chinese commodity might prove a life-threatening trap.

Securing the Manly American Mercantile Man

Immediately following Dr. Young's closing motivational speech on the health risks of consuming tea, the crowd at the Old South Meeting House dispersed to ready for an assault on the tea ships. One group of "North Caucus" men—the heart and soul of "The Body"—met at Benjamin Edes's print shop to blacken their faces. Here they passed around an exquisite Chinese punch bowl, filled and refilled by Edes's grandson with rum punch, the nectar of valiant British traders worldwide. The bowl was decorated with scenes from the daily working life of a family in China (fig. 5.4).[81] In professing their bodily freedom from the thrall of Chinese tea, these Patriots intoxicated themselves from a bowl celebrating the industry of Chinese men and women. Or did they view the foreigners on the side of the bowl as "hewers of wood and drawers of waters"—as menial, subordinated laborers—as slaves, in short?

Historians of American relations with the Far East acknowledge that China has been conceptualized in sharply contrasting ways over the past three centuries, but most concur with Harold Isaacs's characterization of the eighteenth century as the Age of Respect.[82] Some European Enlightenment philosophers had indeed promoted a view of China as ruled under a system of benevolent despotism, guided by natural morality and a successful agriculture-based economy. This impression, however, only briefly glimmered in philosophical circles in the northern colonies and in the early republic.[83] This chapter, like chapters 2 and 4 above, has attempted to pull the curtain back on a much darker view of China in the popular American imaginary. The association of the Chinese with emasculation, bodily punishment, bodily contamination, and death prevailed during the colonial period, overshadowing more erudite opinions that have become better known or are at least better represented in scholarly archives. The use of Edes's finely crafted Chinese punch bowl in exciting

5.4. Chinese porcelain punch bowl, ca. 1730–70, diam. 33 cm. Descended in the Benjamin Edes family. Gift of Mrs. Benjamin Edes, 1871. Collection of the Massachusetts Historical Society.

American *men*, Patriots or not, to destroy property reveals the brutish aggression aroused by a trade in alluring Chinese-produced objects and foodstuff.

Just meters from Griffin's Wharf, where American men insecure in their English identity metamorphosed into Indians—non-Christian, non-European subjects threatened with colonization—and courageously destroyed the colonizer's tool, Chinese "poison," Bostonians would one day christen their own "India Wharf" and never again need to cloak themselves as servile Indians.[84] But that would not come for another quarter-century, and, in this moment, the war for mastery was not yet won. After their unprecedented victories in India, Britain threatened its colonists with a zero-sum game of global capitalism: there would be no room in the world for a safe haven between enslavers and enslaved, masters and the mastered, capitalists and workers. Both those who produced and those who consumed alluring Asian commodities, without mastering the trade, were in danger of becoming Britain's pawns. These commodities—refined and brightly decorated porcelain dishes, richly hued red and black lacquers, and pungent teas, none of which were available in the West and each of which bestowed a Western owner with marks of prestige and sophistication related to the eminence and antiquity of China—all of these commodities became associated, for American Patriots, with the treachery of Britain's mercantile establishment.

Indeed, many Americans had been suspicious all along about the unhealthy, unsavory aspects of Asian commodities. This attitude emerged in the freakish Chinese tormenters in the murals of Newport's William Gibbs; it is evident in the scurrilous treatment of chinaware by Philadelphia preacher Benjamin Lay and in the writings of Americans newspaper contributors. It is certainly evident in the "destruction of the tea" and all the derisive rhetoric that surrounded tea drinking in the decades preceding the revolt. This attitude was nurtured by British officials who made the direct consumption of Chinese commodities a crime on American soil, and by American merchants who turned these same forbidden commodities into delicious booty. In American thought, Chinese commodities became allegorical cousins of the biblical apple that seduced Eve or of the wooden horse that destroyed Troy. China was equally irresistible.

One thing is certain: whether suspicious of Chinese commodities or uncritically in their thrall, Americans from the seventeenth century forward were profoundly impacted by and participated in the economic and cultural undercurrents of the European China trades. Americans elaborated their own set of complex associations to China and china. Most important, as shown in their revolution, they were frustrated by the impediments imposed on them by Britain in their free (and, in their minds, safe) enjoyment of that trade. Benjamin Franklin was well aware of this in 1770 when he wrote in London's *Public Advertiser* that colonists would soon be fitting out ships to sail, themselves, to the coast of China. "[Britain] cannot, I suppose hinder their fitting out Ships" and "prevent smuggling on a Coast of 1500 Miles in Length," he said, and he was exactly right.[85] But it would take an armed insurrection—a major war— for the American colonists to obtain the state status so necessary, from the perspective of the elite who took control of the colonies' new government, to do business in China. Such were the prestige and dangers of the China trade that it called for state-level players.

The successful revolution immediately secured American merchants a place in Canton's Golden Ghetto, where Europeans flocked to compete in the most important trade of its time. But political independence from English taxes did not, evidently, secure the liberty of American bodies from the danger of Asia, whether the threat came in the form of a "Yellow Peril" or contaminated toothpaste.[86] Still today the globe remains more deeply divided between an "East" and a "West" than along almost any other cultural or imaginary fault line. It may be, in fact, the continued relevance of the cultural imperatives of an imagined East in formulating our own Western identity that has obscured our ability to see the important historical role of China and the commerce of potent Chinese objects in the historical formation of the United States.[87]

Epilogue

An East Indies Trade for North America

In the spring of 1783, several months before the signing of the Treaty of Paris concluding the American Revolution, Ezra Stiles, then president of Yale University, gave a noteworthy sermon announcing with enormous pride the entrance of the United States of America, a new sovereign state, onto a global stage of eminent imperial powers. He did not confine his perspective to the Atlantic. The lengthy speech, marking a political election, contained over sixty references to India and the Far East, comprising about a third of his remarks directed toward major geographic locations, including Britain against who the Americans had just fought a long, grueling war. Stiles was looking forward, not backward, and it was East Asia that drew his attention.

> This great American revolution, this recent political phenomenon of a new sovereignty arising among the sovereign powers of the earth, will be attended to and contemplated by all nations. Navigation will carry

the American flag around the globe itself; and display the thirteen stripes and new constellation at *bengal* and *canton*, on the *indus* and *ganges*, on the *whang-ho* and the *yang-tse-kiang*; and with commerce will import the literature and wisdom of the east.[1]

Indeed, within a few months, owners of at least three US vessels had managed to pull together the capital required for the long journey across several seas. According to historian James Fichter, three US "East Indiamen" came into the Cape of Good Hope—the gateway to Eastern ports—in the 1784–85 season, five the year after, nine the next, sixteen in the 1788–89 season, and in the following season nineteen US vessels sailed into the Indian Ocean and beyond. That makes fifty-two recorded US voyages beyond the "Atlantic World" within only six years of American independence from Britain. By way of comparison, there were fifty-six English vessels recorded at Cape Town in those years, indicating the strong showing by the United States in Asia immediately following the war. Moreover Fichter notes that there were likely more American voyages, but it is difficult to get Indian Ocean data for this early period of US mercantile history.[2] Stiles's sermon was anything but boastful hyperbole. The United States developed a competitive presence in the Eastern hemisphere immediately on the heels of independence, just as Stiles had predicted at the close of the war.

On January 14, 1784, the Continental Congress of the new United States of America ratified the Treaty of Paris, establishing its independent statehood, but American merchants had not waited for the formalities of imperial politics or the crush of a postwar economic depression to ready China vessels. A month before the ratification, in December 1783, a fifty-five-ton sloop from Hingham, Massachusetts, the *Harriet*, set sail for China from Boston with a cargo of North American ginseng. This native root was similar to the Asian variety in demand in China as a health supplement. It took months to harvest enough plants to fill a ship's hold, as well as outfit an East Indiaman and find a suitable crew. The captain was able to make good his voyage, trading the ginseng for a cargo of Chinese tea en route at the Cape of Good Hope. The better-known *Empress of China* set sail in February, 1784, a month after the treaty was ratified, but planning for the voyage had been underway since May of 1783, months before peace was concluded with Great Britain. A joint partnership from Philadelphia capitalized the 360-ton vessel and its cargo of ginseng, furs, and specie for $120,000. When it returned to the port of New York from China fifteen months later, it was able to clear a profit of 25 percent, a handsome margin by any measure.[3]

In the fall of 1785, shortly after the successful return of these initial China trade vessels, John Adams sent letters from Paris to several colleagues in the new US government, urging them to set up an official East Indies trade. In one letter he notes that the Chinese would certainly treat the Americans as "the most favoured nation" once they realized that "our factory would treat them with equity and humanity." In November of that year he wrote to John Jay, then foreign secretary, stating "There is no better advice to be given to the merchants of the United States than to push their commerce to the East Indies as fast and as far as it will go."[4] According to Sucheta Mazumdar, recent data from English, Dutch, and French sources show that the number of American vessels coming into Canton and Macao between 1784 and 1814 is almost a third more than the previous figure of 491 based on Canton Factory Records. The new count is 618 American vessels stopping at Canton and Macao in this period (see fig. E.1, porcelain bowl painted in China with depiction of Canton factories flying US and British flags). But even this extraordinary number is only a partial picture of the American onslaught of Asian seas as many vessels gave Bombay, Batavia, Botany Bay, and other non-Chinese Asian ports as their destinations. American vessels—small, light, maneuverable, and guided by opportunistic merchants with superior sailing skills—developed new and profitable methods of trade with Chinese and Indian merchants. The Americans quickly inserted themselves in interregional Asian carrying trades and

E.1. Chinese porcelain "Hong bowl," ca. 1787–94, showing the factories in Canton used by foreign powers, including the United States, the "flowery flag devils." Gift of the Estate of Harry T. Peters Jr., 1982, E81407. Peabody Essex Museum, Salem, MA. Photo courtesy of the Peabody Essex Museum.

often accumulated capital and valuable cargoes in the China trade without even touching at Chinese ports, just as the *Harriet* had done.[5]

As for tea, it became without a doubt US merchants' most important export from China. But the Americans were primarily the "mules," since they reexported the majority of the tea to Europe and perhaps South America. Until 1820 consumption of silk and cotton textiles outpaced all other Chinese commodities within the United States.[6] Americans never became the tea drinkers that their cousins in England were. Nevertheless, by the end of the century, their trade in Asian waters posed a serious challenge to the mooring the English economy depended on in Asia.[7] American vessels were smaller and more efficient to operate than English East Indiamen, and they cost 20 to 50 percent less to build than those constructed in Britain.[8] An abundance of raw materials certainly contributed to the US boon in shipbuilding and foreign trade, but economist Alejandra Irigoin points out other extenuating circumstances. American trade of teas into Europe was first facilitated by high English taxes, and once those routes were established, American neutrality in the Napoleonic Wars served traders very well. By the late 1790s, US merchants were shipping 3 to 5 million pounds of tea a year from Canton, making them second only to the East India Company in the tea export business and all but destroying French and Dutch trade in China.[9] By 1806, Americans shipped over 12 million pounds of tea from Canton each year, and they also brought more goods into the Atlantic from British India than did the English East India Company. Their victory over the Company was thus complete!

Yet, for Americans the suspect quality of Chinese goods, especially tea, continued. American merchants and mariners saw their best defense was to maintain a strong trade position, hence their masculinity. On his first trip to Canton aboard the *Empress of China* as supercargo, Samuel Shaw, a Patriot and major in the Continental Army, was faced with a serious conflict between the British and the Chinese. A British gunner, in saluting an officer with cannon from his ship the *Lady Hughes*, had killed a Chinese sailor below in a sampan. The Chinese governor demanded that the gunner be turned over for trial and the British refused, fearing a death penalty. Tense discussions between the East India Company Council, claiming to represent the entire foreign community in Canton, and the Chinese government, all the way up to the emperor himself, ensued for many days. What is amazing in this affair is how Shaw, far from home, rallied to the side of the state against which he had been at war for nearly a decade. So recently portrayed as malicious and dangerous despots, the British and their East India Company were now, less than a year since the close of war, viewed sympathetically, as compatriots in a just cause. Shaw wrote in

E.2. Detail of Chinese porcelain vase, showing the compression of tea by barefoot coolies, something that concerned prim American consumers of tea. Late Ming dynasty. Golestan Palace, Tehran, Iran. Photo: SEF / Art Resource, NY.

his journal that everyone thought the affair was settled until "experience once more convinced them that there is no trusting the Chinese."[10] Confronting what Americans perceived as a genuinely despotic and pitiless regime, that of China, differences with Britain paled. Shaw felt himself in control of his own affairs, including his own tea trade which he came to China to conduct. The

East India Company no longer threatened his autonomy. But the Chinese tea trade was still capable of vital and threatening consequences. At one point in the *Lady Hughes* negotiations, the Chinese governor invited representatives of the foreign merchant houses, excluding Britain, to a local pagoda. Shaw declined the tea served, suspiciously, but took the bolt of silk offered. When the Chinese official warned he would block all trade, Shaw and the other foreign houses backed down in their defense of the English immediately, no matter how unjust the consequences for the English gunner. Trade resumed once the Chinese realized that the Americans were not actually English.[11]

Shaw was eventually made a consul to China by the infant United States government, augmenting his and the Americans' sense of political and economic mastery, even though the Chinese did not recognize his diplomatic status. On his third and last trip to Canton in 1789, Shaw noted how reckless consumption of tea in Europe and America had caused its price to rise precipitously since his first trip. This should not have surprised him, given the presence of a growing number of US carriers. "The consumption of tea in the western world has increased astonishingly," he notes, adding that Britain's consumption alone had gone from 14 million pounds a year to 21 million, "not one half of which is supplied by her own ships."[12] The Americans had turned the tables on Great Britain since the destruction of the tea in 1773. It was no longer the East India Company bringing tea to US shores but the Americans transporting it to England—at an enormous profit.

Yet the American consul was worried about US consumption of the Chinese beverage. "If it is necessary that the Americans should drink the tea"— and that was not a given for Patriot Shaw—"it will be readily granted that they ought to employ the means most proper for procuring it on the best terms." Shaw's role as a diplomat to China was to find and preserve a trade advantage. By exploiting their colonial experiences in the Indian Ocean, the Caribbean, and the South Atlantic, and by furtively working foreign coastlines rich in valuable trade commodities—India, Africa, the French and Dutch islands, and, especially now, New Spain—Americans were able to do just that. Shaw knew the way ahead. Before not too long, the United States became the main trading partner of Cuba and Mexico, the two richest of Spain's colonies. The valuable commodity Americans procured there was silver, and the silver, of course, was destined for China. As early as 1793 the United States surpassed Great Britain in silver imports into China, and the British never again caught up. In fact, the United States' control of American silver into China became nearly exclusive by 1807.[13] Meanwhile, Americans never bought tea from England again.

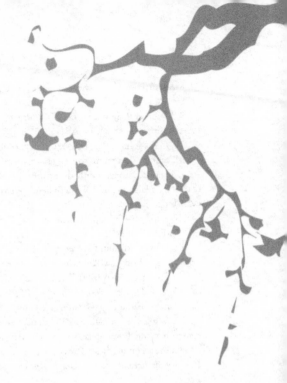

Notes

Introduction

1. Massachusetts Archives, Boston: Massachusetts Probate, Essex County, Salem, vol. 305, pp. 86–88.

2. "Philip English Household Inventory," ca. 1694, box 17, folder 2, Phillips Library, Salem, MA.

3. *Salem Witchcraft Papers: Verbatim Transcripts of the Legal Documents of the Salem Witchcraft Outbreak of 1692*, ed. Paul Boyer and Stephen Nissbaum (New York: Da Capo, 1977), 3:989–1044.

4. A copy of the inventory can be found in Joseph Downs Collection at the Winterthur Library.

5. *Ecclesiastical Records of the State of New York*, compiled by Hugh Hastings et al. (New York: J. B. Lyon, 1901), 1:617–18; Edward Tanjore Corwin, *A Manual of the Reformed Church in America* (New York, 1902), pp. 870–71.

6. See fig. 1.2, which is based on a sample of twenty-four inventories for New York City, 1690–1699.

7. Harold Donaldson Eberlein, *Manor Houses and Historic Homes of Long Island and Staten Island* (Philadelphia: J.B. Lippincott, 1928), pp. 88–89; New York State Archives: Suffolk County Probate Records, Feb. 18, 1704/5.

8. See inventory dated September, 1700, reproduced in *Pennsylvania Magazine* 83 (1959): 265–70.

9. Margaret B. Schiffer, *Chester County, Pennsylvania, Inventories, 1684–1850* (Exton, PA: Schiffer Publishing, 1974).

10. In the John Carter Brown Library, a collecting institution established in the nineteenth century devoted to the Americas, there are hundreds of early modern books about Asia, demonstrating not only the artificiality of the distinct separation that later occurred between an Eastern and a Western hemisphere but also the prevalence of detailed sources available to earlier Americans on the regions of East Asia.

11. Mukhtar Ali Isani, "Cotton Mather and the Orient," *New England Quarterly* 43, no. 1 (Mar. 1770): 47.

12. Sucheta Mazumdar, *Sugar and Society in China: Peasants, Technology, and the World Market* (Cambridge, MA: Harvard University Press, 1998), pp. 66–95; John E. Wills, "Maritime Asia, 1500–1800: The Interactive Emergence of European Domination," *American Historical Review* (Feb. 1993): 83–105; John M. Hobson, *The Eastern Origins of Western Civilization* (Cambridge: Cambridge University Press, 2004).

13. While the overland Silk Roads may predate maritime trade circuits, together now sometimes called the "Spice Route," the maritime route for disseminating East Asian spices and Chinese commodities dates back to at least the Roman Empire. See Himanshu Prabha Ray, *The Archaeology of Seafaring in Ancient South Asia* (Cambridge: Cambridge University Press, 2003).

14. V. G. Scammell, "European Exiles, Renegades, and Outlaws and the Maritime Economy of Asia, 1500–1750," *Modern Asian Studies* (Oct. 1992): 641–61; Robert Richie, "The Sea Peoples," in his *Captain Kidd and the War Against Pirates* (Cambridge, MA: Harvard University Press, 1986), pp. 1–26; S. C. Hill, "Notes on Piracy in Eastern Waters," *Indian Antiquary*, vols. 53, 55: supplements (Delhi: Swati Publications,1985/6). See also Alison Games, *The Web of Empire: English Cosmopolitans in an Age of Expansion, 1560–1660* (New York: Oxford University Press, 2008).

15. The "T map," a medieval vision of the world that gave Asia one half the globe while Europe and Africa equally divided the remaining half, was still in use in Columbus's time. Here the various known oceans are all one basin surrounding the three continents (see Evelyn Edson, *Mapping Time and Space: How Medieval Mapmakers Viewed Their World* [London: British Library, 1997]). Europeans persisted in reifying this global geography culturally, laying the groundwork for modern-day continental and hemispheric myths (see Martin Lewis and Karen Wiggen, *The Myth of Continents: A Critique of Metageography* [Berkeley: University of California Press, 1997]).

16. For work that is pushing us in this direction, see Alison Games, "Forum: Beyond the Atlantic: English Globetrotters and Transoceanic Connections," *William and Mary Quarterly* 63, no. 4 (2006); Games, *Web of Empire*; *Envisioning an English Empire: Jamestown and the Making of the North Atlantic World*, ed. Robert Appelbaum and John Wood Sweet (Philadelphia: University of Pennsylvania Press, 2005), esp. Pompa Banerjee's and Susan Iwanisziw's essays; *The British Atlantic World, 1500–1800*, ed. David Armitage and Michael J. Braddick (New York: Palgrave, 2002); and John H. Hobson, *The Eastern Origins of Western Civilisation* (Cambridge: Cambridge University Press, 2004).

17. Sir Humphrey Gilbert, *A Discourse of a Discoverie of a New Passage to Cataia* (1576) purchased by Franklin in London for his Library Company in Philadelphia. Originally bound with Peter Martyr's *History of Travayle in the West & East Indies*, 1577.

18. *Pennsylvania Magazine of History and Biography* 85 (1961): 67. See also Glyn

Williams, *Voyages of Delusion: The Quest for the Northwest Passage* (New Haven, CT: Yale University Press, 2003). Hopeful Americans continued the search, with Thomas Jefferson beginning plans for an expedition shortly after becoming president. The search for a faster route to Asia *within* America continued in the nineteenth century, faltering, I would argue, more due to a weakening of Chinese global economic strength than from any realization that the short cut did not exist. Captain William E. Parry led one of the most famous series of voyages in search of the passage in the 1820s. By that time the opium trade into China by the English and Americans had precipitated a momentous shift in the global balance of payments, with silver flowing for the first time out of China back to the West, with more focus on the Indian Ocean route. Yet the search continued until Roald Amundsen successfully navigated through the Arctic islands in 1903–6.

19. Alexander Hamilton, *Gentleman's Progress: The Itinerarium of Dr. Alexander Hamilton, 1744*, ed. Carl Bridenbaugh (Chapel Hill: University of North Carolina Press, 1948), p. 154.

20. Their work has also been grouped under the labels "New World History" or "Big History." These authors specifically critique the inevitability of European economic hegemony after industrialization. J. M. Blaut, *The Colonizer's Model of the World: Geographical Diffusionism and Eurocentric History* (New York: Guilford Press, 1993); Andre Gunder Frank, *ReOrient: Global Economy in the Asian Age* (Berkeley: University of California Press, 1998); Kenneth Pomeranz and Steven Topik, *The World That Trade Created: Society, Culture, and the World Economy, 1400 to the Present* (Armonk and London: M. E. Sharpe, 1999); Kenneth Pomeranz, *The Great Divergence: Europe, China, and the Making of the Modern World Economy* (Princeton, NJ: Princeton University Press, 2000); Robert B. Marks, *Origins of the Modern World: A Global and Ecological Narrative* (Lanham, MD: Rowman and Littlefield, 2002); see also Janet Abu-Lughod, *Before European Hegemony: The World System, AD 1250–1350* (New York: Oxford University Press, 1989).

21. In a debate with Robert Brenner, Chris Harman, editor of *International Socialism*, cites the wheelbarrow's spur to agricultural surpluses in the English countryside, and hence the role of this Chinese tool to agricultural capitalism. Both scholars acknowledge China as a technological leader. "Feudalism and a Transition to Capitalism with Robert Brenner and Chris Harman," a debate organized by *International Socialism* and *Historical Materialism*, can be heard online; see also Frank, *ReOrient*, pp. 195–203.

22. Fernand Braudel, *Afterthoughts on Material Civilization and Capitalism* (Baltimore: Johns Hopkins University Press, 1977), pp. 47, 69–71.

23. See Joyce Appleby, "Consumption in Early Modern Social Thought," in *Consumption and the World of Goods*, ed. John Brewer and Roy Porter (London: Routledge, 1993).

24. Robert B. Marks, *Origins of the Modern World: A Global and Ecological Narrative* (Lanham, MD: Rowman and Littlefield, 2002), p. 81.

25. Ibid., p. 80. See also Dennis Flynn and Arturo Giraldez, "Arbitrage, China, and World Trade in the Early Modern Period," *Journal of Economic and Social History of the Orient* 38, no. 4 (1995); and Frank, *ReOrient*. Frank notes that in N. B. Harte's edited volume, *The Study of Economic History: Collected Inaugural Lectures 1893–1970* (Plymouth, UK: Clarke, Doble, and Brendon, 1971), "almost every word is about Europe and the United States and their 'Atlantic economy,' which hardly includes even Africa" (p. 24); Frank is now joined by a rising chorus.

26. Flynn and Giraldez, "Cycles of Silver: Global Economic Unity through the Mid-Eighteenth Century," *Journal of World History* 13, no. 2 (Fall 2002): 391–427.

27. "China clay" was kaolin, which does not exist in Europe. In 1743–44, twenty tons

of South Carolina clay was exported to the newly formed English porcelain manufacturer Bow, which was in search of a natural resource comparable to Chinese kaolin. They described it as "an earth, the produce of the Chirokee nation in America, called by the natives unaker" (Julie Emerson et al., *Porcelain Stories from China to Europe* [Seattle: University of Washington Press with the Seattle Art Museum, 2000], p. 160). The colony of Georgia, in another example, was founded with the explicit purpose of cultivating silk for British textile mills. Unsuccessful experimentation with silk cultivation continued until the middle of the nineteenth century in America.

28. The debate on whether or not Americans used the Company flag as a model for their own has been largely confined to naval historians, with most Americans arguing against imitation. Carington Bowles's 1783 *Bowles's Universal Display of the Naval Flags of All Nations in the World* depicts close to 250 naval flags from all over the world and only two have thirteen red and white stripes: the East India Company (post 1707) and the United States. Three others have six or nine red and white stripes: two German ports (Wismar and Bremen) and Tunis. For a thorough treatment, and an English interpretation, see Sir Charles Fawcett, "The Striped Flag of the East India Company, and Its Connexion with the American 'Stars and Stripes,'" *Mariners Mirror* 23 (Oct. 1938), Cambridge University Press.

29. See Christopher Witmore's argument that we need to make *less* of a distinction between "things" and "people"; materials, refined manufactures, words, texts, human actors are all "folded into humanity" and we should develop methods of analysis that deal with them seamlessly ("Historians and the Study of Material Culture," *American Historical Review* 114, no. 5 [Dec. 2009]: 1360, 1369).

30. Hamilton, *Itinerarium*, p. 8, commenting on the family of a Maryland ferryman. Hamilton continues to remark on the simpleness, and rude and unpolished nature, of the typical Americans he encounters on his five-month voyage through the colonies.

31. On presumed colonial American inferiority vis-à-vis Europeans, see Michal J. Rozbicki, "The Curse of Provincialism: Negative Perceptions of Colonial American Plantation Gentry," *Journal of Southern History* 63, no. 4 (Nov. 1997): 727–52; Richard Bushman, *The Refinement of America: Persons, Houses, Cities* (New York: Vintage Books, 1992); Kariann Yokota, "Post-Colonial America: Transatlantic Networks of Exchange in the Early National Period," PhD diss., University of California, Los Angeles, 2002.

32. Maya Jasonoff demonstrates the connection in the British imagination between Asian objects and status in Anglo-India in *Edge of Empire: Lives, Culture, and Conquest in the East, 1750–1850* (New York: Knopf, 2005). The same can be done for the American side of the British Empire; see also Ralph Bauer, *The Cultural Geography of Colonial American Literatures: Empire, Travel, Modernity* (Cambridge: Cambridge University Press, 2003); and Jim Egan, *Oriental Shadows: The Presence of the East in Early American Literature* (Columbus: Ohio State University Press, forthcoming).

33. "New beverage" is a modifier often used by historical archaeologists to refer to wares designed to consume tea, chocolate, coffee, and certain imported liquors, as opposed to the traditional beverages of ale, beer, grog, warm milk, and so on.

34. Cary Carson, "Why Demand?" in *Of Consuming Interests: The Style of Life in the Eighteenth Century*, by Cary Carson, Ronald Hoffman, and Peter Albert (Charlottesville: University of Virginia Press, 1994), p. 575.

35. Some of the porcelain displayed in colonial homes was Japanese, carried primarily to the Atlantic by the Dutch during the twenty-year period in the mid-seventeenth century when China officially closed its ports to sea trade. Japanese porcelain had a distinct aesthetic

called "Imari," named after the southern Japanese seaport, that was later imitated by the Chinese in an effort to regain market share. Soon most of the popular Imari porcelain in colonial homes was Chinese, not Japanese. The same copying by the Chinese occurred in the style of lacquered screens, a Japanese innovation later mass-marketed to the West by the Chinese and called by Europeans "Coromandel screens."

36. See esp. Gloria Main, "Many Things Forgotten: The Use of Probate Records in *Arming America*," *William and Mary Quarterly*, 3rd ser., vol. 59, no. 1 (Jan. 2002): 211–16, and "The Standard of Living in Southern New England, 1640–1773," *William and Mary Quarterly* 45 (1988): 124–34; Carole Shammas, *The Pre-industrial Consumer in England and America* (Oxford, 1990); for more references, see John Beddell, "Archaeology and Probate Inventories in the Study of Eighteenth-Century Life," *Journal of Interdisciplinary History* 31, no. 2 (August 2000): 223–45.

37. The interpretive division between form, function, and symbolic meaning for artifacts is one archaeologists have worked with since at least the mid-twentieth century. There are very few historians who probe the references contained within objects to the extent that archaeologists and cultural anthropologists do, but a number of literary scholars, familiar with "close reading" and discourse analysis, have turned to the utility of "close reading" objects, including David Porter (*Ideographia: The Chinese Cypher in Early Modern Europe* [Palo Alto, CA: Stanford University Press, 2001]) and David Fliegelman (*Declaring Independence: Jefferson, Natural Language, and the Culture of Performance* [Palo Alto, CA: Stanford University Press, 1993]). For Robert St. George's method of "indirect reference," see *Conversing by Signs: Poetics of Implication in Colonial New England Culture* (Chapel Hill: University of North Carolina Press, 1998), pp. 2–9.

38. See esp. Chris Gosden and Yvonne Marshall, "The Cultural Biography of Objects," *World Archaeology* 31, no. 2 (1999): pp. 169–78; Igor Kopytoff, "The Cultural Biography of Things: Commoditization as Process," in *The Social Life of Things: Commodities in Cultural Perspective*, ed. Arjun Appadurai (Cambridge: Cambridge University Press, 1986), pp. 64–91.

39. Porter, *Ideographia*, p. 138. One curatorial scholar of Chinese porcelain after another has remarked on the lack of interest by early modern Westerners in the Chinese symbols presented on their porcelain, including Claire Le Corbeiller, Alice Cooney Frelinghuysen, John G. Phillips (all from the Metropolitan Museum in New York), Amanda Lange (Historic Deerfield), and Craig Clunas (Oxford, University of Sussex, Victoria and Albert Museum).

40. Ibid. See Porter's chap. 3, "Chinoiserie and the Aesthetics of Illegitimacy," pp. 133–92.

41. Stacey Pierson, *Design as Signs: Decoration and Chinese Ceramics* (London: University of London and the Percival David Foundation, 2001), pp. 5–8; Margaret Medley, *The Chinese Potter: A Practical History of Chinese Ceramics* (London: Phaidon Press, 1989); and Michael Butler et al., *Treasures from an Unknown Reign: Shunzhi Porcelain* (Alexandria, VA: Art Services International, 2002).

42. Julia B. Curtis and Stephen Little, *Chinese Porcelains of the Seventeenth Century: Landscapes, Scholars' Motifs, and Narratives* (Seattle: University of Washington Press, 1995); Stephen Little, *Chinese Ceramics of the Transitional Period, 1620–1663* (New York: China Institute of America, 1983); Medley, *Chinese Potter*, pp. 215–63.

43. Stephen Little, "Narrative Themes and Woodblock Prints and Decoration of the Seventeenth Century," in his *Seventeenth-Century Chinese Porcelain from the Butler Family Collection* (Alexandria, VA: Art Services International, 1990), pp. 21–31.

44. For a full discussion of the symbolism of Chinese design motifs painted on Chinese porcelain, see Pierson, *Designs as Signs*.

45. See, e.g., the inventory of a Philadelphia cordwainer, 1770: his porcelain includes: "14 enamelld China plates £1.5"; "3 Doz. & 10 burnt China Cups & Saucrs £1.15"; 5 burnt China punch bowls, 3 broke £1.7"; 1 burnt China canister & stand"; "1 incompleat sett blue&wht China 11Sh6"; "1 blue&wht punch bowl broke & 14 plates 10 of wch broke 7Sh6." For the use of the terms "India china" and English china," see James Beekman Letterbook (1761, New York Historical Society).

46. A. Owne Aldridge, *The Dragon and the Eagle: The Presence of China in the American Enlightenment* (Detroit: Wayne State University Press, 1993), pp. 23–46.

47. Letter from Stiles to Franklin, Feb. 26, 1766. The Papers of Benjamin Franklin, digital edition, Packard Humanities Institute, 1988–present.

48. See Porter, *Ideographia*, pp. 78–83.

49. Mukhtar Ali Isaani, *The Oriental Tale in America through 1865*, PhD diss., Princeton University, 1962.

50. Cited in ibid., p. 128. Voltaire also called China "le plus sage empire de l'univers." Quoted in Zhang Longxi, "The Myth of the Other: China in the Eyes of the West," *Critical Inquiry* 15, no. 1 (Autumn 1988): 108–31, p. 117.

51. Adolf Reichwein, *China and Europe: Intellectual and Artistic Contacts in the Eighteenth Century* (NY: Barnes and Noble, 1925), p. 77 quoted here. On the importance of China to Western Enlightenment thought, see also Jonathan D. Spence, *Chan's Great Continent: China in Western Minds* (New York: Norton, 1999), chap. 5; Donald E. Lach and Edwin J.Van Kley, *Asia in the Making of Europe: A Century of Wonder* (Chicago: University of Chicago Press, 1978), vol. 2; Qian Zhonshu, "China in the English Literature of the Seventeenth Century," *Quarterly Bulletin of the Chinese Bibliography* 1 (Dec. 1940): 351–84, and "China in the English Literature of the Eighteenth Century," *Quarterly Bulletin of the Chinese Bibliography* 2 (Dec. 1941): 113–52.

52. Mukhtar Ali Isani, "Cotton Mather and the Orient," *New England Quarterly* 43 (Mar. 1970): 46–58.

53. Jonathan Goldstein, *Philadelphia and the China Trade, 1682–1846* (University Park: Pennsylvania State University Press, 1978), pp. 10–17.

54. Charles Thomson, "Preface," Minute Book, American Philosophical Society, *Transactions* (January 1, 1768): vii.

55. Metcalf Bowler, *A Treatise on Agriculture and Practical Husbandry: Designed for the Information of Landowners and Farmers* (Providence: Bennett Wheeler, 1786).

56. Oliver Goldsmith, *Citizen of the World, or, Letters from a Chinese Philosopher Residing in London* (Dublin: J. Williams, 1760–61). On this passage, see also J. H. Bunn, "The Aesthetics of British Mercantilism," *New Literary History* 11, no. 2 (Winter 1980): 313.

57. Mihaly Csikszentmihalyi, "Why We Need Things," in *History from Things*, ed. Steven Lubar and W. David Kingery (Washington DC: Smithsonian, 1993).

58. The adjective "old" is one that is used often for china in places that have been exposed to Chinese commodities for a few generations. In the nineteenth century, Chinese porcelain that is not preceded by the adjective "old" is not considered worthy of a collector's notice (see Alice Morse Earle, *China Collecting in America* [New York: Scribner's Sons, 1906]).

59. This development is attributed to Josiah Spode, although experimentation with ox bone had been going on for several decades in England.

60. R. E. Roentgen, *The Book of Meissen*, 2nd ed. (Atglen, PA: Schiffer Publishing, 1996).

61. Arjun Appadurai, "Commodities and the Politics of Value," in *The Social Life of Things: Commodities in Cultural Perspective*, ed. Appadurai (Cambridge: Cambridge University Press, 1986), p. 15.

Chapter 1

1. Ned Ward, "A Trip to Jamaica: With a True Character of the People and the Island" (London, 1698), in *Caribbeana: An Anthology of English Literatures of the West Indies, 1657–1777*, ed. Thomas W. Krise (Chicago: University of Chicago Press, 1999), p. 88. Ward's observation of the Jamaican people was not dissimilar to comments about northerners, however; he said, "They regard nothing but Money, and value not how they get it, there being no Felicity to be enjoyed but purely Riches. They are very Civil to Strangers who bring over considerable Effects; and will try a great many ways to kill him farely for the lucre of his Cargo" (p. 91).

2. William Beeston, in *Calendar of State Papers 1693–1696* (hereafter referred to as *CalSP*), ed. J. W. Fortesque (London: Mackie and Co., 1903), item nos. 393 and 496, letters of June 10, 1693, and July 28, 1693.

3. Peter Delanoy, in *CalSP 1693–1696*, item no. 1892, letter of June 13, 1695.

4. Ibid., item no. 1916, letter of June 25, 1695.

5. "Red Sea" may have been a catchall phrase for all of western Asia. Most English in the seventeenth century would have been more familiar with biblical Asia, which included places such as the Red Sea, than with the Indian Ocean, its islands and seaports, or the coast of India, even though these destinations were as popular with Atlantic mariners as the "Red Sea."

6. Three influential historical syntheses of colonial American culture see this politicization of goods happening later: T. H. Breen, who argues for a marked change in the nature of consumption only after about 1745 (*The Marketplace of Revolution: How Consumer Politics Shaped American Independence* [Oxford: Oxford University Press, 2004]); Gordon Wood, who argues that the first cracks in an organic traditional society began to appear only in the same mid-eighteenth-century time period (*The Radicalism of the American Revolution* [New York: Vintage Books, 1991]); and Richard Bushman, who argues just as Neil McKendrick does for Britain ("Consumer Revolution in Eighteenth-Century England," in *Consumer Society*, ed. Neva Goodwin et al. [Washington DC: Island Press, 1997]), that consumption was powered by a conflict-free emulation until an Industrial Revolution put goods in the hands of everyone, hence in the nineteenth century for Americans (*The Refinement of America: Persons, Houses, Cities* (New York: Knopf, 1992). *Of Consuming Interests: The Style of Life in the Eighteenth Century*, by Cary Carson, Ronald Hoffman, and Peter Albert (Charlottesville: University of Virginia Press, 1994) remains one of the best historical studies of the highly contested role of goods and consumption in early colonial America. For a good treatment of politicizing consumption earlier, see also Phyllis Whitman Hunter, *Purchasing Identity in the Atlantic World: Massachusetts Merchants, 1670–1780* (Ithaca, NY: Cornell University Press, 2001). Historical archaeologists have generally been more attuned to the global and political dimensions of consumption in this early era of North American colonization. See esp. *Recovery of Meaning: Historical Archaeology in the Eastern United States*, ed. Mark Leone and Parker Potter (Washington DC: Smithsonian Institution Press, 1988); and *Historical Archaeology and the Study of American Culture*, ed. Lu Ann de Cunzo and Bernard Herman (Knoxville: University of Tennessee Press, 1996). The now well-known "debate on luxury" led by authors such as John Sekora and Maxine Berg,

as well as trenchant works on "the culture of consumption" such as John Brewer's edited volumes, focus on the centrality of consumption to social and political change in Europe. We are left to infer relevance to the presumed laggard growth of American civil society. Even Jean-Christophe Agnew, who explicitly seeks to insert an American perspective in Brewer and Porter's Euro-centered *Consumption and the World of Goods*, has difficulty seeing back beyond the nineteenth century. See John Sekora, *Luxury: The Idea in Western Thought, Eden to Smollett* (Baltimore: Johns Hopkins University Press, 1977); Maxine Berg and Elizabeth Eger, *Luxury in the Eighteenth Century: Debates, Desires, and Delectable Goods* (New York: Palgrave, 2003); Maxine Berg and Helen Clifford, *Consumers and Luxury: Consumer Culture in Europe, 1650–1850* (Manchester: Manchester University Press, 1999); John Brewer and Roy Porter, *Consumption and the World of Goods* (New York: Routledge, 1993). For a review of the role of consumption to historical studies of early modern Europe, see Matthew Hilton, "Class, Consumption, and the Public Sphere," *Journal of Contemporary History* 35, no. 4 (Oct. 2000): 655–66.)

7. The various Navigation Acts were continually revised, extended, and strengthened from the 1650s to the 1770s (see Larry Sawers, "The Navigation Acts Revisited," *Economic History Review*, n.s. 45, no. 2 [May 1992]: 262–84). In addition, the government maintained a stake in the East Indies trades, primarily by strengthening and investing in the East India Company. In the early 1690s, though, the government foresaw advantages in letting other groups enter the trade and loosened the Company monopoly. This opened the way for American traders, who proved to be not at all what the king and Parliament had in mind in opening the trade. By 1698 the Crown had capitalized a new powerful East India Company that ultimately merged with the old one under the same monopolistic terms as previously.

8. The *Empress of China*, sent to China in early 1784 by Robert Morris and a group of investors from Philadelphia and New York, is generally hailed as the first American "East Indiaman."

9. For both Americans and Europeans there was a general lack of geographic precision in reference to the regions of Asia, with Japan, China, the Spice Islands, India, and the Middle East all vaguely referred to as the "East Indies" (just as later—and still today—they were also referred to as "Oriental").

10. "Interlopers" was the term used by the East India Company for non-Company traders in the Indian Ocean. Throughout most of the seventeenth century, interlopers were tolerated as an annoying fact of life because they had protection from the Crown, which directly profited from *all* inbound cargoes from the East. In 1698 a group of interlopers formed the New East India Company, with £2 million in state backing! A few years later they merged with the Old East India Company, further consolidating the Company's power and monopoly.

11. For a masterful demonstration of global interconnectedness in the late seventeenth century, see John E. Wills, *1688: A Global History* (New York: Norton, 2001).

12. Madagascar colonist Adam Baldridge alone claims to have met at least twenty-four American sea captains in the eight years he lived in the Indian Ocean, and, as he was under suspicion for his dealings with pirates, he would have had every reason to low-ball this figure (see his deposition of May 5, 1699, in John Franklin Jameson, *Privateering and Piracy in the Colonial Period: Illustrative Documents* [New York: Macmillan, 1923], pp. 180–87).

13. The eighty-five is my figure based on available crew sizes from the thirty-four American vessels listed (see table 1.1 for sources). This is very close to the figure for average crew size of eighty-eight given by Carl Swanson for American privateers in the period 1738–49

("American Privateering and Imperial Warfare," *William and Mary Quarterly* 42, no. 3 [July 1985]: 363). A number of these thirty-four vessels were only lightly armed, or not armed at all, and carried only twenty to thirty men. While this would tend to lower the figure for average crew size, the total number sailing beyond the Atlantic of 2,900 is probably actually higher as many of the listed privateering captains sailed on more than one voyage. It is also unlikely that all American ships making the trip to the Indian Ocean were picked up in the records.

14. The estimated numbers are: Pennsylvania, 2,000; Connecticut, 3,000; New England, 9,500; Rhode Island, 1,200; New York, 3,000 (from "Estimate of the Annual Charge for the Defence of Albany and of Quotas to be Furnished by the Various Colonies" (*Calendar of State Papers, Colonial Series, America and West Indies, 1693–96* [hereafter referred to as *CalSP*], ed. J. W. Fortesque [London: Mackie and Co., 1903], item nos. 173, 611iii.). As a percentage of an estimated total population of about 170,000 in the northeast colonies, 2,795 American mariners in the Indian Ocean is also impressive at 2% of total population (Virginia Harrington, *American Population before the Federal Census of 1790* [New York: Columbia University Press, 1932], pp. 3–4).

15. C*alSP 1697–98*, item nos. 401 and 404, letters of April 25 and 26, 1698.

16. Marcus Rediker, *Between the Devil and the Deep Blue Sea: Merchant Seamen, Pirates, and the Anglo-American World, 1700–1750* (Cambridge: Cambridge University Press, 1987), p. 13.

17. In the fifteenth and sixteenth centuries England and Spain negotiated a number of treaties delineating prize law, and in the sixteenth and seventeenth centuries the French were at the table. England and Holland framed prize agreements at the end of each of their conflicts in the seventeenth century. See Carl J. Kurlsrud, *Maritime Neutrality to 1780: A History of the Main Principles Governing Neutrality and Belligerency to 1780* (Boston: Little Brown and Co., 1936), pp. 26–51; Eliga Gould, "Zones of Law, Zones of Violence: The Legal Geography of the British Atlantic, circa 1772," *William and Mary Quarterly* 60, no. 3 (July 2003): 471–510.

18. Figures for the second half of the seventeenth century; wages tended to rise during wartime. Ralph Davies, *The Rise of the English Shipping Industry* (London: Macmillan, 1962), 135–37; Alexander B. Hawes, *Off Soundings: Aspects of the Maritime History of Rhode Island* (Chevy Chase, MD: Posterity Press, 1999), 18; Rediker, *Between the Devil*, 117–23, 304–05.

19. Constantin de Renneville, *Recueil des voyages qui ont servi à l'establissement et aux progrez de la Compagnie des Indes orientales* (London: W. Freeman, 1703), p. 385.

20. John Bruce, *Annals of the Honorable East-India Company* (London, 1810), quoted in S. C. Hill, "Notes on Piracy in Eastern Waters," *Indian Antiquary* 53 (Jan. 1923–Oct. 1928): 71. Weddell represented the Courteens Company, a London-based rival to the East India Company. See also John Goldsmith Phillips, *China Trade Porcelain* (Cambridge, MA: Harvard University Press, 1956), p. 22; Kenneth R. Andrews, *Trade, Plunder, and Settlement: Maritime Enterprise and the Genesis of the British Empire, 1480–1630* (Cambridge: Cambridge University Press,1984). pp. 278ff. On Courteens, see Shafaat Ahmad Khan, *The East India Trade in the Seventeenth Century (in Its Political and Economic Aspects)* (London, 1923); Holden Furber, *Rival Empires of Trade in the Orient, 1600–1800* (Minneapolis: University of Minnesota Press, 1976), pp. 39ff.

21. Ralph Davies notes that seamen were often paid in colonial currencies, indicating their strong association with America (*The Rise of the English Shipping Industry in the Seven-*

teenth and Eighteenth Centuries [London: Macmillan, 1962], p. 142); on the cosmopolitan diversity of English ships, especially privateers and piratical ships, see Rediker, *Between the Devil*, pp. 155–56.

22. Jacob Judd, "Frederick Philipse and the Madagascar Trade," *New York Historical Society Quarterly* 47 (1963): 356; Robert Ritchie, *Captain Kidd and the War against the Pirates* (Cambridge, MA: Harvard University Press, 1986), 32–36.

23. "Deposition of Samuel Burgess," a New Yorker and *Jacob* crew member, *CalSp 1697–98*, item no. 473ii, dated May 3, 1698.

24. Letters to the East India Company, *CalSP 1697–98*, item no. 473xvii, dated Jan. 15 and Nov. 30, 1696.

25. A *pinke* was generally a narrow-sterned, square-rigged, slow-moving cargo vessel that was suited for coastal sailing in shallow waters.

26. James G. Lydon, "Barbary Pirates and Colonial New Yorkers," *New York Historical Quarterly* 45 (July 1961): 281–89; all of New York was aware of Leisler's capture, and a public collection was made to reimburse him.

27. See, e.g., Jaspar Dankers and Peter Sluyter, *Journal of a Voyage to New York, 1679–80*, trans. Henry C. Murphy (New York, 1867). Dankers says, "[The captain] intended to sail round Ireland, which suited us very well, for although it was said that the Hollanders were at peace with the Turks, there were many English vessels taken by them daily, and under such circumstances we ran some danger of being plundered, fighting with them, and perhaps being carried into Barbary" (p. 381).

28. Commission, *CalSP 1699*, item no. 196, dated Feb. 27, 1635; Lydon, "Barbary Pirates," p. 288.

29. Quoted in Jameson, *Privateering and Piracy*, pp. 154–55.

30. Hill, "Notes on Piracy," p. 69.

31. For a good discussion of such lines in European culture, see Nicolás Wey Gómez, *The Tropics of Empire: Why Columbus Sailed South to the Indies* (Cambridge, MA: MIT Press, 2008).

32. Hill, "Notes on Piracy," p. 100.

33. Hawes, *Off Soundings*, p. 28.

34. A "piece-of-eight" equaled one Spanish dollar, and as it was worth eight *reals*, it was marked with an "8."

35. John Gardiner was the grandson of Lyon Gardiner, who had settled the property in 1639; John's father David established the manor title in 1686. The manor patent, granted by New York Governor Dongan, empowered the lord of the manor to hold "Court Leet and Court Baron," in addition to vesting him with the "Advowson and right of Patronage of all churches within the manor precincts," as well as a number of other rights and privileges. See Harold Donaldson Eberlin, *Manor Houses and Historic Homes of Long Island and Staten Island* (Philadelphia: J. B. Lippencott, 1929), pp. 27–46.

36. Council of Lords of Trade and Plantations to the Lords Justices, CalSP 1697–98, item no. 904, Oct. 19, 1698.

37. Statement, *CalSP 1696–97*, item no. 1098, June 22, 1697.

38. Deposition, *CalSP 1696–97*, item no. 517iv, of August 3, 1696; and John Franklin Jameson, *Privateering and Piracy in the Colonial Period: Illustrative Documents* (New York: Macmillan, 1923), pp. 165–71.

39. Report submitted by Customs Commissioner Edward Randolph, *CalSP 1696–97*, item no. 149, Aug. 17, 1696.

40. Ibid.; Hawes, *Off Soundings*, 27.

41. See Aug. 3, 1696, deposition of John Dann, *CalSP 1696–97*, item no. 517; and Jameson, *Privateering*, pp. 165–67.

42. Karl Marx gave an excellent history of the power block formed by King William's government in supporting the East India Company in "The East India Company—Its History and Results," first published in the *New York Daily Tribune*, July 11, 1853, and reprinted in *Marx-Engels: Collected Works* (New York: International Publishers, 1975–2005), 12:148.

43. As recounted by Alexander Hamilton in *New Account of the East Indies* (1727; facsimile edition, London: Argonaut Press, 1930), p. 132.

44. Robert Brenner, *Merchants and Revolution: Commercial Change, Political Conflict, and London's Overseas Traders, 1550–1653* (London: Verso, 2003), p. 109.

45. *Ahsan alTaqasim, fi ma'rifat al-aaqalim* (Calcutta, 1901), cited in K. N. Chaudhuri, *Trade and Civilization in the Indian Ocean: An Economic History from the Rise of Islam to 1750* (Cambridge: Cambridge University Press, 1985), p. 2.

46. Chaudhuri, *Trade and Civilization*, p. 2.

47. The conquests of Alexander the Great, fourth century BCE, are presumed to have first linked the Mediterranean with Asian trade routes, although knowledge of Chinese silks appears in sixth-century (BCE) Greek texts. See John E. Vollmer et al., *Silk Roads, China Ships* (Toronto: Royal Ontario Museum, 1983), pp. 6–23; and Philip Curtin, *Cross-Cultural Trade in World History* (Cambridge: Cambridge University Press, 1984), pp. 93–96.

48. Robert Finlay, "Pilgrim Art: The Culture of Porcelain in World History," *Journal of World History* 9, no. 2 (Fall 1998): 151; Medley, *Chinese Potter*, p. 103.

49. Sucheta Mazumdar, *Sugar and Society in China: Peasants, Technology, and the World Market* (Cambridge, MA: Harvard University Press, 1989), p. 70; and Andre Gunder Frank, *ReOrient: Global Economy in the Asian Age* (Berkeley: University of California Press, 1998), pp. 197–98.

50. Medley, *Chinese Potter*, p. 170.

51. Bahadur was the ruler of Gujarat in the early sixteenth century. C. R. Boxer, *The Portuguese Seaborne Empire* (London: Hutchinson, 1969), p. 50.

52. Charles Boone, quoted in Chaudhuri, *Trade and Civilization*, p. 3. Of interest here is that by the mid-eighteenth century, the position of gunner, a lower-level officer specifically responsible for armaments, is only found on East Indiamen, whereas the position had long since disappeared on Atlantic vessels (see Davies, *Rise*, p. 112).

53. This piece is now at the British Museum (Medley, *Chinese Potter*, pp. 100–102).

54. Medley, *Chinese Potter*, 97–114; Finlay, "Pilgrim Art," pp. 150–55.

55. Quoted in John Caswell, "Chinese Ceramics from Allaippidy in Sri Lanka," in *A Ceramic Legacy of Asia's Maritime Trade*, ed. Peter Y. K. Lam (Oxford: Oxford University Press, 1985), p. 33.

56. As a testament to the continuing power of Western "China-mania," there is still today a booming market for shipwrecked porcelains, evident in the sales of such reputable auction houses as Christie's and Sotheby's (see Christie's auction catalog "The Nanking Cargo," Amsterdam, April 28-May 2, 1986, on the sale of the mid-eighteenth-century *Geldermalsen* cargo) as well as many less reputable hawkers (see summer 2005 wire service headlines, "Ruby Mining Company Announces Shipwreck Porcelain Auctioned at Nantucket Wine Festival," www.primezone.com/newsroom/news.html).

57. With technological improvements and widespread popular availability of scuba technology, shipwrecks are being discovered (and pillaged) all over the world at an increasing

pace. Antique collector publications and archaeological publications regularly report such finds. See, e.g., a list of some of the shipwreck discoveries from Southeast Asia that has been compiled and uploaded at http://www.seaantique.com/shipwrecks.htm created by S.E.A. Antiques 2002 (updated Nov. 13, 2004).

58. Mazumdar, *Sugar and Society*, p. 71.

59. Medley, *Chinese Potter*, pp. 69–70, 172–78. In Southeast Asia, by contrast, imported porcelain overran native ceramic traditions (Finlay, "Pilgrim Art," pp. 158–61).

60. Gao Jinyuan, "China and Africa: The Development of Relations over Many Centuries," *African Affairs* 83, no. 331 (April 1984): 241–50, at 241; and Basil Davidson, *Old Africa Rediscovered* (London: Gollancz, 1959), pp. 53, 158.

61. Pierre Verin, "Les Echelles anciennes de commerce sur les côtes nords de Madagascar," PhD diss., University of Paris, Oct. 1972; Sucheta Mazumdar, personal communication.

62. Mazumdar, *Sugar and Society*, pp. 86–90.

63. Prior to the eighteenth century, much greater wealth was carried between the Mughal, Safavid, and Ottoman Empires than in the China trade, which may partly explain the general European preference for the Indian Ocean to the Pacific (I am grateful to Sucheta Mazumdar for this point). Awe of Spanish power may have been another reason.

64. Robert Wisset, *A Compendium of East Indian Affairs* (London: E. Cox, 1802).

65. By comparison, Maryland and Virginia only owned 25 percent of their shipping at the end of the century. John J. McCusker, "The Shipping Industry in Colonial America," in *America's Maritime Legacy: A History of the U.S. Merchant Marine and Shipbuilding Industry since Colonial Times*, ed. Robert A. Kilmarx (Boulder, CO: Westview Press, 1979), p. 22.

66. The value of total textiles was £53,314, accounting for 53 percent of total value, and of that £22,444 was woven, thrown, and wrought silk (Nuala Zahedieh, "London and Colonial Consumers in the Late Seventeenth Century," *Economic History Review* [1994]: 239–61, at 251).

67. For a critique of a tightly bounded Atlantic, see Linda Colley's review of Bernard Bailyn's *Atlantic History: Concept and Contours* (Cambridge, MA: Harvard, 2005); Carla Gardina Pestana's *The English Atlantic in an Age of Revolution, 1640–1661* (Cambridge, MA: Harvard, 2004) in "The Sea Around Us," *New York Review of Books*, June 22, 2006; *Atlantic History: A Critical Appraisal*, ed. Jack P. Greene and Philip D. Morgan (New York: Oxford, 2009); and Peter A. Coclanis, "Atlantic World or Atlantic/World," *William and Mary Quarterly* 63, no. 4 (Oct. 2006): 725–42.

68. Earl of Bellomont to Lords of Trade, May 8, 1698, in *New York Colonial Manuscripts*, ed. E. B. O'Callaghan (Albany: Weed, Parsons, 1861), 4: 308.

69. Adolph Philipse, letter to Robert Heysham, May 5, 1698, quoted in Jacob Judd, "Frederick Philipse and the Madagascar Trade," *New York Historical Society Quarterly* 47 (1963): 354–74, at 367–68.

70. "Act for Raising a Sum not to Exceed £2 million . . . for Settling the Trade to the East Indies," Sept. 29, 1698, in *Statutes of the Realm*, vol. 7. Provisions of this act state that no one may trade to the East Indies who has not put up stock in the East India Company (article 54) and that those stockholders have "the sole trade" (article 71); moreover, "Goods from the Indies cannot break bulk before being brought to England" (article 59).

71. "Orders for Capt. Samuel Burgess from Fredryck Flypse," cited in Judd, "Frederick Philipse," p. 366.

72. T*he Embassy of Sir Thomas Roe to the Court of the Great Mogul, 1615–1619, as Narrated in His Journal and Correspondence*, ed. W. Foster (London, 1899).

73. Josiah Child, *The Great Honour and Advantage of the East India Trade to the Kingdom* (London: Thomas Speed, 1697).

74. Frank, *ReOrient*, p. 112.

75. I would like to thank Kee Il Choi for elucidating this point.

76. Craig Clunas, *Chinese Export Art and Design* (Victoria and Albert Museum, 1987), p. 12.

77. In New York City, a second-story chamber contained "3 Chinea cups & saucers, 3 Chinea mustard potts, 3 Chinea cups & 2 Earthen saucers, 1/2 doz. burnt Chinea cups & saucers,1 small burnt Chinea dish, 1 Blue and White Earthen plate, 1 small Blue & White Earthen dish." A "Lower store" contained "6 chinea cups & saucers"; a "small room" had 1 Japan Tea Table, 2 small Chinia bowls, 2 Chinia saucers." The rambling Philipsburg Manor (Yonkers) had Chinese porcelain and lacquers in several rooms. Adolph Philipse, estate inventory of Jan. 24, 1749, now in the Philipse-Gouverneur Collection, New York Historical Society.

78. Clunas, *Chinese Export Art*, p. 16.

79. New York State Inventories, reel 1, New York State Archives, Aug. 25, 1700. Muslin at this time was always Asian as Europeans had not yet mastered the weaving of this textile.

80. Minutes of the Council of New York, *CalSP 1697–98*, item no. 433, May 8, 1698.

81. Ibid.

82. *Documents Relative to the Colonial History of New York*, 4:447. Tew, related to a reputable Newport family, sailed to the Indian Ocean at least twice. He was allegedly killed by "a great Shott from a Moor's Ship" in 1695 (Hawes, *Off Soundings*, p. 34).

83. Minutes of the Council of New York, *CalSP 1697–98*, item no. 433, May 8, 1698,

84. Ibid., item no. 521, letter of May 20, 1698.

85. Caleb Carr of Rhode Island is "illiterate" and William Markham of Pennsylvania is "infirm" (*CalSP 1696–97*, no. 149, Aug. 17, 1696); Walter Clarke of Rhode Island is "ignorant" (*CalSP 1697–98*, no. 521, May 30, 1698).

86. Edward Randolph to Council of Trade and Plantations, *CalSP 1697–98*, item 404, April 26, 1698.

87. Over the course of the seventeenth century the Cootes had been supporters of both Catholic and Protestant kings, and had supported with their lives the republican civil war, the monarchal restoration, and the Whig revolution. They defined the term "court sycophant." See Frederic de Peyster, *Life and Administration of Richard, Earl of Bellomont* (New York Historical Society, 1879); Robert C. Ritchie, *Captain Kidd and the War against Pirates* (Cambridge, MA: Harvard University Press, 1986), pp. 47–48.

88. Some of the foremost historians of colonial America gathered March 30–April 1, 2006, at Harvard University to take on these issues at the conference "Transformations: The Atlantic World in the Late Seventeenth Century," part of the International Seminar on the History of the Atlantic World.

89. Ritchie, *Captain Kidd*, 178–80; Jameson, *Privateering and Piracy*, 227.

90. Edward Randolph to the Lords of Trade, *CalSP 1697–98*, item no. 404, April 26, 1698.

91. Narrative of Capt. Robert Snead, *CalSP 1697–98*, item no. 451i, April 1697.

92. For an excellent book-length account of William Kidd and his relationship with Lord Bellomont, see Ritchie, *Captain Kidd*.

93. Clunas, *Chinese Export Art*, p. 16.

94. The company garnered the patronage of the Mughal emperor and soon overshadowed

the Portuguese, based in Goa and Bombay. It built factories in Surat (1612), Madras (1639), Bombay (1668, ceded in the dowry of Catherine de Braganza), and eventually Calcutta (1690). In 1634 the Mughal emperor extended his hospitality to English traders in Bengal. By 1647 the Company had twenty-three factories and ninety employees in India. It also established fortifications in Bengal (Fort William), in Madras (Fort St. George), and Bombay (Bombay Castle). But it was not able to establish a land presence in China (Canton) until 1711.

95. Also important to the changed relationship between crown and mariners beginning in the reign of King William, of course, is the greater power Parliament wielded.

96. Second Navigation Act,1660. The restricted staples included tobacco and sugar, important cargo items for northern shippers. Like the first Navigation Act of 1651, this one was aimed principally at trade with the Dutch.

97. Under pressure from well-placed "interlopers" who also wanted to establish trading posts in India, King William demonopolized the East India Company in an act of 1694, which allowed any British firm to trade with India. It is not clear what impact this had on the choices made by colonial privateers as they had begun arriving in the Indian Ocean several years before the deregulating act.

98. It might be useful to contextualize the pirates within the broader culture of overseas commerce at this time. Placed next to the atrocities committed in European commerce with Africans and Native Americans, the pirates' robberies and violence emerge as related to a different code, one that targets first and foremost the rich and powerful.

99. T. Volker, *Porcelain and the Dutch East India Company* (Leiden: E.J. Brill, 1971).

100. For an account of the brutality suffered by sailors at the hands of their captains, see Rediker, *Between the Devil*, pp. 212–22. That this practice carried into American vessels of later periods is made clear in the numerous accounts of flogging found in the diary of an American privateersman in the Revolutionary War (see Zuriel Waterman, "Diary of a Doctor-Privateersman, 1779–1781," in *Rhode Islanders Record the Revolution*, ed. Nathaniel Shipton and David Swain [Providence: Rhode Island Publications Society, 1984]).

101. See Elizabeth Mancke, "Chartered Enterprises and the Evolution of the British Atlantic World," in *The Creation of the British Atlantic World*, ed. Elizabeth Mancke and Carole Shammas (Baltimore: Johns Hopkins University Press, 2005).

102. Armenian sailors on board the violated ship, *Quedah Merchant*, reported Kidd's raids directly to emperor Aurengazeb's court. They became the straw that broke the camel's back regarding English piracy. The emperor's officials ordered the imprisonment of Company servants in India until proper restitution had been made for Kidd's acts. See Ritchie, *Captain Kidd*, pp. 127–51.

103. See Sir Dalby Thomas, *An Historical Account of the Rise and Growth of the West-India Collonies, and of the Great Advantages They Are to England, in Respect to Trade* (London: Jo. Hindmarsh, 1690); Sir William Petty, *Political Arithmetick : or, A Discourse Concerning, the Extent and Value of Lands, People, Buildings . . . &c., as the Same Relates to Every Country in General, but More Particularly to the Territories of His Majesty of Great Britain* (London: R. Clavel, 1691). See also Charles M. Andrews, *The Colonial Period of American History* (New Haven, CT: Yale University Press, 1938), p. 338.

104. Robert B. Marks, *Origins of the Modern World: A Global and Ecological Narrative* (Lanham, MD: Rowman and Littlefield, 2002), p. 88.

105. See Howard I. Chapelle, *The Search for Speed Under Sail: 1700–1855* (New York: W. W. Norton and Co., 1967), pp. 53–62.

106. For the national and ethnic fluidity of early eighteenth-century ship compositions, see Rediker, *Between the Devil*, pp. 10–76.

Chapter 2

1. *China-mania* is a nineteenth-century expression applied to those who desperately sought *old* Chinese porcelain, in other words, Chinese objects already in the West and already considered "family heirlooms." The cultural behavior described by the term—competitive acquisitiveness and an effort to enhance one's own family status through display of Chinese objects—aptly suits the behavior of the English and Anglo-Americans toward China in this earlier period as well. See, e.g., the chapter entitled "The China Mania" by Louise Chandler Moulton in *Random Rambles* (Boston: Robert Bros., 1881), pp. 217–24.

2. James Deetz, *In Small Things Forgotten: An Archaeology of Early American Life* (New York: Anchor, 1996), describes the period of greatest cultural distance between England and its American colonies to be the seventeenth century, as do both T. H. Breen in *Marketplace of Revolution* (Oxford: Oxford University Press, 2004) and Richard Bushman in *The Refinement of America* (New York: Vintage, 1993). As for the size of the ocean, by the time colonial engravers were etching political cartoons in the 1760s and 1770s, the Atlantic is depicted as a mere river!

3. Maud Lyman Stevens, *The History of the Vernon House in Newport, R.I.* (Charity Organization Society, 1914), p. 14; and correspondence with Metcalf Bowler, Vernon Papers, Newport Historical Society.

4. Curator Edwin Hipkiss, in a letter to Stephen Luce dated April 9, 1937; cited in Historic American Buildings Survey (hereafter HABS), report RI-34, US Dept. of the Interior.

5. Ruth Ralston, associate curator, Metropolitan Museum of Art, HABS report RI-34, p. 25.

6. Antoinette Downing, *Architectural Heritage of Newport: Rhode Island, 1640–1915* (Cambridge, MA: Harvard University Press, 1952), p. 454. The HABS report states they "can be firmly dated as circa 1760–1775" (see "Historian's Work Sheet," p. 1), but I believe these dates can be extended to after the Revolution as well.

7. This list is very long, but *Magazine Antiques* offers eighty-five years of colonial Americana; see also *The Great River: Art and Society in the Connecticut River Valley, 1635–1820*, ed. William Hosley (Hartford: Wadsworth Athaneum, 1985); George Francis Dow, *The Arts and Crafts of New England, 1704–1775* (New York: Da Capo Press, 1927); the section entitled "America" in *Period Rooms in the Metropolitan Museum of Art*, ed. Amelia Peck (New Haven, CT: Metropolitan Museum of Art and Yale University Press, 1996); and Nancy Carlisle, *Cherished Possessions: A New England Legacy* (Boston: Society for the Preservation of New England Antiquities, 2003).

8. "General Introduction," *Magnalia Christi Americana*, ed. Kenneth Murdock and Elizabeth Miller (1702; Cambridge, MA: Belknap Press, 1977).

9. Thomas Jefferson, *Notes on the State of Virginia*, ed. Frank Shuffelton (1785; New York: Penguin Books, 1999), pp. 68–71, 99, 170. See also Drew McCoy, *The Elusive Republic: Political Economy in Jeffersonian America* (Chapel Hill: University of North Carolina Press, 1980), for a compelling treatment of Americans' perception of themselves as a young, uncorrupted people.

10. Quoted from Gordon Wood's Pulitzer Prize–winning *Radicalism of the American Revolution* (New York: Vintage Books, 1993), p. 6. For a more explicit treatment of the

postcolonial ideological status of the early United States, see Karianne Yokota's unpublished dissertation, "Post-Colonial America: Transatlantic Networks of Exchange in the Early National Period," PhD diss., University of California, Los Angeles, 2002.

11. John Singleton Copley, letter of Sept. 30, 1762, cited in "Copley-Pelham Letters," *Massachusetts Historical Collections*, ser. 1, 71 (1914): 136.

12. Letter of R. G. Bruce in London to Copley in Boston, cited in "Copley-Pelham Letters," p. 136.

13. See Joyce Appleby, "Consumption in Early Modern Social Thought," in *Consumption and the World of Goods*, ed. John Brewer and Roy Porter (New York: Routledge, 1994).

14. Fernand Braudel, *Afterthoughts on Material Civilization and Capitalism* (Baltimore: Johns Hopkins University Press, 1977), pp. 47, 69–71.

15. See Oliver Impey, "Eastern Trade and the Furnishing of the British Country House," in *The Fashion and Functioning of the British Country House*, ed. Gervase Jackson-Stops et al. (Hanover, NH: National Gallery of Art and the University Press of New England, 1989), pp. 177–91.

16. See Eric Wolf, *Europe and the People without History* (Berkeley: University of California Press, 1982), Andre Gunder Frank, *Re-Orient: Global Economy in the Asian Age* (Berkeley: University of California Press, 1998), Sucheta Mazumdar, *Sugar and Society in China: Peasants, Technology, and the World Market* (Cambridge, MA: Harvard University Press, 1998).

17. Robert B. Marks, *Origins of the Modern World: A Global and Ecological Narrative* (Lanham, MD: Rowman and Littlefield, 2002).

18. The colony of Georgia, e.g., was founded with the explicit purpose of cultivating silk for British textile mills and balancing Britain's global balance of trade. See James Oglethorpe, "A New and Accurate Account of the Provinces of South-Carolina and Georgia" (1732), reproduced in *The Publications of James Edward Oglethorpe*, ed. Rodney M. Baine (Athens: University of Georgia Press, 1994), pp. 200–240.

19. David Porter, *Ideographia: The Chinese Cipher in Early Modern Europe* (Palo Alto, CA: Stanford University Press, 2001), p. 1.

20. The English were not yet welcome on the Chinese coast and there is evidence that the Chinese abhorred the Dutch. As this chapter rests on a closer examination of the East-West interactions, however indirect and mediated, that may have been responsible for the content of the Newport wall murals, the Chinese reaction to these northern Europeans is worth noting. *T'ai-wan Fu-chih*, a Chinese gazette compiled in the late seventeenth century, portrays the Dutch in the following light (and the English, of course, were often taken for the same people as the Dutch): "The people which we call Red-hair or Red barbarians are the Dutchmen. They are also called Po-ssu-hu. They live in the extreme west of the Ocean extending from Formosa. . . . They are covetous and cunning and have good knowledge of valuable commodities and are clever in seeking profits. They spare not even their lives in looking for gain and go to the most distant regions to trade. . . . If one meets them in the high seas, one is often robbed by them . . . Wherever they go, they covet rare commodities, and contrive by all means to take possession of land" (cited in John Goldsmith Phillips, *China Trade Porcelain: An Account of Its Historical Background, Manufacture, and Decoration* [Cambridge, MA: Harvard University Press, 1956], pp. 20–21).

21. Roger Williams, "George Fox Digged out of His Burrows, or an Offer of Disputation on Fourteen Proposals Made in the Summer 1672" (Boston, 1676).

22. John Higginson, letter from Salem, Aug. 31, 1698, Higginson Family Papers, Phillips

Library, Salem. Nathaniel never did return to America to satisfy the curiosity of friends and family about his experiences in the East.

23. "East India pictures" show up often in estate inventories from Boston, New York, and Philadelphia in the first two decades of the eighteenth century. Nieuhoff traveled with the Dutch embassy in 1655. The book was first published in French in 1665 and had many successive editions in French, English, and Latin.

24. Probate Records, New York State Archives, Albany, NY.

25. Jane Row, July 8, 1756. The total inventory was £281, so she was quite well off. Cited in E. McSherry Fowble, *Two Centuries of Prints in America, 1680–1880: A Selective Catalogue of the Winterthur Museum Collection* (Charlottesville: University of Virginia Press, 1987), p. 19.

26. Arnold Montanus, *Atlas Chinesi* (London, 1671). Also from Logan's collection, to give just a few examples: Samuel Purchas's voyages, published in 1625, which includes a hundred pages on China; Martino Martini, *Sinicae Historiae Decas Prima* (Amsterdam, 1659); and *La Moral de Confucius* (Amsterdam, 1688). See the catalog "China on Our Shelves," for an exhibit (July–Oct. 1984) at the Library Company, Philadelphia, founded by Benjamin Franklin in 1741.

27. Early American Imprints, ser. 1: Evans, nos. 625 and 1953 respectively.

28. Jesuit Louis Le Comte, *Memoirs and Observations Topographical, Physical, Mathematical, Mechanical, Natural, Civil, and Ecclesiastical. Made in a Late Journey through the Empire of China, and Published in Several Letters. Particularly upon the Chinese Pottery and Varnishing; the Silk and Other Manufactures; the Pearl Fishing; the History of Plants and Animals. Description of Their Cities and Publick Works; Number of People, Their Language, Manners and Commerce; Their Habits, Oeconomy, and Government. The Philosophy of Confucius. The State of Christianity, with Many Other Curious and Useful Remarks* (London: B. Tooke, 1697); for published Jesuit letters, see *The Travels of Several Learned Missioners of the Society of Jesus, into Divers Parts of the Archipelago, India, China, and America* (Paris, 1713, and London: R. Gosling, 1714); Jean Baptiste du Halde, *The General History of China. Containing a Geographical, Historical, Chronological, Political and Physical Description of the Empire of China, Chinese-Tartary, Corea and Thibet* (London: J. Watts, 1736). Many editions, translated and untranslated, circulated in British America. See, e.g., the inventory of books first acquired by Franklin's Library Company (Catalogue of the Library Company of Philadelphia, [1741; Philadelphia: Library Company, 1956]) or Franklin's 16-page "Catalogue of Choice and Valuable Books" (Philadelphia, 1744.) For Newport, see the original collections catalog for the Redwood Library, chartered in 1747.

29. Portrait of Ezra Stiles by Samuel King, Yale University Art Gallery, New Haven, CT.

30. The Chinese emperor initially looked kindly on the Jesuits, who he deemed less disruptive than other sects within his realm. A 1692 decree proclaimed: "The Europeans are very quiet; they do not excite any disturbances in the provinces, they do no harm to anyone, they commit no crimes, and their doctrine has nothing in common with that of the false sects in the empire, nor has it any tendency to excite sedition. . . . We decide therefore that all temples dedicated to the Lord of heaven, in whatever place they may be found, ought to be preserved, and that it may be permitted to all who wish to worship this God to enter these temples, offer him incense, and perform the ceremonies practised according to ancient custom by the Christians. Therefore let no one henceforth offer them any opposition." Cited in Stephen Neill, *A History of Christian Missions* (Harmondsworth: Penguin Books, 1964), pp. 189–90; see also Dun Jen Li, *China in Transition, 1517–1911* (New York: Van Nostrand

Reinhold, 1969), and Kenneth S. Latroutte, *History of Christian Missions in China* (New York: Russell and Russell, 1967).

31. *Boston News-Letter*, May 11 and May 18, 1719.

32. Cited in Dun Jen Li, *China in Transition*, p. 22.

33. *Boston Gazette*, June 13, 1720.

34. See Pierre Stein, "Boucher's Chinoiseries: Some New Sources," *The Burlington Magazine* 138, no. 1122 (Sept. 1996): 598–604.

35. The term "japanning," which describes imitation Asian lacquering, may have originated with mid-seventeenth-century contact between the Dutch and the Japanese. At this time Japanese lacquer screens were held in the highest esteem among Asian lacquer connoisseurs (Oliver Impey and Mary Tregear, *Oriental Lacquer: Chinese and Japanese Lacquer from the Ashmolean Museum Collections* [Oxford: Oxford University Press, 1983]).

36. See esp. Dean A. Fales, "Boston Japanned Furniture," in *Boston Furniture of the Eighteenth Century: A Conference Held by the Colonial Society of Massachusetts, May 11–12, 1972* (Charlottesville: University Press of Virginia, 1974), pp. 49–69; also John H. Hill, "The History and Technique of Japanning and the Restoration of the Pimm Highboy," *American Art Journal* 8, no. 2 (Nov. 1976): 59–84. Hill points out that Dutch japanners actually brought Chinese lacquer artists into Europe for training, and that there was much secrecy and competition that surrounded studio japanning in Europe (pp. 60–61).

37. Skinner's American Furniture and Decorative Arts Auction, Nov. 8, 2004.

38. Willyam is named as the son of Richard (*Records of the First Church in Boston, Collections of the Colonial Society of Massachusetts* 40 [Boston: The Society, 1961], p. 346). Marriage Records of South Congregational Church, cited in HABS RI-34, pp. 2, 6.

39. William S. Appleton, *Boston Births, Marriages, and Deaths, 1630–1699, and Boston Births, 1700–1800* (1883; Baltimore: Genealogical Publishing Co., 1978).

40. A deed for an adjacent property defines its western boundary as "the lot of Mr. Gibbs." The "Gibbs lot" is also cited in the will of Mary Stanton, née Clarke (HABS RI-34, p. 6).

41. The property was originally owned by Jeremiah Clarke (Newport Land Deeds). In 1704 an inventory for a John Clarke, mariner, is recorded in Newport and, a few weeks later, that of his widow Elizabeth (Town Council Book I). These two may have been residing in the house subsequently bought by Gibbs.

42. HABS report RI-34.

43. *Gleanings from Newport Court Files, 1659–1783*, action dated 1727/8, p. 349.

44. Estate of Capt. William Gibbs, Feb. 17, 1728/9, Newport Town Council Book 6, p. 163.

45. Gibbs's inventory of fifteen chairs, two tables, a clock and looking glass, as well as the paint supplies, is clearly a partial account of the household belongings, most of which obviously passed unencumbered to his daughter and son-in-law. Gardner's Dec. 6, 1731, inventory is found in Newport Town Council Book 7, pp. 89–92.

46. Richard Randall, "William Randall, Boston Japanner," *Magazine Antiques* (May 1974): 1127–31; and Robert Emlen, "A Masterful William Claggett Clock," *Magazine Antiques* (Sept. 1980): 502–7.

47. The term is used by Nina Fletcher Little in *American Decorative Wall Painting, 1700–1850*, New England ed. (New York: E. P. Dutton, 1989).

48. "A Notebook and a Quest," *Magazine Antiques* 32, no. 1 (July 1937): 8–9.

49. A section of this paneling was installed in the American Wing of the Metropolitan Museum of Art in 1926. See Charles O. Cornelius, "Colonial Painted Paneling," *Bulletin of*

the Metropolitan Museum of Art 21 (Jan. 1926): 6–7; and Little, *American Decorative Wall Painting*, pp. 12–15.

50. I would like to thank Joseph Cullon for this insight.

51. See Lesley Hoskins, *The Papered Wall: The History, Patterns, and Techniques of Wallpaper* (New York: Thames and Hudson, 2005).

52. In the late seventeenth and early eighteenth centuries the screens were more commonly called "Bantam Work" for another transshipment point, the Dutch port of Bantam in Java; see Sir Henry Garner, "Coromandel Laccuer," in his *Chinese Lacquer* (London: Faber and Faber, 1979), pp. 259–63; and *Two Hundred Years of Chinese Lacquer*, exhibition catalog presented by the Oriental Ceramic Society of Hong Kong and the Art Gallery of the Chinese University of Hong Kong, Sept. 24-Nov. 21, 1993. See also W. de Kesel and Greet Dhondt, *Coromandel Lacquer Screens* (Gent: Snoeck-Ducaju and Zoon, 2002), p. 306.

53. De Kesel and Dhondt, *Coromandel Lacquer Screens*, p. 26.

54. Kung-Hsin Chu, *Transmission of Chinese Lacquer Art to the West: A Study Based on Early Kang-His Lacquer Screen "Spring Morning in the Han Palace"* (Taipei: National Palace Museum, 1995), pp. 35–37.

55. Ibid., p. 8.

56. Daniëlle Kisluk-Grosheide, "Lacquer and Porcelain as en Suite Decoration in Room Interiors," in *Schwartz Porcelain: The Lacquer Craze and Its Impact on European Porcelain*, ed. Monika Kopplin (Munich: Heimer, 2004), pp. 38–49.

57. Ibid., p. 43; and Oliver Impey, "Eastern Trade and the Furnishing of the British Country House," in *Fashioning and Functioning of a British Country House*, Studies in the History of Art, National Gallery of Art (Manchester, NH: University Press of New England, 1989).

58. This room is covered with European japan work. Perhaps the only surviving seventeenth-century Chinese lacquer walls were from the former Stadholder's Court of Leeuwarden dating to 1695, subsequently preserved in the Rijksmuseum, Amsterdam.

59. See, e.g., Kee Il Choi, "Japan and Design in Early Chinese Export Art," *Magazine Antiques* (Sept. 2000).

60. French engraver François Boucher, e.g., may have been influenced by an illustrated 1696 edition of *Yuzhi gengzhi tu*, an ancient Chinese treatise on tilling and weaving (see Perrin Stein, "Boucher's Chinoiseries: Some New Sources," *Burlington Magazine* 138 [Sept. 1996]: 598–604). See also the long list of books that were in the Bodleian Library, Oxford, at the end of the seventeenth century, "Chinese Books in Europe in the Seventeenth Century," www.bodley.ox.ac.uk/users/djh/17thcent/17theu.htm.

61. Richard Rudolph, "Eighteenth Century Newport and Its Merchants," *Newport History* 51, no. 2 (Spring 1978): 21–38.

62. See letter from Bellomont cited in Robert C. Ritchie, *Captain Kidd and the War against the Pirates* (Cambridge, MA: Harvard University Press, 1986), p. 178.

63. Newport Town Council Book 2:354, 247, 265 respectively.

64. I would like to thank Kee Il Choi for this observation. Christian J. A. Jörg argues that the content of Chinese Coromandel screens is too different in subject matter to have served as a model for Gibbs's murals (see "Collector's Notes," *Magazine Antiques* (Feb. 2007): 34.)

65. De Kesel and Dhondt's *Coromandel Lacquer Screens* gives a good overview of the thematic content of these screens, which includes primarily palace scenes, the world of the immortals or of scholars, legendary panoramas, and in the smaller panels flora and fauna and other auspicious symbols.

66. Jonathan Spence, *The Chan's Great Continent: China in Western Minds* (New York: Norton, 1998), pp. 18–19.

67. Ibid., p. 21.

68. Theodor de Bry's *Grand Voyages* concerns Brazil, while the *Petit Voyages* concerns the East Indies. The latter was first published in 1598 with German text and in 1599 with Latin text. These images are also available at http://www.historical-prints.co.uk.

69. See, e.g., Jérôme Bourgon, "Chinese Executions: Visualizing their Difference with European Supplices," *European Journal of East Asian Studies* (Dec. 2003): 151. Bourgon notes, "That the Chinese were singled out by a native cruelty in refined tortures became a widespread representation at the turn of the twentieth century [in Europe]." Even today, the expression "Chinese torture" is used in the United States unthinkingly, although not in reference to bodily injury (*Brewer's Dictionary of Phrase and Fable*, 2000).

70. Downing, *Architectural Heritage*, pp. 453–54.

71. The Taoist hell had ten presiding judges, but the concept of eighteen hells is very common in Chinese popular culture. For information on Buddhist hells, see Anne Goodrich Swann, *Chinese Hells: The Peking Temple of Eighteen Hells and Chinese Conception of Hell* (St. Augustin: Monumenta Serica, 1981), and Wolfram Eberhard, *Guilt and Sin in Traditional China* (Berkeley: University of California Press, 1967).

72. Karil Kucera, "Cliff Notes: Text and Image at Baodingshan," PhD diss., Department of History of Art, University of Kansas, 2002.

73. Tang dynasty–era swords (AD 618–907) and Ottoman era–swords (beginning in thirteenth century) have a similar shape as people of Turkic ethnicity interacted with the military elite of the Tang dynasty (Charles Benn, *China's Golden Age: Everyday Life in the Tang Dynasty* [Oxford University Press, 2002], pp. 2–3). Margaret Medley points out that in the Tang Dynasty "foreign influences are easily discerned in almost every medium" (*The Chinese Potter: A Practical History of Chinese Ceramics* [London: Phaidon Press, 1989], pp. 75–77). Unless Gibbs was extracting elements from a Chinese original, he would have been more familiar with the Turkish material culture.

74. Images of the Baodingshan rock carvings can be seen in Angela Falco Howard, *Summit of Treasures: Buddhist Cave Art of Dazu China* (Trumbull, CT: Wetherhill, 2001).

75. I would like to thank Jérôme Bourgon of the Turandot research project on "Chinese torture, supplice chinois" for giving me the big picture on this complex topic. See also Goodrich Swann, *Chinese Hells*, pp. 43–66, for a comprehensive list of the typical Buddhist hells, based on a temple in Beijing.

76. Raymond T. McNally and Radu Florescu, *In Search of Dracula: The History of Dracula and Vampires* (Boston: Houghton Mifflin, 1994).

77. Michel Foucault, *Discipline and Punish: The Birth of the Prison* (New York: Vintage, 1979).

78. A woodcut print from a German pamphlet. This is only one example of hundreds of similar illustrations.

79. Herodotus, *Inquiries*, trans. Shlomo Felberbaum, book 3, installment 19, text online at http://www.losttrails.com/index.html.

80. Most information today on Dracula comes from pamphlets published in the Holy Roman Empire. The first known example dates to 1488, not long after his death (McNally and Florescu, *In Search of Dracula*), p. 225.

81. See William Layher, "Horrors of the East: Printing *Dracole Wayda* in Fifteenth-Century Germany," *Daphnis* 37 (2008): 11–32.

82. The pope rescinded his bull and the leader was tortured on a burning hot throne, but he ultimately became a martyr. This was one of the "great peasant revolts" cited by Friedrich Engels in his notes to Wilhelm Zimmermann's *History of the Great Peasant War* (1926).

83. Curators today call these objects "European subject." See Kee Il Choi, "Japan and Design in Early Chinese Export Art," *Magazine Antiques* (Sept. 2000); and Choi, "A Chinese Porcelain 'European-Subject' Baluster Vase and Its Export Design Context," *Oriental Art* 48, no. 1 (2002): 17–22.

84. See Choi, "European-Subject Baluster Vase," p. 19.

85. Daniel Updike lived in Newport and Wickford and died in 1757.

86. De Kesel and Dhondt, *Coromandel Lacquer Screens*, pp. 81–83.

87. See Craig Clunas, "Human Figures in the Decoration of Ming Lacquer," *Oriental Art* 32, no. 2 (1986): 172–87.

88. Spence, *The Chan's Great Continent*, pp. 32–33.

89. *American Weekly Mercury*, Philadelphia, April 28, 1720, cited in Fowble, *Two Centuries of Prints*, p. 7.

90. *Annals of Trinity Church, Newport, Rhode Island, 1630–1821*, Newport, 1890.

91. Similar stories were spread about the Jesuits among Native Americans (see Francis Parkman, *Jesuits in North America in the Seventeenth Century* [Boston, 1867]).

92. Downing, *Architectural Heritage*, p. 453.

93. Stevens, *History of the Vernon House*, pp. 44–46.

94. HABS Report-RI 34.

Chapter 3

1. Local and European earthenwares and stonewares were so readily available in the colonial countryside that Livingston, in Albany, would not need to write to her husband in New York City for these types of cups, which were furthermore never used with "saucers." Letters dated July 16, 18, and 21, 1717, from Alida Livingston, Livingston Manor (near Albany), to Robert Livingston, New York City. The Gilder Lehrman Collection, New York, NY.

2. Curator William Sargent at the Peabody Essex Museum in Salem has displayed examples of Delft next to Chinese porcelain where it is impossible to determine, looking through the glass of the display case, which is the authentic Chinese article and which the European imitation. See also figs. 3.2 and 3.3 from the Peabody Essex Museum.

3. Art historian Susan Gray Detweiler states in her book *George Washington's Chinaware* (New York: Harry N. Abrams, 1982), e.g., "Washington—as the most prominent consumer in the new nation—participated in the post-war dissolution of an English monopoly on American taste and trade and the turn to China and France as new sources for porcelain tableware." China was not a "new" source for cultural inspiration, and certainly not for porcelain, in the early republic. This misperception has permeated much of the scholarly literature treating America's relationship to China. Indeed, Detweiler points out that a reconstruction of the Washington estate yields many pieces of Chinese porcelain dating to the years before his marriage in 1759.

4. Colonial American population growth surged in the eighteenth century, and immigration accounted for roughly 20 percent of the white population's increase, or about 270,000 white settlers. Many more immigrants arrived in the middle colonies where land was plentiful than in New England, which partly explains the rise of Philadelphia as a colonial metropolitan center. See Marc Egnal, "The Economic Development of the Thirteen Colonies, 1720 to 1775," *William and Mary Quarterly* 32, no. 2 (Apr. 1975): 195; and US Bureau

of the Census, *Historical Statistics of the United States, Colonial Times to 1957* (Washington DC, 1957), p. 756. For works on eighteenth-century orientalism, see Oliver Impey, *Chinoiserie: The Impact of European Styles on Western Art Decoration* (New York: Scribners, 1977); and "Eastern Trade and the Furnishing of the British Country House," in *The Fashioning and Functioning of the British Country House*, Studies in the History of Art 25 (Manchester, NH: National Gallery of Art and University Press of New England, 1989); also Hugh Honour, *Chinoiserie: The Vision of Cathay* (New York: Harper and Row, 1973); and Donald F. Lach, *Asia in the Making of Europe* (University of Chicago Press, 1965), esp. vol. 2.

5. Robert Finlay, "Pilgrim Art: The Culture of Porcelain in World History," *Journal of World History* 9, no. 2 (1998): 141–87, at 142.

6. A selection would include *The Social Life of Things: Commodities in Cultural Perspective*, ed. Arjun Appadurai (Cambridge: Cambridge University Press, 1986); Mary C. Beaudry, Lauren J. Cook, and Stephen A. Mrozowski, "Artifacts and Active Voices: Material Culture as Social Discourse," in *Archaeology of Inequality*, ed. Randall McGuire and Robert Poynter (Oxford: Basil Blackwell, 1991), pp. 150–91; Cary Carson, Ronald Hoffman, and Peter Albert, *Of Consuming Interests: The Style of Life in the Eighteenth Century* (Charlottesville: University of Virginia Press, 1994); James Deetz, *In Small Things Forgotten* (New York: Anchor, 1996); Mark P. Leone, "Georgian Order as the Order of Merchant Capitalism in Annapolis, Maryland," in *Recovery of Meaning: Historical Archaeology in the Eastern United States*, ed. Mark P. Leone and Parker B. Potter (Clinton Corners, NY: Percheron Press, 2003); Carole Shammas, *Pre-Industrial Consumer in England and America* (Oxford, 1990); Margaretta Lovell, *Art in a Season of Revolution: Painters, Artisans, and Patrons in Early America* (Philadelphia: University of Pennsylvania Press, 2005).

7. See Sucheta Mazumdar, *Sugar and Society in China: Peasants, Technologies, and the World Market* (Harvard University Press, 1998); T. H. Breen, *Marketplace of Revolution* (Oxford: Oxford University Press, 2004); David Hancock, *Citizens of the World: London Merchants and the Integration of the British Atlantic Community, 1735–1785* (Cambridge: Cambridge University Press, 1997); Phyllis W. Hunter, *Purchasing Identity in the Atlantic World: Massachusetts Merchants, 1670–1780* (Ithaca, NY: Cornell University Press, 2001); and Robert St. George, *Conversing by Signs: Poetics of Implication in Colonial New England Culture* (Chapel Hill: University of North Carolina Press, 1998) for works that link the dynamics of trade and commerce with the meaning of commodities and personal possessions within community contexts.

8. Mazumdar, *Sugar and Society*, pp. 60–119; E. H. Pritchard, "Struggle for Control of the China Trade during the Eighteenth Century," *Pacific Historical Review* 3 (1934): 280–94; Holden Furber, *Rival Empires of Trade in the Orient, 1600–1800*, (Minneapolis: University of Minnesota Press, 1976); and Holden Furber, *John Company at Work: A Study of European Expansion in India in the Late Eighteenth Century* (Cambridge, MA: Harvard University Press, 1948).

9. On the packing of porcelain, see the contemporary account of Jean-Baptiste Du Halde, *General History of China* (London, 1736), pp. 342–44.

10. See nn. 56 and 57 in chap. 1 for shipwreck sites yielding Chinese porcelain; also Robert Marx and Jennifer Marx, *Treasure Lost at Sea: Diving the World's Great Shipwrecks* (Buffalo, NY: Firefly Press, 2003).

11. John Goldsmith Phillips, *China Trade Porcelain: An Account of Its Historical Background, Manufacture, and Decoration and a Study of the Helena Woolworth McCann Collection* (Cambridge, MA: Harvard University Press, 1956).

12. T. Volker, *Porcelain and the Dutch East India Company* (Leiden: E. J. Brill, 1971); Phillips, *China Trade Porcelain*; John E. Volmer et al., *Silk Roads—China Ships* (Toronto: Royal Ontario Museum, 1983).

13. Robert Finlay, "Pilgrim Art: The Culture of Porcelain in World History," *Journal of World History* 9, no. 2 (Fall 1998): 141–87.

14. *Spendidum furtum*, Latin for "magnificent theft," was the expression used by King James I for the gifts merchant-adventurers compensated him with for his support of their transoceanic adventures.

15. Sarah Richards, *Eighteenth-Century Ceramics: Products for a Civilised Society* (Manchester: Manchester University Press, 1999), pp. 58–59.

16. K. N. Chaudhuri, *Trading World of Asia and the English East India Company* (Cambridge: Cambridge University Press, 2006), pp. 406–10; Phillips, *China Trade Porcelain*, pp. 39–41. Holden Furber argues that allowing company employees to trade privately deterred them from excessive smuggling, something that had plagued the Dutch East India Company (*Rival Empires of Trade*, pp. 275–76).

17. Supercargo instructions and outgoing letters are contained in Despatch Books at the British Library. The quote is from Nov. 1, 1726, vol. 103, p. 508, cited in Chaudhuri, *Trading World*, pp. 408, 610.

18. Richards, *Eighteenth-Century Ceramics*, p. 59; Furber, *Rival Empires of Trade*, pp. 129, 134.

19. Thomas R. Hazard, *Jonny-Cake Letters* (Providence, 1882); see also Thomas W. Bicknell, "Rhode Island Orchards," *History of the State of Rhode Island and Providence Plantations*, vol. 3 (New York: American Historical Society, 1920); and "Origins of the Rhode Island Greening," *Boston Transcript*, April 14, 1908.

20. See Hancock's *Citizens of the World* for a book-length, biographical examination of several merchants of this new breed.

21. The first tax on Chinese porcelain was issued in 1704 by Queen Anne, but tea had been taxed since 1660. In 1721, importing tea from any foreign parts was outlawed (7 Geo. I c. 21 ¶12). Silk has its own very complex history in Europe as a silk-weaving industry existed there, although supplies of raw silk were meager. Finished Asian textiles were banned in England for much of the eighteenth century (pers. comm., Linda Eaton, Winterthur Museum.)

22. *Boston Gazette*, June 13, 1720.

23. Naval Office shipping lists for Massachusetts' entrances and clearances from 1686 to 1765 record only two instances of porcelain entering Boston, and both times it came off of prize ships rather than merchant ships from London (Naval Office Shipping Lists, Massachusetts Historical Society [hereafter MHS]).

24. Stephen Matchak, "Salem's Trading Partners: A Colonial and Federal Comparison," paper presented at the annual meeting of the Northeast Society for Eighteenth-Century Studies, Salem State College, Nov. 10, 2006; for the importance of southern Europe and the West Indies to Salem, see also Hunter, *Purchasing Identity*, pp. 145–46. John J. McCusker and Russell R. Menard note that, "for certain colonies, at least, exports coastwise rivaled transoceanic commerce in importance" (*The Economy of British America, 1607–1789* [Chapel Hill: University of North Carolina Press, 1985], p. 78). See also Cathy Matson's work on colonial merchants in New York, where she found that only an elite group traded in London: "'Damned Scoundrels' and 'Libertisme of Trade': Freedom and Regulation in Colonial New York's Fur and Grain Trades," *William and Mary Quarterly* 51 (July 1994): 389–418,

and *Merchants and Empire: Trading in Colonial New York* (Johns Hopkins University Press, 1998).

25. See, e.g., correspondence in the 1690s between Major John Higginson in Salem with John Tucker and Thomas Hayler in Bilboa. Higginson Papers, Phillips Library, Salem.

26. Harry E. Cross, "South American Bullion Production and Export, 1550–1750," in *Precious Metals in the Later Medieval and Early Modern Worlds*, ed. J. F. Richards (Durham, NC: Carolina Academic Press, 1983), pp. 397–423.

27. Ibid., pp. 407, 397.

28. Alejandra Irigoin, like Dennis O. Flynn and Arturo Giraldez (eds., "Introduction," *Metals and Monies in an Emerging Global Economy* [Brookfield, VT: Ashgate/Variorum, 1997]), Kenneth Pomeranz (*The Great Divergence: Europe, China, and the Making of the Modern World Economy* [Princeton, NJ: Princeton University Press, 2000]) and Andre Gunder Frank, *ReOrient: Global Economy in the Asian Age* (Berkeley: University of California Press, 1998), considers silver a commodity rather than exclusively as specie ("The End of a Silver Era: The Consequences of the Breakdown of the Spanish Peso Standard in China and the United States," *Journal of World History* 20, no. 2 [June 2009]: 207–44, at 208; and "Bringing the New World back into Global History: Spanish American Silver Bound to China on American Vessels," paper presented at the Boston Area Latin American History Workshop, April 6, 2005).

29. Nuala Zahedieh, "The Merchants of Port Royal, Jamaica, and the Spanish Contraband Trade, 1655–1692," *William and Mary Quarterly* 43, no. 4 (Oct. 1986): 570–93.

30. Nuala Zahedieh, "Economy," *British Atlantic World, 1500–1800*, ed. David Armitage and Michael Braddick (New York: Palgrave, 2009), p. 54.

31. James Henretta and Gregory Nobles, *Evolution and Revolution: American Society, 1600–1820* (Lexington, MA: D. C. Heath, 1987), pp. 116–18; McCusker and Menard, *Economy of British America*, pp. 82–86; Jacob Price, "Economic Function and the Growth of American Port Towns in the Eighteenth Century," *Perspectives in American History* 8 (1974): 121–86.

32. Charles Knowles to the Board of Trade, Nov. 18, 1752, cited in McCusker and Menard, *Economy of British America*, p. 84.

33. For entrances in the years 1751 and 1774 in Salem, Matchak did not find silver mentioned once ("Salem's Trading Partners").

34. Invoice for Robert Livingston Jr., June 1732, Livingston Papers no. 2503, Gilder Lehrman Collection, New York, NY.

35. McCusker and Menard note that after the Molasses Act of 1733 sugar, molasses, and rum were regularly and openly "smuggled" into northeastern ports, diminishing the value of colonial trade records for historians (*Economy of British America*, p. 78). See also customs officials' reports from the colonies, especially after 1763, such as John Temple's reports from Boston ("Great Britain Commissioners of Customs, 1764–74; Letters and Records of John Temple," MHS).

36. Benjamin Greene Ledger, 1734–58, reel 1, MHS.

37. The Browns used Stephen Gregory, who spoke French and signed his name *Gregoire* in Hispaniola; see James B. Hedges, *The Browns of Providence Plantations: The Colonial Years* (Providence, RI: Brown University Press, 1968), p. 41.

38. Ibid., pp. 43–44.

39. Francis Higginson, letter to James Jeffrey dated Nov. 7, 1758; Higginson Papers, box 2, f. 1718–59, MHS.

40. Furber, *Rival Empires of Trade*, p. 129.

41. Ibid., pp. 120–21.

42. Ibid., p. 117.

43. India Office Records, June 9, 1721, cited in ibid., p. 365.

44. Report dated Oct. 2, 1721, cited in Furber, *Rival Empires of Trade*, p. 366.

45. Furber, *Rival Empires of Trade*, pp. 144–46, 226.

46. Ibid., p. 140; see also G. V. Scammell, "European Exiles, Renegades, and Outlaws and the Maritime Economy of Asia," *Modern Asian Studies* 26, no. 4 (Oct. 1992): 641–61.

47. Adam Smith, *Wealth of Nations*, book 2, chap. 7.

48. *New Hampshire Gazette*, July 21, 1761.

49. *American Weekly Mercury*, Philadelphia, July 18, 1723.

50. The captain claims to have served the Compagnie since 1752. Letter in French signed "Gloro," from Henebon near Lorient, January 10, 1777, deposited at the American Philosophical Society.

51. [Benjamin Franklin], "Colonist's Advocate: X," *Public Advertiser*, Feb. 19, 1770.

52. *Boston Gazette*, Oct. 2, 1721.

53. Malachy Postlethwayt, *The Universal Dictionary of Trade and Commerce: with Large Additions and Improvements, Adapting the Same to the Present State of British Affairs in America, since the Last Treaty of Peace Made in the Year 1763* (London, 1774).

54. Wim Klooster, "Curaçao and the Caribbean Transit Trade," in *Riches from Atlantic Commerce: Dutch Transatlantic Shipping, 1585–1817*, ed. Johannes Postma and Victor Enthoven (Boston: Brill, 2003), pp. 203–18.

55. For a masterful account of the global trading network maintained by individual Dutch merchants, see John E. Wills, *1688: A Global History* (New York: Norton, 2001). Lisa Jardine's *Going Dutch: How England Plundered Holland's Glory* (New York: Harper's, 2009) offers excellent background on overlapping English and Dutch circuits of overseas trade. For examples of Jewish trade networks lacing the globe from medieval times forward, see Gedalia Yogev, *Diamonds and Coral: Anglo-Dutch Jews and Eighteenth-Century Trade* (Leicester: Leicester University Press, 1978).

56. Phillip Livingston to Robert Livingston Jr., Sept. and Dec. 1740, Livingston Papers nos. 2602 and 2607, Gilder Lehrman Collection (hereafter GLC), New York, NY.

57. "Store at the Manner," accounting dated May 20, 1735, Livingston Papers, GLC.

58. Thomas Willing to Robert Morris, Nov. 1756, "Charles Willing and Son Letterbooks," HSP.

59. Labels penned by Anne Allen Ives (1810–1884), recorded in an inventory of the bequest taken in 1909, Rhode Island School of Design Museum.

60. See, e.g., the daybook of Obadiah Brown, 1753–54, John Carter Brown Library, Providence, RI, Brown Family Papers, box 1076, f. 5.

61. James Brown daybook, 1745–1750, Brown Family Papers, box 1076, f. 7.

62. Hedges, *The Browns of Providence Plantations*, pp. 8–11.

63. "Memorial on Smuggling," March 12, 1784, cited in Hoh-Cheung and Lorna H. Mui, "Smuggling and the British Tea Trade before 1784," *American Historical Review* 74 (Oct. 1968): 48. See also W. A. Cole, "Trends in Eighteenth Century Smuggling," *Economic History Review* 10, no. 3 (1958): 395–410, for a complete discussion of legal vs. illegal tea trades and the impact of Parliamentary tax laws.

64. "Memorial on Smuggling," in Hoh-Cheung and Mui, pp. 51–53. Carole Shammas estimates, however, that about half the tea consumed in England before 1780 was smuggled

in, but even here the proportion of legal tea is far greater than in the colonies ("Changes in English and Anglo-American Consumption from 1550 to 1800," in *Consumer Society*, ed. Neva R. Goodwin [Covelo, CA: Island Press, 1997], p. 124).

65. John Kidd to Rawlinson and Davidson, Jan. 28, 1757, Kidd Letterbooks 1749–63, HSP.

66. That is true until 1767. O. M. Dickerson, *The Navigation Acts and the American Revolution* (Philadelphia: University of Pennsylvania Press, 1951), p. 88.

67. Thomas C. Barrow, *Trade and Empire: The British Customs Service in Colonial America, 1660–1775* (Harvard University Press, 1967), p. 150.

68. John W. Tyler, *Smugglers and Patriots: Boston Merchants and the Advent of the American Revolution* (Boston: Northeastern University Press, 1986), pp. 16, 20.

69. Peter Randolph to William Peters, July 20, 1750; Letters of the Custom House of Philadelphia, vol. 1, 1750–61, HSP.

70. On Revolutionary-era smuggling, see esp. Tyler, *Smugglers and Patriots*. On the use of the term "free trade" and sugar smuggling in Rhode Island, see Frederick B. Wiener, "Rhode Island Merchants and the Sugar Act," *New England Quarterly* 3, no. 3 (Jul. 1930): 464–500.

71. Barrow, *Trade and Empire*, pp. 84–166.

72. Andrew Brown to the Lords of Commissioners of His Majesty's Treasury, Jan. 21, 1768, Public Record Office, London (hereafter PRO).

73. Quotation from Barrow, *Trade and Empire*, p. 148.

74. The burning of the customs ship *Gaspee* is still celebrated in Rhode Island today as the first act of the Revolution.

75. Will Book 3, 1761–81, pp. 9–16, Warwick Historical Society.

76. See chart 5.2, "American Population and British Imports," in James Henretta and Gregory Nobles, *Evolution and Revolution: American Society, 1600–1820* (Lexington, MA: D. C. Heath, 1987), p. 117.

77. Estimates summarized by Labaree on the extent of illegal tea imports in the years preceding the revolution run as high as 90 percent of imported tea. Benjamin Labaree settles on the conservative estimate of 75 percent smuggled (*The Boston Tea Party* [Oxford University Press, 1964], p. 7).

78. John Kidd to Neate & Neave, June 7, 1750, John Kidd Letterbook, 1748–61, HSP.

79. Boylston Family Papers, box 86, vols. 43–66, MHS.

80. Tyler, *Smugglers and Patriots*, p. 260.

81. The most lavish inventories are found in Williamsburg and Charleston. See Graham Hood, *The Governor's Palace in Williamsburg: A Cultural Study* (Williamsburg, VA: Colonial Williamsburg Foundation, 1999), for a series of impressive estates.

82. See, e.g., Arlene Palmer Schwind, "The Ceramic Imports of Frederick Rhinelander," *Winterthur Portfolio* 19, no. 1 (Spring 1984): 21–36.

83. "Imports from Great Britain and Ireland, 1772–73," MHS manuscripts.

84. Townshend Papers, Harvard University, Lamont Library, Buccleuch Collection, reel 1, bundle 22.

85. John Goldsmith Phillips, *China Trade Porcelain* (Cambridge, MA: Harvard University Press, 1956), p. 42.

86. By comparison, only olive oil at £9,920 had a more valuable drawback, with wine and fruit at £7,000 and £2,500 respectively. Townshend Papers, reel 2, bundle 31.

87. *New York Mercury*, August 24, 1767.

88. See, e.g., George Washington's 1757 porcelain order of about fifty pieces sent to London (Detweiler, *George Washington's Chinaware*, p. 31).

89. Maxine Berg, *Luxury and Pleasure in Eighteenth-Century Britain* (Oxford: Oxford University Press, 2005), p. 317.

90. Letterbook of James Beekman, 1766–99, New York Historical Society.

91. See chart 5.2, "American Population and British Imports," in Henretta and Nobles, *Evolution and Revolution*, p. 117.

92. "Extracts from Letters Etc. to Prove the State of the Tea Trade in America," in *Tea Leaves*, ed. Francis Drake (Boston: A. O. Crane, 1884), pp. 191–98; Labaree, *Boston Tea Party*, pp. 7–14.

93. Labaree, *Boston Tea Party*, p. 12.

94. Tyler, *Smugglers and Patriots*, pp. 8–13.

95. Ibid., p. 13.

96. Jean McClure Mudge, *Chinese Export Porcelain in North America* (New York: Crown Publishers, 1986), p. 140.

97. War of Spanish Succession (1702–13, also known as Queen Anne's War); War of Quadruple Alliance (1718–20); War of Jenkins' Ear (1739–42); War of the Austrian Succession (1742–48); King George's War (1744–48); Seven Years' War (1756–63); French and Indian War (1754–63); Anglo-Cherokee War (1759–63); Pontiac's Rebellion (1763–66); First Anglo-Mysore War (1766–69). See Douglas E. Leach, *Roots of Conflict: British Armed Forces and Colonial Americans* (Chapel Hill: University of North Carolina Press, 1986); and Fred Anderson, *The Dominion of War: Empire and Liberty in North America* (New York: Viking, 2005).

98. During King George's War (1739–48), Bowler's father was among many who fitted out vessels for privateering in Newport. His was the sloop *Duke of Cumberland* of ninety tons and eight guns.

99. Capt. Blue's name is also spelled *Blew*. Howard A. Chapin, *Privateer Ships and Sailors: The First Century of American Colonial Privateering, 1625–1725* (Toulon: G. Mouton, 1926), pp. 135–37.

100. "The Itinerarium of Dr. Alexander Hamilton, 1744," cited in Carl E. Swanson, "American Privateering and Imperial Warfare, 1739–1748," *William and Mary Quarterly* 42, no. 3 (1985): 357–82, at 358.

101. The list of important Americans whose wealth and political power was built on privateering and outright pillaging is impressive, beginning in the seventeenth century with Governor (later Sir) William Phips of New Hampshire and extending through the revolution. It includes William Bingham, the founding father of the first bank of the United States.

102. 1750 estate inventory of John Palmer of Marblehead, Oct. 15, 1750, vol. 329, Essex County Probate Records, 1638–1840.

103. Richard C. Nylander, "The Jonathan Sayward House, York, Maine," *Antiques* (Sept. 1979): 567–78. The Sayward-Wheeler House, with its china closet and plates intact, is open once a month for visitors. See http://fortress.uccb.ns.ca/archaeology/welcome.htm for an online tour of the archaeological remains of the Chinese ceramics used by the French at Louisbourg.

104. The collector was Anne Allen Ives, 1810–84, daughter of China trader Sullivan Dorr and wife to China trader Moses Brown Ives. Her daughter Hope Brown Russell bequeathed the collection to the Rhode Island School of Design Museum of Art in 1909.

105. Items no. 976–79, 984–87 in the 1909 "Invoice" of Hope Brown Russell's bequest to the Rhode Island School of Design Museum of Art.

106. For an account of the loss of the *Geldermalsen*, see J. R. Bruijn, F. S. Gaastra, and I. Schöffer, *Dutch-Asiatic Shipping in the 17th and 18th Centuries*, 3 vols. (The Hague,

1979, 1987); Christie's Amsterdam B.V., *The Nanking Cargo, Chinese Porcelain and Gold, European Glass and Stoneware, Recovered by Captain Michael Hatcher from a European Ship Wrecked in the South China Seas* (Amsterdam, 1986); and C. J. A. Jörg, *The Geldermalsen: History and Porcelain* (Groningen: Kemper Publishers, 1986).

107. By the middle of the first half of the eighteenth century, all merchants carried a letter of marque and arms, regardless of intentions, because they could never be sure when they might be attacked by another vessel. "Flags of truce" were vessels bearing a flag of neutrality, also granted by a sovereign power, and intended for transferring prisoners of war. Presumably such vessels were nonbelligerent and were not to be attacked. However, these flags seem to have afforded little protection from privateers and were raised and lowered at will while raiding other ships (see Alexander B. Hawes, *Off Soundings: Aspects of the Maritime History of Rhode Island* [Chevy Chase, MD: Posterity Press, 1999]; William P. Sheffield, *Privateersmen of Newport*, Address given before the Rhode Island Historical Society [hereafter RIHS], 1883; and the *Oxford English Dictionary*).

108. From 1757 to 1761 Bowler was in a partnership with Newport merchant Christopher Champlin. Information on Bowler and Champlin, and their vessels, is found in the Champlin Papers, MS 20, at the RIHS; the Champlin Account Book, 1757–69, Newport Historical Society; and *Commerce of Rhode Island, 1726–1800*, vol. 1, Collections of the MHS, Boston, 1914.

109. Daniel and Charles Crommelin took the freeman's oath in New York in 1698, and their descendants held prominent positions in both that city and Amsterdam (*Commerce of Rhode Island*, 2:90). In 1757, they sent the brig *George*, then in New York, out on a privateering venture. Their intent was to offer the job to Captain Duncan, who could "go home to Holland in [the *Elizabeth & Mary*] if he declines privateering in George" (Champlin Papers, April 4, 1757).

110. Champlin Papers, Sept. 29, 1757.

111. Ibid., Aug. 4, 1758. This one is addressed to "Metcalf Bowler & Co." from Livingston.

112. Ibid., Aug. 18, 1758.

113. James Duncan to Bowler and Champlin, in ibid., Feb. 14, 1760.

114. Hawes, *Off Soundings*, p. 87.

115. Misc. Manuscripts Collection, MS 9001-F, "Flaggs of Truce," RIHS.

116. In 1762 Bowler is listed as owner of the *Defiance*. A vessel by this name had been the most successful privateer of King George's War (1739–48) and Bowler's is thought to be the very same vessel. James Duncan was captain. Robert Grieve, *Sea Trade and Its Development in Rhode Island and Providence Plantations* (Providence, RI, 1919).

117. Hazard, *Jonny-Cake Letters*; see also Bicknell, "Rhode Island Orchards" vol. 3; and "Origins of the Rhode Island Greening," *Boston Transcript*, April 14, 1908; Metcalf Bowler, Esq., "A Treatise on Agriculture and Practical Husbandry: Designed for the Information of Landowners and Farmers" (Providence, RI: Bennett Wheeler, 1786).

118. During the revolution Bowler both served as speaker of the colonial legislature and raised support for Continental troops while spying for the British. His loyalties clearly lay entirely outside Euro-American nationalizing state politics. I'd like to thank Jim Egan for this perspective.

119. Historical information on both Norden and Cratey can be found in the *Essex Institute Historical Collections*, vols. 4 and 5, vol. 41 (pp. 191, 386), vol. 42 (pp. 117–18, 202, 353–54), vol. 46 (pp. 9, 309), vol. 54 (pp. 71, 83, 281); and in Christine Heyrman, *Com-*

merce and Culture: The Maritime Communities of Colonial Massachusetts (New York: W. W. Norton, 1984), pp. 227, 233–44.

120. Heyrman, *Commerce and Culture*, p. 244.

121. In Cratey's estate inventory, his dwelling house, land, and out houses were valued at £750. Yet Norden purchased them in 1712 from Cratey's son, after a complicated transfer of property that disinherited Cratey's daughter, for a mere £240. See Essex County Probate Records, vol. 305, and Essex Registry of Deeds, book 25, leaf 187.

122. Essex County Probate Records, vol. 319.

123. *American Weekly Mercury*, Philadelphia, Dec. 26, 1732. See also, e.g., two similar auction advertisements, *New England Weekly Journal*, Sept. 11, 1739, and *New York Weekly Journal*, April 14, 1740.

124. There are hundreds of such boxed-out ads in every colonial newspaper. For one example, see the June 28, 1739 issue of *American Weekly Mercury*.

125. Mrs. Pratt of mid-eighteenth-century Newport runs a typical china shop—and it is at home. See Hodge, "A Middling Gentility."

126. See Arthur L. Jensen, *The Maritime Commerce of Colonial Philadelphia* (Madison: University of Wisconsin, 1963), pp. 11–15.

127. For Newport, see Hodge, "A Middling Gentility"; for Boston and Salem, see Hunter, *Purchasing Identity*; for New York, see Cathy Matson, *Merchants and Empire: Trading in Colonial New York* (Baltimore: Johns Hopkins University Press, 1998).

128. Estate inventory of Richard Grafton, Jan. 16, 1743, from the files of Leslie Grigsby, Winterthur Museum.

129. Charles Willing to Robert Hibbert in Manchester, July 30, 1754, in Charles Willing & Son Letterbook, June-November, 1754, Willing Papers, HSP.

130. Charles Willing, letters of August 6 and October 25, 1754, respectively, in Charles Willing & Son Letterbook, June-November, 1754, Willing Papers, HSP.

131. Samuel Powell Jr. daybook, June 28, 1735, collection 232, box 2, Joseph Downs Collection, Winterthur.

132. Quaker merchant William Wilson, also of Philadelphia and selling the same sorts of commodities but twenty years later, wrote often to his captains to avoid any such ill-gotten gains. Quakers were pacifists. William Wilson Letterbook, 1757, Joseph Downs Collection, Winterthur.

133. "Sailing orders to Sam'l Bicknell, Master of *Tryall*, Philadelphia 7/23/1730," Joseph Downs Collection, Winterthur.

134. "July 25, 1755, Persons Licensed to Sell Tea, Coffee and Chinaware the Ensuing Years," Hancock Papers, misc. papers, 1728–1825, reel 2, MHS.

135. *New Hampshire Gazette*, April 3, 1761.

136. Breen, *Marketplace of Revolution*, p. 35.

137. For an excellent study on the use of probate inventories, see *Early American Probate Inventories*, ed. Peter Benes (Boston: Boston University, 1989).

138. Early southern estates were sometimes valued in tobacco and New York estates in guilders or even wampum.

139. Curators are not certain what the adjective "burnt" meant, but our best guess is that it refers to porcelain of the "Imari" palate (Amanda Lange, pers. comm.). Large quantities of Japanese ware from Imari first carried this blue underglaze/*rouge-de-fer* overglaze decorative motif in the mid-seventeenth century. The Chinese subsequently imitated this color scheme, which proved very popular in the West.

140. Adolph Philipse (d.1749), for example.

141. Abbott Lowell Cummings states in *Rural Household Inventories: Establishing the Names, Uses, and Furnishings of Rooms in the Colonial New England Home, 1675–1775* (Boston: Society for the Preservation of New England Antiquities, 1964), "Because a certain wealthy merchant of Boston might have had a brass or crystal chandelier before the Revolution . . . does not mean that every farmer owned one!" He underlines the sparse furnishings of "the average rural yeoman's house."

142. William Newell Hosley, *The Great River: Art and Society of the Connecticut River Valley, 1635–1820* (Wadsworth Athaneum, 1985), p. 428.

143. Inventories of Capt. Peter Brock (1707), Jonathan Bennet (1708), and George Hix (1703), Newport Town Council Book, vol 2.

144. Laurel Thatcher Ulrich calls colonial women "deputy husbands," pointing out that they not only had no legal right to property but no cultural standing as property owners as well (*Good Wives: Image and Reality in the Lives of Women in Northern New England, 1650–1750* [New York: Knopf, 1982], p. 43).

145. McCusker and Menard stress the importance of small private loans—"friend to friend, neighbor to neighbor"—to the colonial economy (*Economy of British America*, p. 334–37).

146. Knowledge of this practice comes to us from nineteenth-century collectors who recorded, on "granny labels" or in family histories, the origins of their china dishes. Anne Allen Ives labeled a set she bought in 1842: "This, and one other cup & saucer formed part of a tea set that was buried in the earth during our Revolutionary war at Wickford, R.I." (1909 inventory of the bequest to Rhode Island School of Design Museum by Hope Brown Russell). See also Alice Earl Morse, *China Collecting in America* (New York: Empire State Book Co., 1892), for tales of hidden and buried china.

147. Breen, *Marketplace of Revolution*, p. 52.

148. Ibid., p. 52.

149. The methods used in this survey were simply to take the first twenty to twenty-five inventories at the beginning of each decade from 1690 to 1770, from five seaport regions, noting the presence of china as well as silver and other items. The probate records used were grouped by county, but in each of the five regions the principal city of the county accounts for at least two-thirds of the inventories with the remaining third or less coming from adjacent rural towns. The cities are Philadelphia, New York, Newport, Boston, and Salem/Marblehead. (The poor preservation of Newport estate records has left me, in some decades, with less than the requisite twenty records and too few records after 1740 to include at all.) Inventories that did not include any dining objects or other household possessions are not counted in this survey (those for travelers, transient sailors, or the dependent elderly may include only money and clothing, e.g.). In each region and in each decade at least two or three widows show up in the sample. While all were identified as "widow," some of these women were clearly carrying on small or large mercantile businesses and died owning household goods as well as merchantable stock. Many other widows' and widowers' estates included only clothing and textiles, and such partial households are not included here. In total, the survey comprises over a thousand inventories, and it focuses on the presence or absence of Chinese porcelain and its co-occurrence with silver.

150. Joseph Dudley became Massachusetts governor following Bellomont, holding the position until 1715. He was accused of working with smugglers and illicit traders, a concern London maintained for almost all successive Massachusetts governors.

151. For the first few decades of Newport and Philadelphia, my data represent almost all inventories available at the Newport Historical Society and the Philadelphia City Archives. By the end of the colonial era, it represents about a third of available inventories. There are much more complete sets of estate records available for Suffolk and Essex Counties, Massachusetts, at the Massachusetts Archives and for New York City and its surrounding counties at the New York State Museum. For these three towns, my data set becomes increasingly less representative as the century progresses.

152. See Richards, *Eighteenth-Century Ceramics*, p.109.

153. See principally Richard Bushman, *The Refinement of America* (New York: Vintage, 1993).

Chapter 4

1. William Sargent, "The Legacy of Imitations: Issues of Connoisseurship in Chinese Export Porcelain," *American Ceramic Circle Journal* 9 (1994).

2. By the second decade of the eighteenth century, Germans were making high-quality hard-paste porcelains, but these were not commercially available to most Europeans or Americans.

3. David Porter, *Ideographia: The Chinese Cipher in Early Modern Europe* (Palo Alto, CA: Stanford University Press, 2001); Sarah Richards, *Eighteenth-Century Ceramics: Products for a Civilised Society* (Manchester: Manchester University Press, 1999); *Exoticism in the Enlightenment*, ed. G. S. Rousseau and Roy Porter (Manchester: University Press, 1990); John Sekora, *Luxury: The Concept in Western Thought, Eden to Smollett* (Baltimore: Johns Hopkins University Press, 1977); Simon Schama. *The Embarrassment of Riches: An Interpretation of Dutch Culture in the Golden Age* (New York: Knopf, 1987).

4. See esp. Porter, *Ideographia*, chap. 3, "Chinoiserie and the Aesthetics of Illegitimacy," pp. 133–92.

5. The term "Celestial Empire" is itself primarily a nineteenth-century usage in the West, often used tongue-in-cheek and originating in the Chinese belief that their emperors were divine (see entry in the *Oxford English Dictionary*, 1989).

6. The *Oxford English Dictionary*, 2005, states that the most plausible etymology relates the term "Yankee" to the Dutch diminutive for John, *Janke*, a name applied to Dutch and English sailors, captains and pirates at the end of the seventeenth century. By the revolutionary era, it was being used as a term of derision by southerners or British regulars for New Englanders. The name stuck with New Englanders, and by the early nineteenth century, the term had acquired many of the positive, defiant qualities it now carries.

7. See, e.g., Samuel Elliot Morison, *Maritime History of Massachusetts* (1922).

8. Dutch people and customs did not disappear after England took over New York in 1664, so even though the colony was English, it still retained a strong Dutch culture and language for many decades—hence the expression "Dutch New York."

9. In colonial America, the term "porcelain" was only used by the early Dutch; see inventories of Jacob de Lange (1697) and Francis Rombouts (1692), Probate Records, New York State Archives, Albany, NY.

10. By the seventeenth century in England, the manor system had lost much of its feudal baggage and in many cases had become merely a "freehold" from the king in exchange for loyalty, although a manor freeholder could exercise certain rights and privileges beyond the norm. Archaeologists have found porcelain at the following seventeenth-century northern colonial estates: the governor's mansion at New Sweden (Tinicum Island); Sylvester Manor,

Long Island; portions of Rennsselaerswyck, including "Schuyler Flats"; Philipse Manor
on the Hudson; Ebenezer Grosvenor Homestead in Connecticut; Updike estate in Rhode
Island; Tyng estate in Massachusetts (see Jean McClure Mudge, *Chinese Export Porcelain
in North America* [New York: Crown, 1986], app. D; and David Sanctuary Howard and
Conrad E. Wright, *New York and the China Trade* [New York: New York Historical Society,
1984]). Other manors associated with porcelain through collections or documentary
evidence are Livingston Manor, granted to Robert Livingston by New York's Governor
Donegan in 1686; Van Cortlandt Manor, granted to Stephanus Van Cortlandt in 1697 by
King William; Lion Gardner's estate on Gardner's Island, with a special patent guaranteeing
independence that was repeatedly reaffirmed by a succession of governors; Daniel Horsemonden's estate in Flatbush, NY; Thomas Paine's estate on Conanicut Island, Rhode Island;
and John and Elizabeth Tatham's estate in New Jersey.

11. See Joyce Goodfriend, *Before the Melting Pot: Society and Culture in Colonial New
York, 1664–1730* (Princeton, NJ: Princeton University Press, 1992), pp. 161–69, 188–98.

12. Marblehead was founded in 1629 as an entrepreneurial venture by English West
Country merchants (Christine Heyrman, *Commerce and Culture: The Maritime Communities of Colonial Massachusetts* [New York: W. W. Norton, 1984]). This depot, and many
small neighboring coastal communities such as Beverly and Ipswich, were a major source
of crewmen for the late seventeenth-century voyages to the Indian Ocean discussed in
chap. 1. For the cosmopolitan, irreligious, and law-breaking character of seventeenth-century
fishing camp-towns, see John William McElroy, "Seafaring in Seventeenth-Century New
England," *New England Quarterly* 8, no. 3 (Sept. 1935): 331–64. Daniel Vickers notes that
one-quarter of all violent crimes committed in seventeenth-century Essex County were in
Marblehead, a rate four times greater than its population size would predict ("Work and
Life on the Fishing Periphery of Essex County," in *Seventeenth-Century New England: A
Conference Held by the Colonial Society of Massachusetts, June 18 and 19, 1982*, ed. David D.
Hall and David Grayson Allen, publication 63 [Boston: Colonial Society of Massachusetts,
1984], pp. 83–117).

13. Such early elite owners of china might include James Logan, who established Sten-
ton, his five-hundred-acre plantation, in 1728, one or two generations after those considered
here along Rhode Island and Long Island Sounds.

14. See Sucheta Mazumdar, *Sugar and Society in China: Peasants, Technologies, and the
World Market* (Cambridge, MA: Harvard University Press, 1998), pp. 83–109; John E.
Wills, *1688: A Global History* (New York: Norton, 2001).

15. A number of works have appeared in the last few years reminding us of the important
role of the Dutch in colonial America, before they were overshadowed by the emergence
of the first British Empire. Much of this work owes a great debt to the tireless Old Dutch
translator, Charles T. Gehring, who over the last twenty-five years has translated into English
several volumes of legal, official, and personal papers from New Amsterdam (see the website
of the New Netherland Institute: http://www.nnp.org/nnp/publications/index.html); see
also Charlotte Wilcoxen, *Dutch Trade and Ceramics in America in the Seventeenth Century*
(Albany, NY: Lane Press of Albany, 1987); Cathy Matson, *Merchants and Empire: Trading
in Colonial New York* (Baltimore: Johns Hopkins University Press, 1997).

16. Samuel Greene Arnold, "Dutch Disturbance at Warwick," *History of the State of
Rhode Island and Providence Plantation*, vol. 1, 1636–1700 (New York: D. Appleton and
Co., 1859), pp. 240–42.

17. *New Haven Town Records*, ed. Franklin Bowditch Dexter, vol. 1 (New Haven Historical Society, 1917), p. 200.

18. Wilcoxen, *Dutch Trade and Ceramics*, p. 13.

19. Russell Shorto, *Island at the Center of the World: The Epic Story of Dutch Manhattan and the Forgotten Colony that Shaped America* (New York: Doubleday, 2004), pp. 160–61; Neil Dunay et al., *Smith's Castle at Cocumscussoc: Four Centuries of Rhode Island History*, Cocumscussoc Association, 2003. Anne Hutchinson also traveled first to New Amsterdam in search of religious freedom.

20. Cotton Mather, *Magnalia Christi Americana*, ed. Kenneth Murdock and Elizabeth Miller (1702; Cambridge, MA: Belknap Press, 1977). Perry Miller, *Errand into the Wilderness* (Cambridge, MA: Harvard University Press, 1956).

21. Patricia E. Rubertone and Charlotte Taylor, *Historical Archaeology at Cocumscussoc: The 1991 Field Investigations*, report submitted to the Rhode Island Historic Preservation and Heritage Commission, Providence, RI, 1992; Caroline Frank, "Tea and Trade: Porcelain from Cocumscussoc," *Castle Chronicle* 15, no. 2 (Summer 2006).

22. Architectural historians conjecture that the date the manor house was constructed was probably immediately after King Phillip's War, ca. 1678.

23. On the Dutch East India Company, see esp. C. R. Boxer and J. H. Plumb, *The Dutch Seaborne Empire, 1600–1800* (New York: Penguin Books, 1990); and H. L. Wesseling, *Imperialism and Colonialism: Essays on the History of European Expansion* (Santa Barbara, CA: Greenwood Press, 1997).

24. T. Volker, *Porcelain and the Dutch East India Company* (Leiden: E. J. Brill, 1971), pp. 50–66, 108–10, 125–28.

25. Mudge, *Chinese Export Porcelain*, p. 280.

26. Wilcoxen, *Dutch Trade and Ceramics*, p. 13.

27. While a large supply does not necessarily determine demand or the nature of demand, in the case of the Anglo-American colonies, where any supply of Chinese goods has been generally denied to have existed at all, it was certainly necessary to the development of a locally contingent, cosmopolitan orientalist taste.

28. Rensselaerswyck was the largest patroonship; others included Vriessendael and Colen Donck (today's Yonkers). Manor estates could approach 200,000 acres and were held by families such as the Livingstons, Van Cortlandts, Philipses, and Schuylers. Many of these estates are maintained as historic properties today.

29. Robert St. George, *Conversing by Signs: The Poetics of Implication in Colonial New England Culture* (Chapel Hill: University of North Carolina Press, 1998), p. 65.

30. On the importance of private land holdings to the English mode of settlement, see Donna Merwick, *Possessing Albany, 1630–1720: The Dutch and English Experiences* (Cambridge: Cambridge University Press, 1990); Anne Keary, "Retelling the History of the Settlement of Providence: Speech, Writing, and Cultural Interaction on Narragansett Bay," *New England Quarterly* 69, no. 2 (1996): 250–86; K. Ryzewski, C. Frank, and K. Deslatte, "Our Site Is Alive, Intimate, and Discomforting! Digging with Descendants on Private Property," *Norwegian Archaeological Review* (forthcoming).

31. Quoted in Harold Donaldson Eberlein, *Manor Houses and Historic Homes of Long Island and Staten Island* (Philadelphia: J. B. Lippincott, 1928), pp. 88–89.

32. The extent of Smith's or any other colonial manor holder's self-rule, within the official dictates of English imperial structures, was technically only local, at the most "micro" level, and dependent on the manor's distance, in all senses of the word, from the appointed colonial governor presiding over the colony.

33. "What's Colonial about Colonial America," in *Possible Pasts: Becoming Colonial in Early America*, ed. Robert B. St. George (Ithaca, NY: Cornell University Press, 2000), p. 61.

34. Feb. 18, 1704/5, Suffolk County Probate Records.

35. See, e.g., 2004–6 reports on the "Greene Farm Archaeology Project" on Warwick, RI, submitted by K. Ryzewski et al. to the Rhode Island Historic Preservation and Heritage Commission. Archaeology has uncovered a complex, worldly culture, including ivory teeth and an iron-making operation, on a seventeenth-century manor estate that was ostensibly a rural backwater overseen by someone Lord Bellomont called "a brutish man" ("Report on the Irregularities of Rhode Island," 1699, *RI Colonial Records* 3:385–88).

36. Robert Blumenfield, *Blanc-de-Chine: The Great Porcelain of Dehua* (Berkeley, CA: Ten Speed Press, 2002).

37. *Diary of Samuel Sewall*, vol. 2, 1699/1700–1714, *Collections of the Massachusetts Historical Society*, vol. 6, ser. 5, Boston; see, e.g., p. 159 in 1700.

38. See David D. Hall, *Worlds of Wonder, Days of Judgment: Popular Religious Beliefs in Early New England* (Cambridge, MA: Harvard University Press, 1990).

39. Marcia Pointon, "Quakerism and Visual Culture," *Art History* 20, no. 3 (Sept. 1997): 397–431; Phyllis Whitman Hunter, *Purchasing Identity in the Atlantic World* (Ithaca, NY: Cornell University Press, 2001); St. George, *Conversing by Signs*; Elizabeth Kowaleski-Wallace, *Consuming Subjects: Women, Shopping, and Business in the Eighteenth Century* (New York: Columbia University Press, 1997).

40. Quoted in Thomas Michie, *The China Trade on Narragansett Bay, 1750–1850* (Providence: Rhode Island School of Design Museum of Art, 1992), p. 8.

41. Mercy Otis Warren, *History of the Rise, Progress, and Termination of the American Revolution,* (Boston, 1805).

42. St. George, *Conversing by Signs*, pp. 42–45.

43. Christiaan J. A. Jörg, *Chinese Ceramics in the Collection of the Rijksmuseum, Amsterdam, the Ming and Quing Dynasties* (London: Scala Publishers, 1997), pp. 299–300. John Goldsmith Phillips, *China Trade Porcelain: An Account of Its Historical Background, Manufacture, and Decoration* (Cambridge, MA: Harvard University Press, 1956), pp. 22–28.

44. Updike descendants remained at Smith's Castle for 120 years, and in Wickford until the present. They include well-known author John Updike of *Rabbit* and *Witches* fame.

45. Christian J. A. Jörg, "The Dutch Connection: Asian Export Art in the Seventeenth and Eighteenth Centuries," *Magazine Antiques* (March 1998).

46. Ivor Noël Hume, *A Guide to Artifacts of Colonial America* (New York: Random House, 1969), p. 261; Frank, "Tea and Trade," p. 12.

47. T. H. Breen, *Marketplace of Revolution* (Oxford: Oxford University Press, 2004), pp. 166–72, and "An Empire of Goods: The Anglicization of Colonial America," *Journal of British Studies* 25, no. 4 (Oct. 1986): 467–99; James Deetz, *In Small Things Forgotten* (New York: Anchor, 1996), pp. 62–63.

48. Take Captain John Boit from Boston, e.g., who was nineteen years old on August 1, 1794, when he set sail in the eighty-nine-ton (sixty-three-foot) sloop *Union*, which circumnavigated the globe in less than two years with a crew of twenty-two. (Phillips, *China Trade Porcelain*, p. 32; see also Mary Malloy, *Boston Men on the Northwest Coast: The American Maritime Fur Trade, 1788–1844* (Kingston, Ontario: Limestone Press, 1998).

49. *Pennsylvania Gazette*, March 25, 1742.

50. See entry on Lay in *American National Biography*.

51. Wm. Wilson Letterbook, 1757, Joseph Downs Collection, Winterthur.

52. See, e.g., the July 24, 1740, issue of the *Pennsylvania Gazette*, which contained

reports of Spanish privateers along the coast. From this date forward, almost every issue of every colonial paper contained news of privateering battles in the western Atlantic.

53. See Sophia Hume, *Extracts from Divers Ancient Testimonies of Friends* (Wilmington, DE: James Adams, 1766), p. 67.

54. "The moment when, together, the work of art and madness are born and fulfilled is the beginning of the time when the world finds itself arraigned by that work of art and responsible before it for *what it is*" (Michel Foucault, referring to artists gone mad in *Madness and Civilization: A History of Insanity in the Age of Reason* [New York: Random House, 1965], p. 289). On the utility of madmen to cultural analysis, see also Jean and John Comaroff, who confess, "we learnt our most profound lesson about consciousness in rural South Africa from a madman" ("The Madman and the Migrant," in *Ethnography and Historical Imagination* [Boulder, CO: Westview Press, 1992], p. 155).

55. See, e.g., the first page of the inventory of Peter Oliver's estate taken after he fled Massachusetts in 1775; Hutchinson-Oliver Papers, Inventories of Estates, MHS, Boston.

56. See, e.g., *New England Weekly Journal*, Nov. 13, 1727.

57. *Boston News-Letter*, June 16, 1739.

58. [Benjamin Franklin], *New England Courant*, Sept. 3, 1722. On Franklin's exposure to brother James's imported publications, see Claude-Anne Lopez and Eugenia Herbert, *The Private Franklin* (New York: Norton, 1975), pp. 10–14.

59. Franklin Papers, July 20, 1776. Franklin uses the metaphor again when writing from Paris to David Hartley on the eve of the signing of the Peace of Paris: "There is enough sense in America to take care of its own china vase" (Oct. 22, 1783). Papers of Bemjamin Franklin, digital edition, Packard Humanities Institute, 1988–present.

60. Virginia Cowles, *The Great Swindle: The Story of the South Sea Bubble* (Hindsight Books, 2002).

61. *Benjamin Franklin's Autobiography*, chap. 8.

62. John L. Cotter et al., *The Buried Past: An Archaeological History of Philadelphia* (University of Pennsylvania Press, 1992), pp. 86–96, 142–43.

63. Excerpted from Thomas Makin, "A Description of Pennsylvania," reprinted in *Pennsylvania Magazine of History and Biography* 57 (1913): 371–74.

64. See Graham Hood, *Bonnin and Morris of Philadelphia: The First American Porcelain Factory, 1770–1772* (Chapel Hill: University of North Carolina Press, 1972).

65. Kowaleski-Wallace, *Consuming Subjects*, pp. 19–36.

66. Samuel Johnson, *The Literary Magazine or Universal Review* (London: J. Wilkie, 1757), 2:163. Dr. Johnson, of course, offers an endless stream of wisdom regarding the use of tea. One moment he is telling us, "tea is not a liquor proper for the lower classes, as it supplies no strength to labor" (p. 166), and in the next he is singing its praises, "So hear it then, my Rennie dear, Nor hear it with a frown; You cannot make the tea so fast As I can gulp it down. I therefore pray thee, Rennie dear, That thou wilt give to me ... another dish of tea." Dr. Johnson, evidently, had others to supply the "labour" he certainly lacked after all that tea!

67. Simon Mason, *The Good and Bad Effects of Tea Considered* (London: M. Cooper, 1745).

68. John Adams, draft letter to Colonel Josiah Quincy, dated summer 1759, in *Diary and Autobiography of John Adams*, ed. L. H. Butterfield (Cambridge, MA: Belknap Press, 1961), 2:114.

69. Mason, *Effects of Tea*, passim.

70. See esp. Margaret Newell, *From Dependency to Independence: Economic Revolution in Colonial New England* (Ithaca, NY: Cornell University Press, 1998), pp. 17–35.

71. See Jonathan Prude, "To Look upon the 'Lower Sort': Runaway Ads and the Appearance of Unfree Laborers in America, 1750–1800," *Journal of American History* 78, no. 1 (June 1991): 124–59.

72. Quoted in William Smith, *A History of the Late Province of New York* (New York Historical Society, 1830), vol. 4, pt. 2, p. 281.

73. See Christina Hodge, "A Middling Gentility" PhD diss., Boston University, 2006, pp. 136–50.

74. The Puritans saw themselves as being "elect," as persons who were set apart by God. See Perry Miller, "The Marrow of Puritan Divinity," in his *Errand into the Wilderness*, pp. 48–98; and *The Diary of Samuel Sewall*, vols. 1 and 2, ed. M. Halsey Thomas (New York: Farrar, Straus, and Giroux, 1973).

75. Letter from John Francis to John Brown, dated Sept. 1787, regarding the loading of the ship *General Washington*. Private collection.

76. Quoted from Robert Wallace, *A Dissertation on the Numbers of Man* (1753).

77. Benjamin Franklin, printed in [William Clarke], *Observations on the Late and Present Conduct of the French, with Regard to Their Encroachments upon the British Colonies in North America. . . . To Which is Added, Wrote by Another Hand; Observations concerning the Increase of Mankind, Peopling of Countries, &c.* (Boston: S. Kneeland, 1755).

78. This assumption is contrary to that proposed by Franklin, above, in which the exporting country experiences healthy growth. Margaretta Lovell, *Art in the Season of Revolution: Painters, Artisans, and Patrons in Early America* (Philadelphia: University of Pennsylvania Press, 2005), pp. 248–51.

79. The legacy of this sexist ethos is apparent in the way historic homes are named in the northeastern United States, *always* after the male owner or architect.

80. A single John Goddard carved mahogany roundabout chair, ca. 1760, claimed an exorbitant $1,696,000 in January 2007, at Sotheby's New York. A japanned chest by Robert Davis, ca. 1735, sold for $1.8 million in December 2004, at a private auction in Lowell, Massachusetts. A Joseph and Nathaniel Richardson coffee pot, ca. 1780, sold for $74,250 at Neal Auctions in New Orleans in 2002, and one silver ladle, ca. 1760, marked "JR" recently sold for $1,495 through Pook and Pook. These prices speak for themselves.

81. Men are also depicted, usually in a group, around porcelain punch bowls, such as in the Greenwood painting "Sea Captains Carousing in Surinam" (1757). Moses Marcy is seen with a punch bowl (1760), a sign of his engagement with standards of male sociability. In these cases porcelain forms part of the scene rather than being a central object-symbol associated with the man as Revere's silver teapot is.

82. See Arjun Appadurai, "Commodities and the Politics of Value," in *The Social Life of Things: Commodities in Cultural Perspective*, ed. Appadurai (Cambridge: Cambridge University Press, 1986), on the nature of demand. Appadurai also states, "The treatment of the commodity in the first hundred or so pages of *Capital* is arguably one of the most difficult, contradictory, and ambiguous parts of Marx's corpus." Yet 150 years ago Marx revealed a relationship between social practices and larger, less visible economic structures that has been useful to material culture scholars ever since. See also Immanuel Wallerstein, *Mercantilism and the Consolidation of the European World-Economy* (London: Academic Press, 1980), and "Household Structures and Labour-Force Formation in the Capitalist World Economy," in his and Etienne Balibar's *Race, Nation, Class* (London: Verso, 1991).

Chapter 5

1. This ship, the *Dartmouth*, belonged to the Rotch family of Nantucket, not to the East India Company that had commissioned it. I do not know whether it flew the red-and-white striped ensign of the Company, but it may well have, given its close association.

2. "Heathen" is a term applied in modern times to people of polytheistic beliefs, but in this period Muslims were considered "heathen" (*Oxford English Dictionary*). It was an expression regularly applied in the seventeenth and eighteenth centuries not only to so-called Barbary pirates from North Africa but to all trade partners from Africa and the Middle East. It is also applied to all East Indians, whether from India, the Philippines, or China. Clothing was an essential category of difference in the European cosmography, manifesting the moral, class, and racial distinctions that underlay the expression *heathen*. See Roxann Wheeler, *The Complexion of Race: Categories of Difference in Eighteenth Century British Culture* (Philadelphia: University of Pennsylvania Press, 2000), pp. 17–21.

3. The *Dartmouth* carried 114 chests of tea, and the *Eleanor* and *Beaver* similar quantities. For the quoted terms, see especially "TEA destroyed by Indians," a broadside printed in Boston a few days after the Tea Party; "Proceedings of ye Body respecting the Tea," a first-hand account found in the Sewall Papers in the Public Archives of Ottawa and reproduced in "Notes and Documents" by L. F. S. Upton, *William and Mary Quarterly* 22, no. 2 (1965): 287–300; as well as newspaper accounts in the days immediately preceding and following the event. For a reconstruction of events that evening, see "Letters of John Andrews, Esq., of Boston, 1772–1776," in *Proceedings of the Massachusetts Historical Society*, ser. 1 (July 1865): 323–29; "Diary of John Rowe," in *Letter and Diary of John Rowe*, ed. Anne Rowe Cunningham (Boston, 1903), pp. 255–59; *The Selectmen's Minutes from 1769–April 1775* (Boston, 1893), pp. 201–203; Benjamin Labaree, *The Boston Tea Party* (Oxford: Oxford University Press, 1964), pp. 126–45; Alfred Young, *The Shoemaker and the Tea Party* (Boston: Beacon Press, 1999), pp. 99–107; Francis Drake, *Tea Leaves* (Boston: A. O. Crane, 1884).

4. Gary Nash, "Poverty and Politics in Early America," in Billy G. Smith, *Down and Out in Early America* (University Park: Pennsylvania State University Press, 2004), pp. 1–40; Wikipedia also calls it "the spark," http://en.wikipedia.org/wiki/Boston_Tea_Party; Labaree, *Boston Tea Party*, calls it "the catalyst" for the revolution, p. 256; the *Boston Gazette*, 1774, writes the importation of tea is called the match that will light a fire.

5. March 1765. New Yorkers refused to comply with the terms of the Quartering Act and it lapsed in 1770.

6. Christopher A. Bayly, "The British Military-Fiscal State and Indigenous Resistance, India 1750–1820," in *An Imperial State at War: Britain from 1689 to 1815*, ed. Lawrence Stone (New York: Routledge, 1994), p. 338; David Armitage, *The Ideological Origins of the British Empire* (New York: Columbia University, 2000), pp. 2–3; Tony Ballantyne, *Orientalism and Race: Aryanism in the British Empire* (New York: Palgrave Macmillan, 2002), p. 18.

7. Peter D. G. Thomas, *The Townshend Duties Crisis: The Second Phase of the American Revolution, 1767–1773* (Oxford: Oxford University Press, 1987), p. 157; Robert J. Chaffin, "The Townshend Acts Crisis, 1767–1770," in *The Blackwell Encyclopedia of the American Revolution*, ed. Jack P. Greene and J. R. Pole (Malden, MA: Blackwell, 1991), p. 138.

8. Evidence that most Americans were unsympathetic to the victims of the "massacre" in Boston comes from Annapolis, printed in the *London Evening Post* (July 28, 1770): "The late riots at Boston are regarded with a very cool eye all over America, except in New England" (Thomas, *Townshend Duties Crisis*, p. 198).

9. John Adams, letter to Abigail Adams, 1759, in *Diary and Autobiography of John Adams*, vol. 2 (Cambridge, MA: Belknap Press, 1961), p. 114.

10. See Robert St. George, *Conversing by Signs: The Poetics of Implication in Colonial New England Culture* (Chapel Hill: University of North Carolina Press, 1998), pp. 242–68; Benjamin Carp, *Rebels Rising: Cities and the American Revolution* (Oxford: Oxford University Press, 2007).

11. For an overview, see Larry Sawers, "The Navigation Acts Revisited," *Economic History Review* 45, no. 2 (May 1994): 262–84; also Patrick O'Brien, "The Political Economy of British Taxation, 1660–1815," *Economic History Review* 41, no. 1 (Feb. 1988): 1–32; O. M. Dickerson, *The Navigation Acts and the American Revolution* (New York: A. S. Barnes, 1951), and "Use Made of the Revenue from the Tax on Tea," *New England Quarterly* 31, no. 2 (June 1958): 232–43; Hoh-Cheung and Lorna H. Mui, "Smuggling and the British Tea Trade before 1784," *American Historical Review* 74, no. 1 (Oct. 1968): 44–73; and Arthur M. Schlesinger, "Uprising against the East India Company," *Political Science Quarterly* 32, no. 1 (Mar. 1917): 60–79.

12. For a detailed description of the tea ritual, see Rodris Roth, "Tea Drinking in Eighteenth-Century America: Its Etiquette and Equipage," *Smithsonian Bulletin* (1961).

13. See introduction and St. George, *Conversing by Signs*, p. 5.

14. T. H. Breen, *The Marketplace of Revolution: How Consumer Politics Shaped American Independence* (Oxford: Oxford University Press, 2004); Benjamin Carp, *Rebels Rising: Cities and the American Revolution* (Oxford: Oxford University Press, 2007); John W. Tyler, *Smugglers and Patriots: Boston Merchants and the Advent of the American Revolution* (Evanston, IL: Northeastern University Press, 1986); Robert St. George, *Conversing by Signs: Poetics of Implication in Colonial New England* (Chapel Hill: University of North Carolina Press, 1998). See also Margaretta M. Lovell, *Art in a Season of Revolution: Painters, Artisans, and Patrons in Early America* (Philadelphia: University of Pennsylvania Press, 2005); and Alfred F. Young, *Liberty Tree: Ordinary People and the American Revolution* (New York: NYU Press, 2006). For an interpretation of revolution in the Chesapeake, see Michael McDonnell, *The Politics of War: Race, Class, and Conflict in Revolutionary Virginia* (Chapel Hill: University of North Carolina Press, 2007).

15. See Herbert Sloan, review of Marc Egnal, *Mighty Empire: The Origins of the American Revolution*, in *Business History Review* (1989).

16. Joyce Appleby, "Liberalism and the American Revolution," *New England Quarterly* 49, no. 1 (March 1976).

17. Nash, "Poverty and Politics." Before the mid-nineteenth-century expression "Boston Tea Party," the event was called the "Destruction of the Tea" in all sources—see the Currier and Ives print of 1846 called *Destruction of the Tea in Boston Harbor*, for example.

18. See St. George's analysis of the Stamp Act house attacks, for example. He acknowledges that, yes indeed, there were specific economic and social pressures within colonial society that underlay rebellious acts, but by also "reading" the form those acts took and revealing how they functioned as metaphors, he is able to tell us much more about the relationship between colonial society and the course of broader political events. In hanging effigies, entering imposing Georgian mansions, destroying luxurious properties, men and women denuded and degraded an emasculating hegemonic body within their community, seizing control and, ironically, publicly restoring a sense of lost dignity. "The significance of the house assaults derived in part from the parallelism of effigy as body, house as body, society as body," St. George points out. Those in the "mob" also described themselves as "the Body"

throughout the prerevolutionary period. The house attacks can be read as "an expressive form of planned symbolic violence" in which perpetrators and victims engaged in primitive bodily struggle, revealing the persistent influence of Puritan and millennial iconography amid Enlightenment ideals (*Conversing by Signs*, pp. 208–95).

19. In early modern Europe, *Leviathan* was a commonly employed biblical reference carrying connotations of a sea demon sent by Eastern states such as Egypt or Assyria to attack God-fearing (Judeo-Christian) communities. In the book of Enoch, Leviathan is described as female. It is found paired with "Oriental tyrants" in seventeenth-century Reformist texts advocating religious liberties. See, e.g.: "A representation of the threatning dangers, impending over Protestants in Great Brittain With an account of the arbitrary and popish ends, unto which the declaration for liberty of conscience in England, and the proclamation for a toleration in Scotland, are designed," by Robert Ferguson (Edinburgh 1687).

20. See letters of Hannah Winthrop and Mercy Otis Warren, e.g., Nov. 10, 1773 (Warren-Winthrop correspondence, MHS, Boston) for rural women; the account of Hewes (Alfred Young, "George Robert Twelve Hewes," *William and Mary Quarterly* 38, no. 4 (Oct. 1981): 561–623) for poor artisans; and local newspapers for resolutions of towns such as Sudbury, Massachusetts, in the countryside.

21. See Labaree, *Boston Tea Party*, p. 26.

22. See David Porter, *Ideographia: The Chinese Cipher in Early Modern Europe* (Palo Alto, CA: Stanford University Press, 2001).

23. Appleby, "Liberalism," p. 24.

24. Lester C. Olson, *Benjamin Franklin's Vision of American Community* (Columbia: University of South Carolina Press, 2004).

25. Jeremy Belknap, *A History of New Hampshire* (1784–92), quoted in T. H. Breen, "Ideology and Nationalism on the Eve of the American Revolution: Revisions Once More in Need of Revising," *Journal of American History* 84, no. 1 (1997): 13–39, at p. 28.

26. Eliga H. Gould, *Persistence of Empire: British Political Culture in the Age of the American Revolution* (Chapel Hill: University of North Carolina Press, 2000), chaps. 2, 3; Fred Anderson, *Crucible of War: The Seven Years' War and the Fate of the British Empire in North America* (New York: Knopf, 2000), p. 502; Stephen Conway, "From Fellow-Nationals to Foreigners: British Perceptions of Americans circa 1739–1783," *William and Mary Quarterly* 59, no. 1 (2002).

27. Anderson, *Crucible*, p. 521.

28. Ibid., p. 490.

29. Britain controlled Manila, at least in the eyes of Europeans, from November 1762 to May 1764. Anderson, *Crucible*, pp. 515–17.

30. See, e.g., the *Georgia Gazette*, May 31, 1764.

31. *New London Gazette*, Dec. 9, 1763; *Boston Post-Boy*, 1763–64.

32. *Boston Post-Boy*, Feb. 13, 1764.

33. Ibid. The view expressed by nineteenth-century historian Lord Macaulay that "Clive brought peace, security, prosperity, and such liberty as the case allowed to millions of Indians" was perpetuated into the twentieth century in Britain; see the 1911 issue of the *Encyclopaedia Britannica* for example. Clive, an opium addict, militarized the East India Company's territorial expansion and exploitation of peasants. He was even suspected of abusing his authority vis-à-vis the Company.

34. Holden Furber, *Rival Empires of Trade in the Orient, 1600–1800* (Minneapolis: University of Minnesota Press, 1976), p. 131.

35. The uprising later spread all the way to the Great Lakes and was called "Pontiac's Rebellion" after one chief whose role is still unclear. David Dixon, *Never Come to Peace Again: Pontiac's Uprising and the Fate of the British Empire in North America* (Norman: University of Oklahoma Press, 2005); Gregory Evans Dowd, *War under Heaven: Pontiac, the Indian Nations, and the British Empire* (Johns Hopkins University Press, 2002); Anderson, *Crucible*, pp. 527–34.

36. The Treaty of Paris was signed Feb. 10, 1763, by Great Britain, Spain, France, and Portugal, and involved a series of land transfers around the globe, with Britain walking away with a lion's share. Many Indians in formerly French territory, however, were not happy with the new sovereign. The Proclamation Line was a temporary attempt by King George to quell the discontent. See Colin Calloway, *The Scratch of a Pen: 1763 and the Transformation of North America* (Oxford: Oxford University Press, 2006).

37. Jack Greene, "An Uneasy Connection: An Analysis of the Preconditions of the American Revolution," in *Essays on the American Revolution*, ed. Stephen Kurtz and James Hutson (Chapel Hill: University of North Carolina Press, 1973), pp. 32–80, at p. 35.

38. *Oxford English Dictionary*, 2002.

39. See chap. 4, n. 47.

40. Elizabeth Mancke, "Empire and State" in *The British Atlantic World, 1500–1800*, ed. David Armitage and Michael Braddick (New York: Palgrave Macmillan, 2002), pp. 175–95.

41. Stephen Sayre, "The Englishman Deceived," pp. 12, 17. Author Sayre was a literary "soldier of fortune," throwing himself into any revolutionary cause he could find, comparable perhaps to Thomas Paine whose rhetoric so resonated with Americans. This thirty-eight-page pamphlet was listed in a number of colonial libraries, and the sections cited here ran in the *Providence Gazette* on Oct. 22, 1768.

42. Stephen Conway, "From Fellow-Nationals to Foreigners: British Perceptions of the Americans, circa 1739–1783," *William and Mary Quarterly*, ser. 3, 59 (2002): 23–24.

43. Letter from Thomas Hutchinson to unknown person, Dec. 30, 1773, quoted in T. C. Barrow, "The American Revolution as a Colonial War for Independence," *William and Mary Quarterly* 25 (1968): 457.

44. Thomas Jefferson, *Notes on the State of Virginia*, written in 1781–84 as a response to the French minister François Marbois regarding assertions by an important late eighteenth-century natural scientist, Comte de Buffon, a proponent of Montesquieu (ed. Frank Shuffelton [New York: Penguin Books, 1999]).

45. Martin Howard, "A Letter from a Gentleman at Halifax to His Friend in Rhode Island," 1765.

46. *New York Journal, or General Advertiser*, Dec. 2–9, 1773.

47. "Appendix Stating the Heavy Grievances the Colonies Labour under from the Several Acts of the British Parliament," in *A Sermon Containing Scriptural Instructions to Civil Rulers*, given by Rev. Samuel Sherwood in Fairfield, CT, Aug. 31, 1774.

48. *Pennsylvania Packet*, Oct. 18, 1773.

49. *New York Journal*, Oct. 28, 1773. "Hampden" was a pseudonym used by James Otis Jr.

50. *Pennsylvania Chronicle*, Nov. 15, 1773.

51. Joshua 9:21–23.

52. Adams Papers, vol. 19, *Diary*, Dec. 16, 1772–Dec. 18, 1773, MHS.

53. See, e.g., Breen, *Marketplace of Revolution*, pp. 47, 151–58, 206.

54. Drake, *Tea Leaves*, pp. 191–202; Labaree, *Boston Tea Party*, pp. 6–8.

55. Drake, *Tea Leaves*, p. xi.

56. Quoted in Esther Singleton, *Social New York under the Georges* (New York: D. Appleton, 1902), pp. 378–79; emphasis added.

57. See the excellent discussion of eighteenth-century tea literature in Beth Kowalski-Wallace, "Tea, Gender, and Domesticity in Eighteenth-Century England," in *Studies in Eighteenth-Century Culture* 23 (1994): 131–45; and David Porter, "'A Peculiar but Uninteresting Nation': China and the Discourse of Commerce in Eighteenth-Century England," *Eighteenth-Century Studies* 33, no. 2 (2000): 181–99.

58. Simon Paulli, *A Treatise on Tobacco, Tea, Coffee, and Chocolate*, trans. D. Jones (London, 1746), quoted in Kowalski-Wallace, "Tea, Gender, and Domesticity," p. 136. This text is today found in scores of American libraries, indicating its probable strong presence in the colonial period.

59. Jonas Hanway, *An Essay on Tea* (1756). Its full title read, *An Essay on Tea, Considered as Pernicious to Health, Obstructing Industry, and Impoverishing the Nation*. The *Essay* appeared as an appendix to *A Journal of Eight Days Journey from Portsmouth to Kingstown upon Thames*, written as a series of letters to "two ladies," London, 1756. A copy appears in the original inventory of the Redwood Library in Newport.

60. Ibid., p. 213.

61. This discourse bears striking resemblance to the news headlines of our time, accusing the Chinese of contaminating every ingestible item exported to the West, from pet food to toothpaste to baby toys.

62. Hanway, *Essay on Tea*, pp. 216–22.

63. The account of this observer, unsigned and titled "Proceedings of ye Body respecting the Tea," was found in the Sewell Papers in the Public Archives of Canada, Ottowa. A later note on the account compares the handwriting to that of a certain "Coleman," perhaps a cousin of Judge Samuel Sewell. See L. F. S. Upton, "Proceedings of Ye Body Respecting the Tea," in "Notes and Documents," *William and Mary Quarterly* 22, no. 2 (April 1965): 287–300, at pp. 293, 298–300. For an in-depth treatment of Dr. Young and his espousal of bodily health as a revolutionary cause against tyrannical rulers, see Pauline Maier, "Reason and Revolution: The Radicalism of Dr. Thomas Young," *American Quarterly* 28, no. 2 (Summer 1976): 229–49.

64. *Boston Gazette*, Dec. 13, 1773. Smallpox had broken out on the third tea ship to arrive at Boston Harbor, the *Beaver*, which arrived on Dec. 6 but was quarantined away from Griffin's wharf until Dec. 15.

65. John Adams wrote, "The Revolution was effected before the war commenced. The Revolution was in the minds and hearts of the people." Letter to H. Niles, Feb. 13, 1818, *John Adams Papers*, Massachusetts Historical Society.

66. Numbers 22:2–24:25. In other words, Balaam came from the gateway to the Orient. P. Kyle McCarter, "The Balaam Texts from Deir Allā: The First Combination," *Bulletin of the American Schools of Oriental Research*, no. 239 (Summer 1980): 49–60; Meindert Dijkstra, "Is Balaam Also among the Prophets?" *Journal of Biblical Literature* 114.1 (Spring 1995): 43–64.

67. Emerich de Vattel, *Law of Nations* (1758), drew on the seventeenth-century defense of liberalism by Dutch jurist Hugo Grotius, *The Rights of War and Peace: Including the Law of Nature and Nation*, trans. A. C. Campbell, reprint ed. (Westport, CT: Hyperion, 1979).

68. Richard Horowitz, "International Law and State Transformation in China, Siam, and the Ottoman Empire during the Nineteenth Century," *Journal of World History* 15 (Dec. 2004).

69. *Elements of International Law* (Philadelphia, 1836; reprint Cambridge, MA: Da Capo Press, 1972).

70. Although English volunteers participated in a series of European conflicts against the Ottomans in the seventeenth century, England as a state, much less an empire, had never declared war on an Asian sovereign. In the first and second Carnatic wars in India in the decade preceding the Seven Years' War, the French and English East India Companies had fought each other, but without a declaration of war against an Asian state. King Philip's War in New England involved English colonists in a declared war against Native Americans but not the English crown.

71. James William Johnson, "The Meaning of the 'Augustan,'" *Journal of the History of Ideas* 19 (Oct. 1958): 507–22.

72. "The Orderly Book of Capt. Trent at Ft. Pitt," entry of June 24, 1763. Quoted from A. T. Volwiler, "William Trent's Journal at Fort Pitt, 1763," *Mississippi Valley Historical Review* (1924): 390–413, at p. 400.

73. Quoted from Elizabeth Fenn, "Biological Warfare in Eighteenth-Century North America: Beyond Jeffrey Amherst," *Journal of American History* 86 (March 2000): 1552–80, at p. 1554.

74. Amherst letters of July 7 and July 16, 1763; Bouquet's letter of July 13, 1763. Quoted from Fenn, "Biological Warfare," pp. 1555–57. Fenn points out that a published transcript of Amherst second letter is inaccurate. Originals found in *Official Papers 1740–1783* under "Jeffrey Amherst."

75. Fenn, "Biological Warfare," pp. 1572–73. She quotes Americans Josiah Atkins, William Feltman, and Robert Livingston as being aware of this strategy. Benjamin Franklin, "Retort Courteous," 1786, *Writings of Benjamin Franklin*, vol. 10, ed. Albert Henry Smyth (Macmillan, 1907), p. 111.

76. Furber, *Rival Empires of Trade*, pp. 258–59.

77. Sermon by Samuel Sherwood, cited in n. 47.

78. Sermon by Samuel Sherwood, *The Church's Flight into the Wilderness*, New York, 1776. While the expression "whore of Babylon" (Book of Revelations 17, 18) was a common metaphor among early Protestants for the Catholic Church, the whore herself was nevertheless depicted as Asian in much of the imagery related to her throughout the early modern period, especially at its end (see, e.g., William Blake's 1809 watercolor in the British Museum).

79. Ibid.; Sherwood even cites the era of Governor Andros and the competitive greed of England ninety years earlier.

80. See esp. Tyler, *Smugglers and Patriots*; Arthur Schlesinger Jr., "Uprising Against the East India Company," *Political Science Quarterly* 32 (March 1917): 60–79; Thomas C. Barrow, *Trade and Empire: The British Customs Service in Colonial America, 1660–1775* (Cambridge, MA: Harvard University Press, 1967).

81. See a letter from Edes's grandson dated Feb. 16, 1836, in which he recalls the role of the punch bowl in readying the patriots for the "destruction of the tea" (*MHS Proceedings*, ser. 1, 12 [1871]: 174–76). Edes was the printer of the *Boston Gazette*, the patriots' preferred newspaper and the one that carried so many diatribes against Chinese tea.

82. See Stuart Creighton Miller, *The Unwelcome Immigrant: The American Image of the Chinese, 1785–1882* (Berkeley: University of California Press: 1969), pp. 3–15.

83. See Jonathan Goldstein, *Philadelphia and the China Trade, 1682–1846* (University Park, PA: Pennsylvania State University Press, 1978), pp. 13–17.

84. India Wharf, a large-scale speculative project, was established in the 1790s using profits from the trade of Northwest Coast furs to China. Nancy Seasholes, *Gaining Ground: A History of Landmaking in Boston* (Cambridge, MA: MIT Press, 2003). Roger Abrahams points out colonial Bostonians used the term "Indian" in the same breath as "Turk" or "Moor," as seen in the broadside quotes in the opening scene of this chapter, to mean bogey men or masquerading mobs, and such usage was also common in England dating back to the early eighteenth century ("Mohawks, Mohocks, Hawkubites, Whatever," *Common-Place* 8, no. 4 [July 20, 2008]).

85. [Benjamin Franklin], "Colonist's Advocate: X," *Public Advertiser*, Feb. 19, 1770.

86. "Yellow Peril" was a popular expression in the late nineteenth century for Chinese immigrants. In *New York before Chinatown: Orientalism and the Shaping of American Culture* (1999), John Tchen takes us on a well-researched excursion through the history of how nineteenth-century Americans defined themselves as Western vis-à-vis an imagined corrupt and contaminated oriental East Asia. For articles on contaminated toothpaste, see, e.g., "China Investigates Tainted Toothpaste," *New York Times*, May 22, 2007, or "Toxic Toothpaste Made in China Found in US," *New York Times*, June 2, 2007.

87. The proposal that an "Orient" is useful to underpinning a Western identity was most forcefully articulated by Edward Said in his *Orientalism* (New York: Vintage Books, 1978)

Epilogue

1. Ezra Stiles, "The United States Elevated to Glory and Honor," sermon given before the Connecticut General Assembly in Hartford, May 1783.

2. James R. Fichter, *So Great a Proffit: How the East Indies Trade Transformed Anglo-American Capitalism* (Cambridge, MA: Harvard University Press, 2010), pp. 35–39.

3. For information on these vessels, see Jonathan Goldstein, *Philadelphia and the China Trade, 1682–1846* (University Park, PA: Pennsylvania State University Press, 1978), pp. 25–33; Samuel Elliot Morison, *Maritime History of Massachusetts* (Boston: Houghton Mifflin, 1921), pp. 44–45.

4. John Adams to John Jay, letter, in *Memoir of the Life of Henry Lee and His Correspondence* (Philadelphia: H. C. Carey and I. Lea, 1825): 2:142–44; and Donald Dalton Johnson with Gary Dean Best, *The United States and the Pacific: Private Interests and Public Policies* (Westport, CT: Greenwood, 1995), p. 13.

5. Sucheta Mazumdar, "Slaves, Textiles, and Opium: The Other Half of the Triangular Trade," paper presented at the John Carter Brown Library at the *Asia-Pacific in the Making of the Americas* symposium, Sept. 27, 2010.

6. Jacques Downs, *Golden Ghetto: The American Commercial Community in Canton and the Shaping of American China Policy, 1784–1844* (Bethlehem, PA: Lehigh University Press, 1997), p. 72.

7. F. Crouzet, "America and the Crisis of the British Imperial Economy, 1803–1807," in *The Early Modern Atlantic Economy*, ed. John J. McCusker and Kenneth Morgan (Cambridge University Press, 2000).

8. "American Ships and Shipbuilding," by the editors of *Scientific American* 2, no. 2, n.s. (Jan. 7, 1860): 26.

9. Downs, *Golden Ghetto*, p. 67; Alejandra Irigoin, "Westbound for the Far East: North American's Intermediation in China's Silver Trade," paper presented at "America and the China Trades," as part of *Asia-Pacific in the Making of the Americas* research initiative, Brown University, Sept. 28, 2010.

10. *The Life and Journals of Major Samuel Shaw: The First American Consul at Canton*, ed. Josiah Quincy (Boston, 1847), p. 187.

11. Shaw, *Life and Journals*, pp. 187–93. On the *Lady Hughes* affair, see also Li Chen, "Law, Empire, and Modern Sino-Western Relations," *Law and History Review* (Spring 2009): 1–47.

12. Shaw, *Journals*, pp. 305, 298.

13. Alejandra Irigoin, "The End of a Silver Era: The Consequences of the Breakdown of the Spanish Peso Standard in China and the United States, 1780s–1850s," *Journal of World History* 20, no. 2 (June 2009): 207–44; see chart on p. 211.

Index

253